JUKI GIRLS, GOOD GIRLS

❖ ❖ ❖

Juki Girls, Good Girls

*Gender and Cultural Politics in Sri Lanka's
Global Garment Industry*

CAITRIN LYNCH

ILR Press *an imprint of*
CORNELL UNIVERSITY PRESS
Ithaca and London

First published 2007 by Cornell University Press
First printing, Cornell Paperbacks, 2007

Printed in the United States of America

Library of Congress Cataloging-in-Publication Data

Lynch, Caitrin.
    Juki girls, good girls : gender and cultural politics in Sri Lanka's global garment industry / Caitrin Lynch.
        p. cm.
    Includes bibliographical references and index.
    ISBN 978-0-8014-4556-9 (cloth : alk. paper) — ISBN 978-0-8014-7362-3 (pbk. : alk. paper)
    1. Women clothing workers—Sri Lanka—Case studies. 2. Sexual division of labor—Sri Lanka—Case studies. 3. Sex role in the work environment—Sri Lanka—Case studies. 4. Sex role—Sri Lanka—Case studies. 5. Globalization—Social aspects—Sri Lanka—Case studies. I. Title.

    HD6073.C62S755 2007
    331.4'8—dc22

2006101123

Cornell University Press strives to use environmentally responsible suppliers and materials to the fullest extent possible in the publishing of its books. Such materials include vegetable-based, low-VOC inks and acid-free papers that are recycled, totally chlorine-free, or partly composed of nonwood fibers. For further information, visit our website at www.cornellpress.cornell.edu.

Cloth printing   10 9 8 7 6 5 4 3 2 1
Paperback printing   10 9 8 7 6 5 4 3 2 1

To Nick, Cormac, and Nicola,
and to the workers at Shirtex and Serendib

CONTENTS

ACKNOWLEDGMENTS

I have accrued many debts in the years that I have been working on this book. The first person to direct me on this long road was Steven Kemper at Bates College, whose course on South Asia was my introduction to the region and the discipline. It is thanks to Steve that I became interested in anthropology and Sri Lanka . . . and I never turned back.

This project was made possible by the generosity and kindness of many people in Sri Lanka. Owing to concerns about confidentiality, I employ pseudonyms for the factories and all people connected to them. I regret that I cannot thank individuals by name, but special thanks are due the many workers and managers at Shirtex and Serendib whom I describe in this book and particularly the workers I have named Rohini, Mala, and Geeta, whose essays are printed here. I am deeply grateful to Tissa Gunasekera and Asanka Perera (alas, pseudonyms) for allowing me into their factories and providing me with better access to these workplaces than I had anticipated. I also thank the many other investors I interviewed in Colombo, as well as the many managers and investors who welcomed me into their factories in Colombo, the Katunayake Free Trade Zone, and in villages throughout the country. At the Board of Investment, I thank H. B. Masinghe, N. N. Kumaratunga, and Mrs. Pestonjee. Thanks are also due Susil Sirivardana, Sirisena Cooray, Anthony Fernando, Dayan Jayatilleka, and others for illuminating discussions about President Premadasa and the 200 Garment Factories Program.

I am grateful to numerous scholars at the University of Peradeniya and the International Centre for Ethnic Studies (ICES) in Kandy, the two institutions with which I was affiliated during my field research. These scholars include K. M. de Silva, R. A. L. H. Gunawardana, Ashley Halpe, Sirima Kiribamune, Udaya Meddagama, Walter Perera, Gerald Pieris, Sisira Pinnawela, Sudarshen Seneviratne, Tudor Silva, and Carmen Wickremagamage. Scholars in Colombo who provided help include Sunil Bastian, Janaka Biyanwila, Radhika Coomaraswamy, Malathi de Alwis, S. T. Hettige, Tissa Jayatilaka, Kumari Jayawardena, Pradeep Jeganathan, and Darini Rajasingham-Senanayake. I should also mark my appreciation for the valuable comments I received from audiences at presentations of elements of my field research at ICES Colombo, ICES Kandy, the Sri Lankan Federation of University Women (Kandy Branch), and the British Council in Kandy.

Athulya Meddagama was my primary research assistant. Her enthusiasm and kind spirit were always appreciated and facilitated warm relations with factory workers who would ask after her when she wasn't around. Her translation and transcription skills were invaluable. I also thank the numerous other people I employed as research assistants at various stages of the field research: S. A. P. Benedict, Rosemary Chunchie, Mevna de Silva, Mrs. Nandana Galpaya, Mihiri Herath, Michael Joachim, Iyanka Karunaratne, Indu Meddagama, Rizmia Naushad, Kanchana Ratnasara, Gayatri Samarakoon, and Udeni Samarakoon. In the final hour of book preparation, I recruited Nilam Hamead, Upali Lionel, and Sriyani Mallika Ranawana for help in Sri Lanka. Special thanks to Rosemary Chunchie, Yolanda Foster, Susila and Gamini Gunawardane, Cricket Keating, and Saku Richardson for their friendship and assistance during fieldwork. Thanks also to the ISLE Program for providing me with a home for part of my stay, as well as to Bertram Tittawala for being a great landlord for the other part and for helping me locate Hansard Reports and other documents on the 200 Garment Factories Program. I also thank the staff at the Sarvodaya office in "Udakande" for allowing me to use their offices for occasional interviews.

My debts in the United States have been incurred at several institutions. This project began as a Ph.D. dissertation at the University of Chicago. My adviser, Arjun Appadurai, saw it through all the dissertation stages; and his influence has carried on through to this book, which represents a substantial revision of that material. My other three committee members were invaluable: Leora Auslander provided critical assistance throughout the years; Nadia Abu El-Haj was a fabulous late arrival who provided a new perspective that challenged me in productive directions; and the humor and insight of the late Bernard Cohn will never be forgotten. Other important assistance at Chicago came from Carol A. Breckenridge, Sheldon Pollock, Susanne Rudolph, and David Scott.

At Johns Hopkins University, my deepest thanks are owed to Veena Das for inviting me to join the Program for the Study of Women, Gender, and Sexuality as a Mellon Postdoctoral Fellow. For critical comments on earlier versions of chapters, I thank Veena as well as Aaron Goodfellow, Naveeda Khan, Ruby Lal, Gyan Pandey, Jennifer Robertson, Deniz Yükseker, and audiences at seminars where I presented my work.

Administrators, students, and colleagues at Olin College of Engineering have provided me with support that allowed me to finish this book. In particular, I thank Holly Bennett, Helen Donis-Keller, Rob Martello, Mike Moody, and Lynn Andrea Stein for help during the last stage of manuscript preparation. Lynn and Rob both read the entire manuscript at different critical junctures. Lynn, my "work buddy" during the summer of 2005, put her brilliance to work identifying problems and solutions. Rob, the smartest and funniest midnight email buddy one could want, sacrificed his own writing time for a detailed read of my manuscript. Students in my classes at Olin College and Wellesley College read most or all of the manuscript in 2005 and 2006. I thank them for being a test audience: I wrote this book with undergraduates in mind, and these students helped me identify what was needed. Several Olin students provided critical assistance: Sutee Dee provided valuable editing help; Sylvia Schwartz helped at the very end; and this book simply wouldn't have been completed without the humor, patience, insightful comments and queries, and hard work of Jerzy Wieczorek, who was my research assistant during the summer of 2005.

Other friends and colleagues who read versions of my work or provided other help that was needed for it to come together include Marc Boglioli, Cindy Caron, Joslyn Cassady, Jane Collins, Elizabeth Emma Ferry, Michele Gamburd, Rosanna Hertz, Alan Keenan, Steve Kemper, Jeanne Marecek, Dennis McGilvray, Janet McIntosh, Sonya Michel, Diane Mines, John Rogers, Kate Schechter, H. L. Seneviratne, Ajit Serasundera, Deborah Winslow, and Michael Woost. I am also grateful to discussants and audiences at various venues where I presented this work over the years. Seamus Walsh and Dennis McGilvray kindly gave me permission to publish their photographs. Critical assistance on book chapters in the summer of 2005 came from Eliza Kent and especially from Sarah Lamb, whose close reading of many chapters was just what I needed.

Sadly, among my teachers of Tamil and Sinhala, I must name several who have passed away since I met and learned from them. My Tamil teachers were the late Norman Cutler, the late A. K. Ramanujan, and James Lindholm. My Sinhala teachers included the late Kamini de Abrew, Visakha Dharmadasa, Jim Gair, John Paolillo, and Milan Rodrigo. I am grateful for the important help with my Sinhala translations that I received from Deepani Ambalangodage, Steve and Imali Berkwitz, Eardley Mendis, and the late Tamara Mendis (a victim of the December 2004 tsunami who is deeply mourned by many people). Thank you to Janak Ambalangodage who translated the three worker essays. Akila Weerapana at Wellesley College deserves special mention for generously helping with translations and transliterations in the summer of 2005 and in May 2006 (when he tolerated my last-minute schedule).

I gratefully acknowledge financial support from the National Science Foundation for a Dissertation Improvement Grant; the Fulbright Foundation for a Fulbright IIE Research Grant; the Committee on Southern Asian Studies at the University of Chicago; the Joint Committee on South Asia of the Social Science Research Council and the American Council of Learned Societies, with funds provided by the Ford Foundation and the Andrew W. Mellon Foundation; and the Woodrow Wilson National Fellowship Foundation, which awarded me a Woodrow Wilson Dissertation Grant in Women's Studies. I thank the Andrew W. Mellon Foundation for a Mellon Postdoctoral Fellowship at Johns Hopkins University. Important support at the very end came from the Research Fund of Olin College.

Portions of this book are revisions of previously published articles. The work has been substantially revised in light of comments I received from reviewers and editors during production and from colleagues after publication. Portions of chapter 1 appeared as "Good Girls or Juki Girls? Learning and Identity in Garment Factories," in a special issue of *Anthropology of Work Review* on "New Trends in the Culture of Work in Sri Lanka" in the spring of 1999. The introduction, chapter 2, and chapter 5 contain material first published in "The 'Good Girls' of Sri Lankan Modernity: Moral Orders of Nationalism and Capitalism," *Identities: Global Studies in Culture and Power* 6, 1 (1999). Sections of chapters 3 and 4 first appeared in "The Politics of White Women's Underwear in Sri Lanka's Open Economy," *Social Politics: International Studies in Gender, State, and Society* 9, 1 (2002). Earlier versions of my arguments in chapters 2, 3, and 4 appeared in "Economic Liberalization, Nationalism, and Women's Morality in Sri Lanka," in *Economy, Culture, and Civil*

War in Sri Lanka, edited by Deborah Winslow and Michael Woost (Bloomington: Indiana University Press, 2004).

Fran Benson at Cornell University Press has been a wonderful editor. In spite of knowing me for far too long, she sustained interest and then saw the project through to the end. I also am grateful for the comments from three anonymous reviewers whose vastly different reads helped me identify and address problems I had not seen. At the press, I also thank Cameron Cooper, Karen Laun, Carolyn Pouncy, and many others behind the scenes who guided this book through the publishing process. Other critical editorial help came from Will Elison, a friend from the University of Chicago. Among other important contributions to this book, Will first led me to H. L. Mencken.

My parents, Kathy and Frank Lynch, have never wavered in their encouragement of my unconventional pursuits—unconventional, that is, to a family of engineers. They must now breathe a sigh of relief that I teach at an engineering college! I also offer my thanks for many years of interest and assistance to my grandparents Esther McCann-Leopold and Carl Leopold and to my parents-in-law Joan and Hugh Collier. Nick Collier allowed himself to be uprooted from Chicago to accompany me to Sri Lanka. Since I began thinking about this project in 1992 he has had to suffer through my immersion in it, but he has always remained supportive, enthusiastic, and encouraging. I have benefited throughout from Nick's moral support, technical computer support, and critical comments. This book definitely would not exist without Nick's love. I dedicate this book to him and to our children Cormac and Nicola, who are the sweetest things imaginable. I hope they will someday read this book and understand why it's been so important to me.

I also dedicate this book to the workers at Shirtex and Serendib. This book is ultimately about their struggles, dreams, and victories. My wish for them is to achieve more of the second and third and to encounter fewer of the first.

INTRODUCTION

Kumari had one of the shortest commutes of all the workers at Shirtex and Serendib. Workers standing outside the Shirtex canteen had a clear view of Kumari's house and its neatly swept yard, where on most days her laundry or recently harvested peppercorns and cardamom seeds could be seen drying in the sun. A ten-foot-high chain-link fence separated her yard from the factory property, and when forced to work overtime Kumari could shout across to her mother that she would be home late. Kumari had grown up in the very house where she now lived with her mother and eight-year-old daughter. Her husband lived there a few months every two years, when he was between contracts in Saudi Arabia, where he worked as a driver.

On a Thursday morning in September 1995, Kumari awoke at 5:15 a.m. to the sound of her neighbor's roosters. After dressing, she lit the fire and cooked breakfast and lunch for her small family. Kumari's mother would bring her daughter to school an hour or so later. And so, with her rice and curry lunch, a bottle of boiled water, and a folded umbrella tucked into her bag, Kumari set off to work shortly after 6:30 a.m. Because of the fence that surrounded the factory complex, Kumari had to walk ten minutes to get to the entrance, soon joining a growing procession of coworkers. The narrow dirt road, already heating up from the morning sun, wound up and down gentle hills. Kumari's cohort passed paddy fields and threshing grounds; coconut and avocado trees; rose and bougainvillea bushes; and a dozen or so small homes, some of concrete with tile roofs, others of wattle and daub with palm thatch roofs. The factory entrance abutted a collection of buildings: an office for a rural development organization; a nursery school; and a *kadē*, one of the tiny ubiquitous shops that sold rice and flour and lentils, fresh fruits and vegetables (invariably bananas and onions), soaps, chocolate, and various household staples.

By the time Kumari reached the factory gates, a steady stream of workers was already filing through. The vast majority of the workers were women, who waited their turn to open their bags for inspection by the female guards on duty just inside. The male workers walked on the driveway side of the guardhouse and showed their lunch bags to the male guards, whose other task at that time of day was to open the gates for the managers as they arrived in cars or on motorcycles.

Thirty-seven years old and heavyset, Kumari was both older and larger than most of the other 350 Shirtex workers. Always jolly, and always loud, she stuck out from the crowd. Kumari greeted the guards, the managers, and her coworkers, making occasional jokes. She paused to pray at the Buddhist shrine to the side of the driveway and entered the Shirtex canteen where she placed her bag in a cupboard. She went into the production area from the back door, by the canteen and directly opposite her own house, where she could see her mother seated outside the front door brushing her daughter's hair. After punching her time card a few minutes before 7:00, Kumari set to work in the cutting room, where she had been employed for more than two years. She and a coworker on the opposite side of a wide table walked the length of the table in unison, positioning layer upon layer of fabric that they unrolled from a long bolt. After they placed each layer, another pair of workers would follow to smooth down the fabric with a metal rod. When dozens had been placed in this manner, another set of women would trace the pattern on paper lining the top layer, and then the male cutter would carve through the thick stack with the upright cutting machine to make the individual collars, sleeves, cuffs, and other components of what would be assembled into shirts.

It was in the midst of this routine that Kumari saw Samarakoon Sir, the assistant production manager, talking on the phone in the office.[1] The large glass window was meant to provide a quick view of the production area for managers located in the office. But it also provided the opposite view for the workers, and thus relayed information that could be put to good use. For instance, if the production managers were deep in conversation behind the glass, workers knew it was safe for them to talk for a moment.

It was unusual to see Samarakoon Sir on the telephone. As soon as he hung up, Kumari could see that he was crying. Samarakoon Sir promptly left the

JUKI GIRLS, GOOD GIRLS

factory instead of taking his place at a desk in the middle of the production floor. The news quickly spread through the factory that Samarakoon Sir's father had died early that morning, in the capital city of Colombo, a nearly four-hour journey from Udakande, the village where Shirtex and Serendib are located.[2] Kumari recalled when we spoke later that when she had seen Samarakoon Sir crying, she instantly remembered the pain she had felt only a year previously when her own father had died. Samarakoon Sir had come to her father's funeral. Kumari turned and told her cutting-room coworkers, who by now were gathered together, "I don't care who doesn't go, but I am going to Samarakoon Sir's father's funeral." Immediately the other cutting room workers said, "If *akka* [elder sister] is going, we are also going. Let's rent a bus."[3]

This plan swept through the factory quickly with the aid of Podi Menike, the sweeper. Podi Menike was one of the few illiterate workers at Shirtex, but because her job authorized her to move through every area of the factory, she was an informal courier of words, a messenger who transported news in either oral or written form. Throughout the day, workers from other sections began to approach Kumari when she was heading toward the bathroom, when she was sitting in the canteen, when she was trying to do her job in the cutting room. According to Kumari, because the cutting-room supervisor would send them away, the workers started to send secret notes. The notes, which arrived via Podi Menike and other mobile workers, all said the same thing: "*Akka*, we are also coming."

Kumari and three other women were always the ones to organize activities at Shirtex. Once again they joined together, and by noon the next day they had arranged for the entire factory to close on Saturday and for 190 workers, more than half the workforce, to make the journey to the *mala gedara* (funeral house). Kumari and most everyone else at Shirtex and Serendib were Sinhala Buddhists, among whom it is the custom for the deceased to lie in state at home for two to three days prior to cremation.[4] They rented four buses. Although the workers would bring their own rice packets for lunch, Shirtex management would provide a morning snack en route. The Shirtex managers, office workers, supervisors, and mechanics would join the convoy in the factory's air-conditioned van. After visiting the funeral house, the workers would make a visit to Kelaniya Temple, one of the country's holiest Buddhist sites. This would be an all-day trip: leaving early in the morning, they would return in the evening, perhaps even after dark.

This is how it happened that on Saturday morning at 7 a.m. I was standing at a corner by the lake in Sri Lanka's hill capital of Kandy. Despite the early hour, a fair amount of traffic occupied the streets of the crowded city. Eventually I saw four buses and a van turn the corner by the Dalada Maligawa, the Temple of the Sacred Tooth Relic, and proceed in my direction. On the first bus, painted on a white banner tied across the grille, large black letters proclaimed in Sinhala: "Kandy's Shirtex Corporation, with profound sorrow." In the upper right corner was a drawing of an eye, tears dripping to form the letters below. I boarded this first bus, which held Kumari and the rest of the cutting-room workers.

I had visited Shirtex and Serendib nearly every day for six months to conduct field research for my doctorate in anthropology. Despite the sorrowful circumstances, I had been eager for the trip to begin. There were several reasons for this. This was the first time I was traveling with so many workers at once and, given their excitement and enthusiasm, I thought it would be fun. I also was interested in seeing how a journey taken with managers and supervisors would differ from the numerous trips I had already taken with workers on their own. Moreover, I wanted to understand why the workers had been so determined to make this funeral trip. I had been quite surprised to hear of these plans because they seemed to complicate one of the themes emerging in my research at that time. Many workers did not like the harsh manner with which Samarakoon Sir enforced the hourly production targets. In fact, quite a few workers who had quit since my arrival told me that they did so because of the way either Samarakoon Sir or Yohan Sir, the production manager, had treated them. They would tell me this within a few minutes of our accidental meeting in the market in Kandy, on a bus, or on a village path. I knew what they meant, because I personally witnessed some of this ill treatment. At the extreme, the managers would shout crude comments at workers or throw damaged garments at them.

I had never heard of anyone expressing these concerns to management, although they were continually discussed in hushed tones within the factories or quite candidly elsewhere. Under these circumstances, why would so many workers—including some who had previously complained to me about Samarakoon Sir—plan to attend this funeral? What could this tell me about the relationship between "traditional" Sri Lankan social relations and factory production?[5] Could the trip help me understand how laborers negotiated and made sense of their different social roles in their villages—among relatives, neighbors, and friends—and in their workplace? Did the fact that most of these workers were women have anything to do with their efforts to go to the funeral? These are only some of the questions that preoccupied me over the course of the trip and continued to demand my attention as I wrote this book.

When I was doing field research in 1995 and 1996, Sri Lankans of diverse social positions—politicians, industrialists, laborers, students—were struggling to make sense of the social changes that accompanied economic shifts. In the postcolonial period, but especially since the economic liberalization of 1977, the country has undergone considerable change. Such changes do not simply settle on people. Rather, as subjects, people work to make sense of their new worlds and the accompanying shifts in priorities and values.[6] Often politicians, teachers, and professionals take it upon themselves to shape the way others in their society will understand change. But that does not mean that these world-making projects are always achieved in the ways in which the elites intend. Elite projects must be understood and made sense of by people in their daily lives and social worlds. One task of the anthropologist is to examine how subjects craft meaning; in the case under discussion, my task was to examine the meaning of life in different economic arrangements. Kumari and her coworkers drew me into their lives and allowed me to see their daily efforts to understand the world around them. I am grateful for their generosity, and I hope to convey the texture of their world in these pages.

Mala's Ambivalence

Kumari stood on the forefront of a new economic and social project in Sri Lanka. She was a villager who had found industrial employment without migrating to the capital city Colombo or its outskirts. When Shirtex and Serendib opened in 1992, Mala, a woman from a village close to Udakande, had been trying for several years to find a job that suited her educational qualifications and allowed her to stay with her family until she married.[7] Mala had taken her exams at the end of high school and received high marks. But, in a country offering too few openings for qualified students, she was not admitted into university. Just a few years earlier a youth revolt had paralyzed her village, surrounding towns, and much of the southern part of Sri Lanka. Mala and her family survived the revolt, but fellow villagers were killed or disappeared; during the revolt and the ensuing government crackdown everyone she knew lived in fear. Among other concerns, the rebels argued that the government paid insufficient attention to generating jobs for educated youth and that liberal economic strategies adopted since the late 1970s had benefited the urban, English-educated elite to the detriment of most others in Sri Lankan society. Mala did not speak English, hailed from a poor family that did not have access to powerful people, and despite her good exam results was still unable to find a job several years after completing high school.

Mala, like many Sri Lankans who read newspapers and watched television regularly, would have been well acquainted with a state project begun in early 1992 that founded garment factories throughout the country in response to the revolt. The 200 Garment Factories Program was a decidedly new economic strategy that reversed previous patterns of industrialization by bringing factories to villages. Mala would have heard that two factories were slated to open in her district, just a few villages away in Udakande. But she would have been ambivalent about seeking employment there. While some newspapers touted this new industrialization program as a panacea for rural unemployment and poverty, she had been reading reports for many years about how employment of young women in garment factories led to the disintegration of Sri Lankan society. Articles with titles such as "First to the Free Trade Zone, Second to Party Culture" exposed the ways in which young women not only were overworked, underpaid, and subjected to abuse at these factories but also began to adopt new modes of dress, speaking, and socializing that defied Sri Lankan expectations for women's behavior. Mala did not want to be exploited inside or outside the workplace and did not want to associate with women who did not share her moral values.

Even so, working in a factory in nearby Udakande was attractive to Mala. She would not need to leave her family, and the well-paid jobs offered benefits such as free breakfast and overtime pay. In factory opening-ceremony speeches that were widely publicized on television and radio and in newspapers, the president, industrialists, Buddhist monks, and ordinary people praised the program and asserted that it would bring important benefits to the nation. The program's champions explicitly articulated a vision in which economic development would be accompanied by cultural preservation. This vision would have comforted Mala, who was concerned about the ways in which men would take advantage of urban garment factory women and about how some women seemed to forget their values on becoming garment workers.

Thus, although she supported the opposition political party, Mala would have been tempted by some of the president's arguments about this program. Employment in these factories held the promise of a job and respect. These benefits could be attained in her village, where parents and fellow villagers ensured that morality prevailed. She would have read text from President Ranasinghe Premadasa's factory speeches such as this, quoted in a national newspaper:

> I thought I should first bring about a situation where the latent talents and skills of our poor village youth could be brought up to the surface for due recognition. That is why I planned to start factories in villages first. Now the high quality of work of our village youth has won acceptance even of foreign investors. Our village youth were treated with disdain for long. They were called good for-nothing "Kalakanniyas" (miserables). I wanted to rid the social psyche of this long-held misconcept. And I have succeeded in achieving this through the Two Hundred Garment Factories Program. . . . For our village youth, who had developed the moral and physicl [*sic*] strength to stand strain or stress and who are used to hardwork, garment manufacture is mere child's play. . . . We are discovering the richness of our poor and holding it out to the gaze of the entire world. You can feel proud that the government you braved terror to elect is doing this, for the first time. (A. S. Fernando 1993, n.p.)

Mala would have noted favorably how the president linked moral and physical discipline, activity, and work. It was obvious from this and other speeches that the president aimed to provide opportunities to villagers and involve them in the development process so they would not attempt another revolt. He tried to do this while also emphasizing the importance of moral and physical discipline for the nation. He argued that villagers' inherent knack for hard work was not only good for the nation but also conveniently aligned with capitalist discipline. As it turns out, the youth for whom "garment manufacture is mere child's play" were mostly women; employing women was consistent with nationalist and capitalist expectations about women's inherent discipline. Twenty-two-year-old Mala was the perfect candidate for one of these jobs. She cared about the nation's future, her excellent high school performance meant she had the requisite skills and discipline, she was ready to work hard, and she was poor. By the end of 1992 she had obtained a job as a sewing-machine operator at Shirtex, where she was poised to achieve her, and the president's, goals—or so she thought.

With the elaborate discourses that accompanied the 200 Garment Factories Program, President Premadasa offered a resolution to the dilemmas many Sri Lankans faced during this time when the state was implementing various economic liberalization policies.[8] Premadasa was careful to give liberalization a particular Sri Lankan spin—to make it meaningful to citizens who were concerned about neoimperialism. Although these concerns arise in new nations across the globe, they are always articulated in locally meaningful terms. Thus, although these pages tell a story about postcolonial struggles over globalization and neoliberalism, some aspects of the story are not generalizable because of important Sri Lankan particularities. That difference between the general and the particular is the material of everyday life that concerns anthropologists and fills the pages of this book.

The state's attempts to reconcile economic development and cultural preservation are important for understanding the experiences of Kumari, Mala, and their fellow workers. At the same time that these economic and cultural issues were being skillfully negotiated by the state, most Sri Lankans also tried to negotiate them in various ways. Premadasa's discourses had a direct effect on the workers at Shirtex and Serendib. Some of the managers took Premadasa's imperatives to heart and tried to model their factories on values like "the spirit of caring and sharing" that he invoked in his speeches. Furthermore, the discourses also affected how the workers made sense of their factory experiences, because they often embraced Premadasa's vision. His promises and dreams affected many of their own daily movements and decisions.

Thus there is a correlation between state priorities and investment programs, managerial strategies, and the experiences of laborers as they sit and sew collar seam after collar seam day after day. This book is an attempt to ensure that we see those Sri Lankans who are engaged daily with global production as creative agents in their own lives, not simply as pieces in some global Monopoly game played by capitalists and state representatives. I move back and forth between state policies and workers' arguments, and between managers requiring overtime and workers who need to get home to cook dinner. I do so in order to demonstrate the complex relationships among economic processes, cultural meanings, and the day-to-day struggles and triumphs of the workers in the global economy.

While I do not find it a stretch to move from Kumari and Mala to the Sri

Lankan nation, my move does require some explanation. I am relying on certain anthropological conceptions of "the everyday" and power, or of agency and structure. The hallmark of anthropological method—participant observation—yields minute details on individual experience, behavior, and meaning. However, the best anthropological analyses do not stop at the minutiae of daily life. The next step is to move from the individual to the contexts within which individuals live and make sense of their lives. In this book, I attempt to be constantly attentive to the political-economic structures within which individuals act on and understand their worlds. Anthropological contributions to debates about structure and agency have helped me conceptualize the importance of simultaneous attention to questions of political economy and to the voices of individuals such as Kumari and Mala. In concluding her ethnography on so-called mail-order marriages, the anthropologist Nicole Constable (2003, 225) describes the "ethnographic challenge" of situating people in historical and political context while also focusing on individual choices and feelings. Throughout this book, I endeavor to balance an analytic emphasis on power (to show how it circumscribes experiences) and on empowerment (to show how subjects are agents who live and make meaning of those experiences).

Women's Morality, Nation's Modernity

In Sri Lanka, post-independence political discourse, but especially post-liberalization discourse, has focused on how to reconcile modernity and morality, or economic gain and social obligation. Sri Lankans have been asking: "How can our country be economically strong and competitive but still follow its age-old traditions?" This common postcolonial question comes with a distinctly nationalistic edge for many contemporary Sinhala Buddhists in light of two perceived threats to the nation. A separatist movement by the Liberation Tigers of Tamil Eelam has threatened the integrity of the nation-state's borders since the early 1980s, and Westernization threatens the integrity of the nation's culture.

In the face of these twin threats, many Sinhala Buddhists consider women to be the agents who will hold the nation together. Women have been invested with such a responsibility because—as is the case in many societies throughout the world—they are imagined to be at the core of Sri Lanka's moral identity. Many Sinhala Buddhists are thus especially concerned about the social implications of women's central role in the liberalized economic arrangements. Garment workers have become a chief focus of societal concerns, and there is a definite stigma that attends to garment factory employment.

Garment workers in Sri Lanka are often stigmatized as "Juki girls" (*jukiyō* or *juki kello*), "Juki pieces" (*juki käli*), or "garment pieces" (*gäment baḍuwa*). The word "Juki" in these nicknames is derived from a Japanese industrial sewing-machine brand commonly used in Sri Lankan factories.[9] These are derogatory nicknames that originated in reference to women who work in factories in and around Colombo. Both the terms *juki käli* and *gäment baḍuwa* objectify the women in question by making them seem like nothing more than things or pieces of dry goods. As one newspaper editorial notes, the term *juki käli* indicates that these women "are treated like some expendable commodity" (*Daily Mirror* 2005, n.p.; cf. Hewamanne 2002, 7–8). The term *baḍuwa* has powerful sexual connotations, and all these nicknames connote sexual promiscuity.

The stigma of being a garment worker is so damaging and widespread that Sinhala newspaper marriage proposals sometimes disqualify garment workers with the phrase "no garment girls" or "no Juki girls" (Tambiah 1997). In the face of globalized economic and cultural processes, concerns about how women should behave are central to how Sri Lankans understand the effects of economic liberalization on their society. In many times and places, women have become symbols of the nation; the situation is no different in postcolonial Sri Lanka. In association with the symbolic elevation of women, daily practices have emerged to monitor and control female modesty and respectability as a measure of national status and prestige. The Juki-girl stigma must be understood in this national context.

Unlike urban garment workers, Kumari, Mala, and their village coworkers were not automatically stigmatized as Juki girls. In the face of the Juki stigma, Shirtex and Serendib women struggled daily to show everyone around them that they were "Good girls." Sinhala speakers use the English term or the Sinhala equivalent: *honda lamay* or *honda kello*. Good girls are respectable women who embody cultural expectations for women's behavior. And Good girls at Shirtex and Serendib were not only respectable women, they were also good industrial workers. Managers and workers alike used the term *Good girls* to refer to women who possessed good character and who were productive factory laborers (everyone expected that these categories would map onto each other). Managers and workers alike frowned on "bad girls," a characterization that, like its opposite, referred to both character and productivity. To refer to bad girls, Sinhala speakers used the term *naraka lamay* or the English terms *bad girls* or *naughty girls*. Just as often they would simply use the adjective *honda nä* ("not good") when describing a woman who was "bad."

In these pages, I discuss how and why people considered particular women to be Good girls or bad girls, and the ways in which Shirtex and Serendib women often evaluated urban Juki girls as straightforwardly bad. I repeatedly use the unadorned words *good* and *bad*, even when I consider the subtle and shifting meanings of various Sinhala Buddhist concepts that Good girls are expected to exhibit, such as *läjja-baya* (shame-fear, modesty, respectability) and *sanwara* (discipline, decency, control). These stark and straightforward terms are what Sri Lankans often use. They repeatedly referred to women as "good" or "bad," expecting others to infer all the subtleties packed into those terms—for example, "morally upright," "respectable," "upstanding," "proper," "productive," or "conforming to social norms." In this book, I mark off the term as *Good girls*, with a capital G. This idiosyncratic style choice flags the contingent nature of "good," a concept that connotes different meanings for different people but is consistently used in Sri Lanka without explanation.

This book is not a study of Juki girls per se. It is not a study of urban garment factories where all women workers are tarnished with the Juki-girl stigma. Rather, as an ethnographic study of village factories, this book offers insights into the far reaches of gender norms and expectations in the context of globalization—norms and expectations so strong that they had tangible effects on women who remained in their villages where parents, husbands, or other villagers were expected to watch over them. In mass-media representations, government speeches, and everyday conversations, many Sri Lankans look to pairs of oppositional concepts as they try to understand the social transformations they are encountering with the advent of economic liberalization. These oppositions include *Sri Lankan* and *foreign*, *tradition* and *modernity*, *East* and *West*, *us* and *them*, *rural* and *urban*, and, of course, *good* and *bad*. This book questions many of these dichotomies by interrogating them through the lens of anthropological and gender-studies theories. Attention to minute details of discursive representations *and* everyday life allows us to see how inequalities of class, caste, ethnicity, and gender disrupt and complicate these relations. It is clear that in daily practice people struggle to understand them in their complex, overlapping, and often contradictory aspects.

Field Research Design and Setting

This book is based on intensive qualitative fieldwork in Sri Lanka from 1995 to 1996: eighteen months of participant observation and interviews in and around Shirtex and Serendib; extended tours of other garment factories throughout the island; and interviews with politicians, industry leaders, and journalists. My project also relies on a decade (1996–2006) of analysis of fieldwork data, secondary sources, and developments in the status of garment workers and the 200 Garment Factories Program, as well as ongoing correspondence with close contacts in Sri Lanka.

The factories I call Shirtex and Serendib shared the same complex and were located in the small village of Udakande, five miles outside the town of Kandy in the center of Sri Lanka. Shirtex was owned by a Sinhala Buddhist investor and produced dress shirts. During my field research period, Shirtex employed 350 workers. Management was entirely Sinhala Buddhist and male, and half the supervisors were male and half were female. Serendib, also owned by a Sinhala Buddhist, produced women's knitwear and unisex T-shirts and sportswear, and during my field research it employed 600 workers. While the management was also entirely male, and primarily Sinhala Buddhist, the supervisors were all female.

The owners, managers, and workers in both factories were all Sri Lankan, and of these thousand people, only ten or so were not Sinhala (there were Muslims and Christians and one Tamil). Thus the arguments I make in this book pertain to Sinhalas, and particularly to Sinhala Buddhists. I am confident that my analysis of the experiences of the many people involved in these factories would be different if they employed significantly more members of minority ethnic groups, such as Tamils or Muslims, or if the factories were owned or managed by foreigners.

Ninety percent of the workers at both factories were women ranging in age from eighteen to thirty-six, both married and unmarried. The people I refer to as workers were the production workers: sewing- and cutting-machine operators, quality checkers, ironers, mechanics, and so forth. They were clearly differentiated from staff members (office staff and supervisors) and managers. These women most often referred to themselves and were referred to by supervisors and managers as *lamay*, literally "children," but perhaps best translated as "girls."[10] When managers referred to the "workers" in English they would usually refer to them as "the girls." The majority—about 80 percent—were eighteen- to twenty-four-year-old single women.

Most workers lived with their families in Udakande and surrounding villages. Most came to the factories by foot—some walked more than an hour each way on paths that wound through paddy fields and spice gardens. Others combined walking with travel by bus or train. A large portion of Serendib workers lived farther off, because Serendib had previously been located in another village about one-and-a-half hours away by bus. These commuters traveled by bus or train, some for more than two hours each way. A few Serendib workers rented rooms from families in Udakande to avoid the long trip.

I went to the complex almost daily to speak with and observe workers, supervisors, and managers as they worked and during their breaks. I spoke to the owners and foreign buyers who visited. I also participated in simple production activities like buttoning shirts, checking garments for damage, numbering cut components prior to sewing, and attaching price tags. My activities were essentially unconstrained by management, and I spent a lot of time sharing work benches with women, talking as they worked. Some days I spent all my time at one factory or even in one work section; on other days, I alternated between canteens to the rhythm of the two firms' staggered breaks—morning tea, lunch, and afternoon tea.

My conversations with workers were in Sinhala (plus smatterings of Tamil or English); conversations with management were often in English. I also taught English to a group of Shirtex workers in the canteen, and I sewed (or attempted to sew) full-time for one week in the production lines at Serendib. My field research was centered on the factories, but I also socialized with and interviewed workers, their families and friends, other villagers, and managers on holidays. I went with workers and managers on their shopping trips; to rugby games and cricket matches; to weddings, temples, parties, and funerals; to their homes for informal visits; and—along with Athulya Meddagama, my main research assistant—for formal interviews. Factory- and village-based ethnographic research was complemented with archival work on the garment industry and on the economic and social policies that led to the factories' creation. I also conducted interviews with government and industry officials as well as industrialists; and I visited numerous factories in Colombo, the Katunayake Free Trade Zone, and villages throughout the country.

A significant portion of this research consisted of informal interviews and conversations too numerous to count. I routinely observed and spoke to the workers, staff, and management at both factories; and I frequently met and conversed with local villagers as well as workers and their families and friends outside the workplace. Of the approximately one thousand factory workers at both factories, I probably spoke to close to nine hundred and sustained on-going conversations with two hundred. I conducted formal tape-recorded interviews with forty-nine individuals. These people included former or current workers, supervisors, and managers; villagers who did not work in the facto-ries (including local politicians as well as parents, siblings, and boyfriends of workers); national government officials; and local and foreign investors in the 200 Garment Factories Program. I also distributed a questionnaire to all the workers at both factories at the beginning of my field research, and I con-ducted approximately ten formal non-recorded interviews with management, local investors, and one foreign investor. I employed one primary research as-sistant and numerous other aides.

The owners who allowed me into their factories were more generous than I had anticipated. In contrast with the workers' situation, I was allowed re-markably free reign in the factories. Although Yohan Sir, the Shirtex produc-tion manager, would occasionally ask me to stop talking to a particular worker if he perceived a problem with her production, I was otherwise never con-strained by management. Some workers no doubt regarded me with suspi-cion because of the power differences that were evoked by the fact that I am a white, American woman; a few thought I was nothing more than the factory photographer. Nonetheless, I enjoyed a certain degree of popularity, in large part because a visit from me meant being allowed to have a conversation while working (hence the production manager's concerns). Often, after entering the production area at Serendib early in the morning, I would pause for a mo-ment. Soon I would hear my name from various corners of the factory—people who were eager to have a chat were summoning me to their worksta-tions.

I began my field research at Shirtex and developed strong bonds with many workers there, especially with Kumari and her coworkers in the cutting sec-tion. A gesture from the section soon after my arrival cemented these bonds. In my first weeks of field research I wandered both factories carrying in my hand a handkerchief (for wiping my continual sweat), a pen, and a small note-book. On my birthday, the Shirtex cutting-room workers presented me with a gift. It was wrapped in brown paper that had once been a shopping bag and was decorated with roses fashioned from scraps of the same cotton fabric that was being transformed into men's dress shirts on the production floor. Inscribed in Sinhala and English on the brown wrapper were the words "Happy birthday to you from your loving cutting section." This package contained a small black imitation leather purse in which I carried my ethnographer's toolkit from that day on.

One might say in a cursory way that the "loving cutting section" bought my affection. But that would be a simplistic analysis. The factory workers had certain interests in befriending me, as I did in befriending them. Thus the gifting incident and my own position in the factories raise questions of the dynamics of power and subjectivity in anthropological research (Behar 2003; Clifford and Marcus 1986; Rosaldo 1989; M. Wolf 1992). As a feminist anthropologist, I was attentive to the myriad power dynamics within the factories between workers and supervisors, workers and managers, and between myself and all of them. I have no pretence of objectivity—who I am and who I was perceived to be affected what I saw and have influenced my analysis. I have been careful to be aware of my positionality but to balance this awareness with conscientious data gathering and analysis, as well as attention to the perspectives different people bring to bear on the topic. My own positionality shows through in the emphasis I have placed on how women struggle to be perceived as Good girls despite the Juki stigma. The garment workers whom I spoke to the most often told me how good they perceived me to be. They would often cite my long braided hair, "modest" clothing style, and the presence of my husband in Sri Lanka, contrasting these indicators with their perceptions of foreign tourist women they would see in Sri Lanka. Their perception of my moral probity influenced conversations we had about their own struggles to be considered good.

Serendipity and the Resident Anthropologist

In a Persian fairy tale called *The Three Princes of Serendip* (also spelled "Serendib"), which uses one of Sri Lanka's precolonial names in its title, the princes make fortunate discoveries by accident. The English word *serendipity*, denoting the state of affairs that produces such discoveries, originated with this tale. My own route to this project consisted of many serendipitous events.

I arrived at Shirtex and Serendib in 1995 as a graduate student at the University of Chicago, but I had been preparing for this research for years. I trace its roots to my experiences growing up near New Bedford and Fall River in Massachusetts. Starting in the early nineteenth century, these had been important mill towns. During my childhood in the 1970s, the once-flourishing local textile and garment industry was struggling to compete with cheaper labor costs in the U.S. South. This was the period when most of the industry was moving to the southern states, prior to the next move, relocation abroad—to the sort of situation I encountered in Sri Lanka in the mid-1990s, when Sri Lankan women were producing clothing for export to the United States, Europe, and Japan (Collins 2003; Rivoli 2005). Back in the 1970s my mother did a lot of sewing; she made clothing or toys for our own family and for community fundraisers. I still remember the "designer" outfits on my Barbie dolls. The best place to get inexpensive sewing supplies was in the New Bedford and Fall River factories. We would walk through the production area, past women laboring in the steamy, high-ceilinged rooms, our feet clicking on the rickety wooden floors, as we headed to the area where extra materials and overproduced or damaged items were sold. My sister and I would play hide-and-seek among the stacks of fabric and notions as my mother made her purchases. Obviously my mother's sewing and the sewing of women at the Fall River mills and at Shirtex and Serendib are vastly divergent forms of productive labor. Even so, when I walked among the production lines as an anthropologist, I was continually reminded about how women's sewing spoke to me from my past.

The next important step toward my arrival at Shirtex and Serendib came when I was in college in the 1980s. When it came time to register for second-year classes, I decided to take an anthropology course called "Peoples and Societies of South Asia." My father had been a U.S. Army officer in the Vietnam War when I was an infant. I wanted to learn more about Vietnam, to augment the war-centered information I had learned from my father and in high school. The first thing I learned in that class was that South Asia was *not* Southeast Asia! I still remember the perplexed one-word query that ran through my head as the professor unrolled the map that hung from above the chalkboard: "India?" The professor (Steven Kemper, who specializes in the anthropology of Sri Lanka) asked us to guess the annual per capita income of India. This was 1986. Before going to college, and instead of finishing high school, I had spent a year working as a bookkeeper in a restaurant, where I earned $18,000. I reasoned that if a U.S. teenager without a high-school diploma could earn that kind of money, then adults in India would at least earn the same. When the answer turned out to be $300, I was simply confounded. How could people survive on so little money? How different must our lives, our societies, and our economies be? I decided to stick with the class, Vietnam's absence from the syllabus notwithstanding. The following year I went to Sri Lanka on a semester abroad program, and soon after that I found myself in graduate school studying Sinhala and Tamil and preparing for my dissertation research.

My interest in the 200 Garment Factories Program was less random, but the immediate impulse also contained an element of serendipity—a rural traffic jam, of sorts. Since my first trip to Sri Lanka, I had been interested in questions of women, work, and economic and social change. I began to formulate this research project in September 1992 when I was on a bus tour of a desolate area that was the site of a state-sponsored irrigation and colonization program called the Accelerated Mahaweli Development Scheme. Our bus had to stop when hundreds of women factory workers began to stream out of the gates of a newly established village factory. In this sparse, deserted, and dry area this factory seemed incongruous: a shiny, newly built structure on lush, landscaped grounds, separated from the community by a wall topped with shards of glass. I wondered if what I perceived as incongruous would have struck Sri Lankans in the same way. What did they think of these factories located in remote areas? And why were the factories located there anyway? Who were those women, why were they working there, and what was the work like?

I was not sure how to obtain permission to conduct ethnographic research in the factories; I realized that owners and managers were often concerned that researchers were trying to expose labor violations, and so I feared that they would not give me access unless they considered me legitimate in some formal sense. When I arrived for my field research in early 1995, I went first to the government official in charge of the 200 Garment Factories Program to explain my interests and request assistance in obtaining access to a factory. The official phoned the owner of Shirtex and asked if I could study his factory. A week later I found myself taking a tour with the personnel manager. I was allowed to wander alone inside the factory even on that first day to talk to workers, who wanted to know as much about me as I did about them.

A few days later I met the owner of Serendib, and I began my research there as well. After work on that first day at Serendib, I went with hundreds of workers to a nearby Buddhist temple to participate in a *bodhipūja* for the benefit of the factory manager's daughter, a three-year-old whose entire body from neck down had mysteriously become paralyzed (she was eventually healed).[11] During those days at Serendib, two of the assembly lines were producing flowered-print dresses. In preparation for the *bodhipūja*, workers used leftover cloth from these lines to sew mats that resembled multicolored lotus flowers and would be placed on the temple's altar. They also cut triangular flags to hang on the bodhi tree. The flowered flags would be conspicuously vibrant among the faded monochrome flags that already hung from the tree.

And so my field research began.

ROHINI

Young Women and Garment Life

First, I would like to give you a brief description about our village. Our village is beautifully placed between the Asgiriya hill range and the Hanthana hill range. The village we live in is full of fertile land with trees full of fruits, lakes, hills, and a river going through the village.

For a couple that is enjoying a modest but happy life in such a village, adding a child to their nest is a joyful thing.

Nevertheless, for them life is a struggle. They have to do hard physical labor as day laborers to earn their daily bread. Their main objective is to keep the child out of hunger. They are not concerned with the nutritional value of the food they provide.

Children grow up malnourished because the parents are just managing to keep them from going hungry. This hinders the physical and mental development of the child. When children in such families start to attend school, it is obvious that they are mentally not ready for the educational challenges they have to face. Their powers of comprehension are very low, due to malnutrition. You cannot blame the children for problems beyond their control.

Should the poor people be allowed to suffer this way?

We, as children who had to go through this social, economic and class struggle, and all other difficulties in our society and country, understand the enormous suffering our parents undergo.

In order to bring down the tension and stress amongst the educated unemployed youth, former Sri Lankan President Honorable R. Pre-

madasa initiated a project to build two hundred garment factories in Sri Lanka. However, some employers and managers are exploiting the unemployed youth to their benefit.

Some of the youth who work at garment factories are trying their best to help their parents' economic struggle. We are working in garment factories to help our siblings continue their studies. It is unimaginable to think of the unfair treatment we receive at the hands of some of our employers. They could make you feel so negative about yourself by scolding you or punishing you with a salary cut.

If we do not want to go through what most of us endure at these torture houses, we have to stay home. But God, how can we do that when we realize so many loved ones are dependent on us? We all are going through this mental agony of deciding which way we should move.

I hope none of my helpless sisters [women like me] will face this kind of agony and these hardships in the future. May happiness reign in their hearts.

1. GLOBALIZATION, GENDER, AND LABOR

Within a few weeks of my arrival at Shirtex and Serendib, I distributed an informal questionnaire to the workers. The final query was simply "additional information for me to know about you or the factory." On one returned questionnaire, in tiny, neat Sinhala letters, jammed into the allotted space, I found the following response:

> A lot of people in society think garment factories are places without any culture [*sanskrutiya*]. Because I also thought that, at first I did not like coming here. But it was only after coming inside the factory that I could see the skills of the valuable women who work here. That cannot be seen by the outside world since it is enclosed within the four walls. But when we come to work amidst society we are subjected to the insults of young people just like us. It would be a great resource if there arose in the world a movement that would be able to properly direct the cross-eyed way society looks at the valuable services of valuable male and female workers. Can a person's character [*caritaya*] be concluded from a job?

The author was Mala, whom I had spoken with but had not yet known by name. Although I didn't understand its full implications when I first read it, I remember being very excited about her response. This was a dream for me: here was a worker I had barely met volunteering this insight in a questionnaire at the start of my field research! From that day on, visiting Mala at her sewing machine became an important part of my daily rounds at Shirtex. On Sinhala

New Year a few weeks later, I visited her and her family in their home in a nearby village. A few months later, she was the first of many workers I formally interviewed, and over time Mala became a close friend and valuable research contact. Her provocative and moving questionnaire response altered the course of my research. Mala's short essay that is reproduced in this book is a brief articulation of her insight and concerns.

When I first read Mala's response, I did not know what it meant. Why was Mala writing about "character"? Why "culture"? And what "insults" did she mean? She was referring to the Juki-girl stigma, which tarnishes many female garment workers with a reputation for engaging in what is considered inappropriate moral behavior (the concern centers on sexuality, from premarital or extramarital sex to, at the extreme, prostitution). In her questionnaire response she referred to societal concerns about garment workers that center on how Sinhala Buddhist women should behave. Contemporary Sri Lankans live complicated lives in which they often weigh what it means to be a moral person—in local terms, to be "good" (*honday*). They map those evaluations onto attributes they dichotomize as either authentically Sri Lankan or foreign. They also often map them onto gender norms and expectations. These sometimes ambivalent, sometimes straightforward moral evaluations, which look significantly different for Sinhala Buddhists than they do for other Sri Lankans, are historically situated in the postcolonial Sri Lankan political economy.

This chapter provides conceptual tools for understanding the lives of women such as Mala. I describe the larger issues about gender, globalization, and labor that this book engages: the relationship between globalization and localization; how global production is localized; the work of producing meaning in the labor process; the centrality of gender to struggles over modernity and globalization; and the relationship between gender and the reconfiguration of sociality by globalization. I ask why it is that as nation-states become increasingly involved in the global economy, nationalists often debate the cultural effects of economic shifts. And why is gender so often deployed in these debates? I then go on to address whether or not self-fashioning always involves "resistance," and I explore the relationship between agency and resistance.

Moving closer to real people's lives in the second half of the chapter, I focus on the "work" of producing meaning and identities at Shirtex and Serendib. I return to analyze the funeral trip that Kumari organized. Careful attention to these Shirtex women's motivations to attend the funeral allows me to discuss how to move beyond questions of Third World factory laborers as simply vic-

JUKI GIRLS, GOOD GIRLS

tims or agents. I then propose the framework of *learning* as a means for us to appreciate the complicated work of subject production in which these women were engaged in their daily lives inside and outside the factories.

Globalization and Localization

Sri Lanka is one of many postcolonial and Third World societies that adopted economic liberalization policies in the mid- to late twentieth century. Sri Lanka's economy was liberalized in 1977, and the following year a predominantly female workforce was hired in the nation's first Free Trade Zone. Other scholars have argued that in postcolonial nations the dominant response to economic and cultural globalization is often cultural fundamentalism: local people conceive of the entry into their nation of foreign goods, people, ideas, and commodities as a threat to revered cultural traditions. The struggle in Sri Lanka has been not simply between the foreign and the local, but between a foreign and a local constructed in terms of gender and sexuality.

Economic and cultural interests are tightly interwoven and mutually constitutive, but as subjects act on and make sense of their worlds, they often cannot reconcile these interests and instead experience them as deeply contradictory. Sri Lankan debates over globalization and gender emerge from tensions that result when two models for proper living come into conflict. The situation of women garment workers is one of many cases in post-liberalization Sri Lanka in which one set of rules or values (proper gender roles) comes into conflict with another (economic gain) (Dickey 2003). Societal concern about garment workers is focused on women's entry into *globalized* economic processes, where new global economic and cultural forms overtly challenge women's symbolic role as carriers of national tradition.

Globalization involves the transnational movement of people, images, goods, information and ideas, and labor. Although there has been transnational movement for a very long time (for instance, with the eighteenth-century slave trade or the even older spice trade), I join others who argue that there are important distinctive features of the current era of globalization, which began in the 1970s and 1980s with the liberalization of Third World economies enacted through the International Monetary Fund's structural adjustment programs. The period of economic liberalization begun in the 1970s inaugurated changes that still unevenly affect people throughout the world. Compared with past transnational movement, the current era is characterized by the following key features: increasing speed and volume of movement (e.g., the near-instantaneous exchange of information across multiple time zones through email); more permeable national borders; and people's sense of shrinking space ("the world is getting smaller"), which is accompanied by their increasing reflexivity about what it means to live in a globalized world (Waters 2001; cf. Beynon and Dunkerley 2000, 5–6). A central question that anthropologists consider is whether globalization has led to cultural homogenization. Is cultural diversity under threat of erasure because we inhabit an era of global "Coca-colonization" (Hannerz 1992, 217)? For many people, especially in postcolonial nations, "Coca-colonization" is a deeply felt and historically situated fear. In such a vision there is "a recolonization of the non-Western world by fetishized Western goods carrying with them hugely invasive connotations of Western success and affluence" (Beynon and Dunkerley 2000, 23).

All these characteristics are features of post-liberalization globalization in Sri Lanka. Since the 1977 economic reforms, there has emerged a deep-seated fear of neocolonialism in response to a huge increase in the amount of foreign trade the country participates in and in the speed and volume of movement of people, things, and ideas into and away from the island. Sri Lankans perceive the world as getting smaller—many have relatives abroad and speak about the world as being readily at hand to those given the right opportunities. Borders are permeable, both in terms of the movement of people and finances (tourists, development workers, foreign investors, and funding to the Liberation Tigers of Tamil Eelam flow in; refugees, housemaids, and elite college-aged students flow out) and in terms of the entry of goods and images that did not exist in Sri Lanka prior to the economic reforms (e.g., Pepsi, Kentucky Fried Chicken, U.S. and Australian television programs). Finally, Sri Lankans are deeply reflexive about what it means to live in a globalized world: that is precisely what is at stake in the debates over how to engage in economic development without sacrificing cultural distinctiveness.

In this book, I not only describe processes of globalization in Sri Lanka, but I also analyze the politics of these processes. Social transformations that have occurred in Sri Lanka since the liberal economic reforms reveal processes much more complicated than the simple erasure of Sri Lankan culture in the face of globalization. In regard to the 200 Garment Factories Program (henceforth, "the 200 GFP," per local usage), I describe these processes in terms of the *localization of production*. I also analyze the politics of Sri Lankan concerns about cultural homogenization and neocolonialism. Within Sri

Lanka, who is raising the alarm about cultural homogenization, what are their interests, and what precisely do they identify as modes of cultural homogenization and neocolonialism? By understanding the politics of these responses to globalization, we can also understand the ways in which specific Sri Lankans localize production. We thus can appreciate that all Sri Lankans do not experience and understand globalization in the same way.

Rather than assume that globalization in Sri Lanka means cultural homogenization, I join other anthropologists who examine how global consumer culture and economic structures interact with local cultures and economies. For while it is true that national and local cultural identities are influenced by global culture, they are not completely reconstituted. Furthermore, there are numerous ways in which global processes are changed by local processes. Coca-Cola and Sony use the term *global localization* to describe marketing strategies in which they embed their products in local cultures and promote them in locally meaningful ways (Beynon and Dunkerley 2000, 20). "Localization" could serve as a helpful concept for understanding specific cultural responses to globalization, but it is necessary to identify the angles from which I approach this multifaceted phenomenon. The term *localization* here means both how local people make something locally meaningful out of the global, and in so doing often change the global, and how nonlocals embed their global processes and products in local culture.

Thus, in these pages I examine the localization of global production. There are marked similarities in certain aspects of garment production in sites throughout the world. For instance, in the Sri Lankan industry, as in other countries, there is a priority on "greenfields practices"—factory management's continual efforts to find fresh, inexperienced labor (Collins 2003, 13). The search for cheaper labor is also an important push factor. These practices in part account for the movement of industrial production across the world. Many similarities are only surface deep, however. Close contextual analysis allows one to dig below the surface to see the profound differences in meaning of the local forms of global practices and processes.

Localization of Production

The detailed 200 GFP rules issued by President Premadasa mandated a majority female workforce: outside of the staff and managerial workforce, each factory was to employ 450 women and 50 men. (A similar ratio also characterized the non–200 GFP garment factories on the island.) Based on data from different times and places, scholars have noted that assumptions about women's "nimble fingers" have contributed to the global feminization of industrial labor practices (Elson and Pearson 1981; Fuentes and Ehrenreich 1983; Mills 2003; Ong 1987, 1991; Wright 2001).[1] Industrialists and managers alike assume that women have more nimble fingers than men and thus are more suited to factory production than men. On the face of it, attributing nimble fingers to women implies that they are dexterous and thus physically suited to manipulating small things on the production line. However, the concept of nimble fingers is often accompanied by two other important assumptions: that compared to men, women are more patient (and thus can tolerate monotonous jobs) and more obedient (and thus easier to manage and control).

Sri Lankan industrialists and managers share these assumptions about women and men with their counterparts around the world. In conversations with me they invoked all three of these concepts (nimble fingers, patience, and obedience). For instance, when I asked one investor why he employs mostly women, he simply held up his hand, wiggled his fingers, and said, "These." After further questioning, he explained that women were more dexterous than men. One manager explained to me in an interview in English that men's aggressiveness suited them better for other trades, such as food manufacturing:

> Men can't concentrate on a small job. Because . . . they are aggressive. They want to do it and finish it fast. They want to do it quickly and they might damage the garment. But girls are not like that. They want to concentrate very carefully. . . . Even in the ironing, if you give some shirts to girls to iron they will do it neatly, nicely. . . . The garment factory is not only speed-oriented. Quality is very important. . . . Because everybody wants to wear a neat garment, a nice-looking garment. Right? But if you have a food manufacturing trade, sometimes the boys may be better . . . like if you have to pound something. You can just keep on pounding faster and faster.

The most common explanations given to me for employing women over men were that men were too difficult to control, troublesome, and likely to strike. As one investor succinctly noted, "Men are SOBs." Some investors and managers contended that men *could* sew and would be better to employ because they could travel after dark. Sri Lankans often assume that forced or consensual sexual activity usually happens when it is dark outside; concern about sexual activity centers on women and not men. However, these same people then argued that this advantage was overshadowed by the difficulties of disciplining aggressive men for garment labor.

On the surface, these managers and industrialists seem to be owning to the very same assumptions about gender that have contributed to the feminization of labor across the globe. However, the government's ongoing war with the Liberation Tigers of Tamil Eelam (LTTE) provides a key context for the Sri Lankan employment of women in the garment industry. A significant reason that the garment industry in the 1990s was targeted toward women employees was because the government needed men to enlist to fight in the war (there is no military draft). Many workers understood that because garment revenues are a major source of foreign exchange for the state, and because the war is a major expense, garment revenues are used by the state to fight the war. By this reasoning, many garment workers claimed that they were doing a service to the country by working in the 200 GFP factories. Explaining the importance of earning foreign exchange, they proudly compared their national service to that of their boyfriends, husbands, and brothers who were in the army. It was Sinhala Buddhists who made these claims; how Tamil or other minority women experienced this involvement in this state development program remains an important question.

The Sinhala expression *gäni juki, pirimi tuwakku* sums it up: "Juki for women, guns for men." I heard this point, in different words ("women work in garment factories, men work in the army"), numerous times during my field research from people in all strata of Sri Lankan society (cf. Abeysekera 2005). Since the war began in 1983, the military has provided large numbers of young Sri Lankan men with employment, and poverty has often been a push factor in their motivation to enlist (Gamburd 2004). Therefore, when we see industrialists and managers speaking of women and wiggling their fingers, we must understand that the capitalist need for cheap and docile women laborers coincides with the nationalist need for aggressive army men. Admittedly, both employment fields require workers to be disciplined; but there seems to be a sense in which aggression—albeit controlled aggression, directed toward the enemy—is compatible with army discipline, whereas factory owners clearly told me that there is no place for aggression on the factory floor.

Labor practices in factories across the world exhibit similarities—but even these similarities are only surface deep. One could stand in a factory in Colombo one day and in Istanbul the next and experience an uncanny similarity. Managers in both locales might use the same techniques of scientific management.[2] For instance, at any one moment managers in both cities might be timing workers with stopwatches to corroborate hourly production target rates. In both places, the production may be organized in the same way—according to the progressive bundle system, for example (Collins 2003, 31).[3] Both factories might even be producing the same style of Liz Claiborne jeans or Gap tank tops, sewn from fabric of identical color and design. But there would also be something very different about the two factories, and it is the difference that interests me. Do the jobs mean different things for the workers in both places? What do the workers do with their wages? Would workers in Turkey bring a manager a gift when the manager marries, as they sometimes do in Sri Lanka? Would the Turkish workers attend the funeral of a manager's father, as workers insisted they be allowed to do at Shirtex?

The end goal is the same for investors and managers throughout the world: they all want to ship the order on time and at minimal expense. But what are the means through which production is realized in specific locales? In her study of "localization strategies" and the globalization of the garment industry, the anthropologist Jane Collins (2003, 151) explains why it is that production is localized wherever it occurs: "Wherever workers enter into production, they bring with them their needs for subsistence, the needs of their families, their commitments to other activities outside the workplace, and their ideas of what is right and fair. Because of this, in every site where production touches down, it is instantiated differently. It must work through local institutions and establish the necessary web of social relationships to get the job done." Such a formulation highlights the ways in which local subjects at local sites influence global processes. But not only are global economic forms invested with local meaning and incorporated into local cultural practices, they also transform local social relations.

Collins uses the term *localization strategies* to discuss the strategies that apparel firms use to work in local sites. I would modify this concept to deemphasize the "strategic" aspect; global forms are not always "strategically" incorporated into local sites. Responses to globalization are often more subtle and naturalized than strategic. I would also add here the importance of considering how the needs of managers, investors, and state representatives interact to influence the particular forms of production seen scattered across the globe. What were the specifically Sri Lankan social relationships that were established and negotiated in Shirtex and Serendib? How did the grand aims of the 200 GFP affect the day-to-day operations of the factories? Of particular interest to me are the nuances of how state discourses, managerial strategies, and workers' experiences reflected and engaged with local ambivalences and struggles over globalization.

Sri Lankan discussions of globalization often came down to how to preserve what was distinctly Sri Lankan in the face of foreign influences. The anthropologist Lisa Rofel (1999, 18) has argued that modernity "is a struggle that takes place in specific locations and a process that knits together local/global configurations." The discussions that occurred around the 200 GFP reveal various ways in which Sri Lankans were struggling to bring together their understandings of local distinctiveness and global involvement, and in so doing to fashion a distinctively Sri Lankan way of being. It is helpful also to think of the 200 GFP as a "scale-making" project. The anthropologist Anna Tsing (2000; 2002, 472) describes scale-making projects as "relatively coherent bundles of ideas and practices as realized in particular times and places" that "maintain a commitment to localization." The 200 GFP was remarkable in its commitment to a vision of the world that incorporated global and local vantage points at the same time. As is often the case when local subjects make sense of global processes, the creators and proponents of the 200 GFP articulated the program in terms of being simultaneously modern and traditional.[4]

To analyze the local impact of global forms, I consider how subjects who are "forced" to deal with globalization often try to preserve local distinctiveness. Variously situated subjects experience multiple levels of coercion: by the International Monetary Fund, by their economic position in the world, by their president, by their desire to get tax concessions from the government, by their poverty, by their husbands, by their desires for consumer items. In their attempts at preserving locality, subjects invoke discourses of national distinctiveness and purity that reach beyond themselves, but they also engage daily in small but significant practices that have the effect of constituting and maintaining their own persons as modern subjects. I inquire into the nuances of such work for Sri Lankans involved in diverse ways with the global garment industry by examining the production of subjectivity in the context of everyday interactions with such globalized forms as industrial modes of production, scientific management, consumer products, and mass-media images. Here I follow Michel de Certeau (1984), for whom examining the "everyday" involves analyzing how small and mundane practices are smuggled into larger structures of power as subjects create worlds of meaning for themselves. This work of self-fashioning can be seen in the myriad ways in which workers made something of their own out of the repetitive and anonymous labor process of a garment production line. It is also evident in the efforts of government officials, investors, managers, and machine operators to bring together in meaningful ways different kinds of social relations from those expected in "traditional" forms of Sri Lankan life and in the daily operations of capitalist factories. This work of producing meaning and identities was done amid intense ambivalence about Sri Lanka's increasing involvement in global flows of capital; identity building attempted to resolve, or at least ease, this ambivalence.

Two different kinds of *work* are relevant to this study. Against the backdrop of the work of producing garments for export, I concentrate on the work of producing meaning and identities—and this includes the meaning that is brought to the labor process and to the processes of globalization. Especially in postcolonial nation-states concerned about neoimperialism, the advent of globalization can be met with suspicion. People in localities challenged by the encounter with global forms often struggle to make sense of them in terms of their own subject positions at the national level—that is, as citizens of a distinctive nation-state. Modern subjectivity integrates this compulsion of subjects to fashion themselves in relation to different frames—as men and women, as citizens, as laborers and so on—toward different ends.

Gender and Globalization

Ever since the economy was liberalized in 1977, Sri Lankans have debated a perceived tension between economic globalization and cultural preservation. In the face of new economic arrangements and the accompanying reconfiguration of sociality, foremost in the minds of many Sri Lankans is the question of what it means to be "good." The answer is different for women and men, and here the definition of proper Sinhala Buddhist femininity has emerged as a major focus of these debates. If gender is a primary category of analysis in this book, that is in part because ideologies of gender played a central role in the 200 Garment Factories Program.

Initially the 200 GFP interested me because of the complicated negotiations in which it involved the state, its supporters, and factory laborers in attempting to achieve the simultaneous goals of economic development and

JUKI GIRLS, GOOD GIRLS

cultural preservation. Under the program, the Sri Lankan state tried to harness not only the productive activities but also the consumer practices of villagers in the service of the state. The state expected that through their involvement in global capitalist industry, the new worker-citizens would become fully committed to the government in power and thus to the status quo. Within this picture, the worker-citizens were also understood as consumer-citizens: Premadasa and his supporters in the mass media often spoke about how in spending their wages workers would assist the state, become further satisfied with the government, and hence become less likely to join rebel groups. But these modern citizens, whose production capabilities and consumption potentials were being harnessed by the state, were also expected to embody certain "traditional" values. Importantly, the bodies that bore the brunt of this inscription were those of women: the state mandated that each 200 GFP factory employ women as 90 percent of its workforce, which was roughly the same gender breakdown as that shown by the garment industry as a whole in Sri Lanka.

Men and women were differently positioned in these processes of subject production under the 200 GFP, and Sri Lankan notions of femininity and masculinity profoundly affected the experiences of the program's participants. However, my interest in gender is not merely a matter of analyzing how women and men are differently affected by their involvement in global processes. I do not simply ask how women experience modernity. Gender is central to my analysis because, in the words of the historian Joan Scott (1999, 45), "gender is a primary field within which or by means of which power is articulated." As such, I position myself in alignment with Rofel (1999, 19), who has called for scholars to be more attentive to "the centrality of gender in shaping the forms by which and force with which desires for modernity take hold." In her research on silk-weaving factory workers in China, Rofel argues that gender provides a window through which one can examine how modernity is imagined and desired. As she notes, "Gender . . . is not just 'about' women and men, but is about the state, the nation, socialism, and capitalism" (1999, 20).

Gender has been a central arena in which Sri Lankans struggle over modernity and globalization—and hence, power. Globalization has affected women and men in profoundly different ways, and so any study of the everyday impact of globalization on Sri Lankans must examine how people deploy gender in local understandings of the interplay between global and local processes. By analyzing these gendered dimensions of globalization, we can learn much about how the meaning of globalized production becomes localized in specific places. We can simultaneously examine how modern subjects produce themselves in the face of the new social and cultural forms that accompany globalization.

Other scholars have shown how the reconfiguration of sociality by globalization affects men and women differently. Quite simply, societal expectations for the behavior of men and women differ. For Sinhala Buddhists, village women in particular are invested with attachment to tradition. Given this long-standing association, some critics were concerned that village women were targeted as the centerpiece of the state's new rural industrialization program. These concerns ultimately led to a transformation of the 200 GFP. The state originally argued that the 200 GFP aimed to prevent youth unrest (which was assumed to be largely perpetuated by men). Soon after a highly effective critique by the political opposition, the state changed its tack: now the program was said to have been intended to protect women's morality by eliminating the necessity for women's urban migration (framed as a morally suspect move, per the Juki-girl stigma).

In this book I show how debates about gender and globalization in Sri Lanka, which focused on women, were not simply arguments *about* women; yet I continually return to the lived effects of these debates on real women. I would be wrong to assume that discursive representations have no effect on material circumstances. I consciously focus more on women than on men, because Sri Lankans worry about women and not men, and therefore I heard and read about women every day during my field research. Men's roles, norms, and behavior—and the relative silence that attends to them—are worth studying in detail, and other scholars have done so (Abeysekera 2005; Gamburd 2000, 2004; Ismail 1991; Jeganathan 1997).

To understand the state's struggles with questions about the meaning of women's labor for the nation, I examine the discourses and practices of the 200 GFP. To understand the negotiations of those who represented the factories, I analyze the particular forms of managerial paternalism in these factories, as well as situations in which investors and managers deliberated about issues such as who makes a good worker and why. But the main focus of my inquiry is on the lives of women workers. In the face of national debates over globalization and women's behavior, the workers engaged daily in complex social negotiations. These negotiations were evident even as the Shirtex workers set off for Samarakoon Sir's father's funeral on that September 1995 morning. Attending funerals is an important social activity in Sri Lanka, and it is through the number of funeral attendees that one gauges respect for and the respectability of the deceased and his or her family. The factory workers were performing what is considered a traditional social obligation for someone who constantly subjected them to new forms of capitalist discipline in the name of industrial productivity. The arrival of four buses from Shirtex would give a boost to Samarakoon Sir's own social status, and by attending the funeral the workers would thus be doing something positive for their manager.

It is important not to end the analysis there but also to realize that the women would have been doing something for themselves. Indeed, attending funerals in Sri Lanka always involves an element of reciprocity. So what would they get in return? Some women spoke to me about the possibility of immediate tangible favors in the workplace. Partly jokingly, some even told me that when Samarakoon Sir would scold them in the future they would say, "We went to your father's funeral." What interested me more was that many women also seemed to be concerned about more diffuse favors to be garnered through their demonstration of appropriate femininity. The question of motivation raises the issues of agency and resistance, topics to which I now turn.

Women, Labor, and "Resistance"

Manufacturing for the global market has myriad effects on the lives of those whose produce globally distributed goods. Newly available industrial labor opens up new opportunities to factory workers, but they do not simply land on static, preexisting social relations and identities. Global factory work also changes workers' understandings of themselves in profound ways; in the process of learning how to be a garment worker, one learns how to be a new person, a member of a new "community of practice" (Lave and Wenger 1991). Furthermore, while managers may tailor global production practices to the specificities of local sites, global production also changes those local sites and meanings. Politicians and investors, managers and sewing-machine operators bring particular histories, social relations, and senses of self into the global marketplace—and all those are subject to change in the process.

I offer one small example of changing social relations and meanings at Shirtex and Serendib. Prior to working in these factories, many of these workers might have worked as day laborers in the paddy fields scattered throughout Udakande and nearby villages. On one level, the repetitive motions required for transplanting and harvesting rice are similar to those required for sewing garments: both operations require practitioners to lean forward, grab something, manipulate it, place it elsewhere, and repeat. But beyond the similarities in mere physical gesture, there are profound differences in what this work means for workers. There is something different about working in a factory instead of a paddy field; about producing for export rather than producing for the local landowner; about wearing a somewhat fancy dress to work that might get covered with cotton dust, which can be brushed off quickly, rather than a casual skirt and blouse that will get covered in mud. How does the way in which people think of the world, and of their place in the world, change when they move from paddy fields to garment factories? How does employment in global industry affect the formation of identity? What are the everyday ways in which we can see women struggle to make sense of their new lives?

By focusing on garment workers' struggles to lead meaningful lives, I am engaging with a body of feminist scholarship on Third World women that moves beyond questions of victimization. Today many scholars agree that there has long been a common misrepresentation of Third World women as mere victims and not as agents who have motivations for acting as they do (cf. Kabeer 2000; Mahmood 2001, 2005; Mohanty 1991a, 1991b). Scholarly, media, and policy analyses of Third World women have all perpetuated this problem, and it is particularly evident in regards to Western analyses of Muslim women who wear headscarves, women who practice female "circumcision," or even women whose lifelong aspirations are to be good wives and mothers.

Studies of women's experiences in global factories are no exception. In her analysis of Bangladeshi garment workers in Bangladesh and London, the economist Naila Kabeer (2000, 8) argues that 1980s feminist scholarship on Third World women laborers focused so much on the obvious negative aspects of factory employment that "the possibility that access to such employment might have any positive implications tended to be ruled out a priori." The importance of moving beyond the language of victimization to understand Third World women factory laborers was discussed in a conversation published in 2001 between Patricia Fernández-Kelly and Diane Wolf, two feminist sociologists whose research centers on issues of gender and globalization. At one point Fernández-Kelly noted that "the simple dichotomy between exploitative corporations and exploited victims does not go far enough in accounting for women's activities and creative responses to the global onslaught." Wolf's response points to the issues I am concerned with:

Some feminist scholarship is relentless about the exploitative nature of global capital without bringing in what workers think or experience. We thus get a one-dimensional view of women as victims, but we also need to have an understanding of the way those women attempt to subvert their circumstances. A feminist author writing about Indonesian workers argued that, although women factory workers could now afford to pay for a haircut, we should not be distracted by the benefits of such petty consumption; what really mattered was that they were still being exploited. It is easy to make such arguments when you can afford to pay for a haircut (and more), but such arrogance ignores the actual conditions surrounding the women about whom we are arguing. (Fernández-Kelly and Wolf 2001, n.p.)

A too-narrow focus on exploitation can result in a dismissal of the importance for the women workers of their new access to consumer culture. To understand these women's experiences it is crucial to comprehend what makes them happy, what they desire, what they hope for and dream of. Factory workers' consumption practices mean much more than women merely reproducing exploitative capitalist market relationships—along with new-found consumerism, there is likely to be a social life beyond the confines of women's homes and villages. Women also probably feel a concomitant sense of pride in their work, independence, and earning capacity. Furthermore, even if women are not overtly "subverting" their circumstances, we need to pay attention to why and how they may have desires that are counter to those of some scholars and analysts.

The political scientist Cynthia Enloe argues that "Without women's own needs, values, and worries, the global assembly line would grind to a halt" (Enloe 1989, 16–17, quoted in Mills 1999, 9). In her ethnography of Thai women factory workers, the anthropologist Mary Beth Mills (1999, 9) agrees with Enloe that it is crucial to understand that women choose to work at low-waged, harshly disciplined, and unhealthy jobs not only because of the money they will earn. They also do it to "achieve more complex social goals." She then explores what these more complex social goals might be for women who work in Bangkok factories, arguing that "attention to these complex motivations as they converge and collide in the course of migration may, in turn, illuminate women's diverse, often ambivalent responses to their urban sojourns" (9–10).

When the Shirtex women organized the funeral trip, at first it appeared to me that they were condoning managerial abuse and reproducing their oppression. In retrospect, I attribute this interpretation to my liberal feminist expectations. Having read the works of Aihwa Ong (1987, 1991), James Scott (1985), and others in preparation for my fieldwork, I had come to Sri Lanka expecting to find the assertion of power by capitalists but also various covert and overt responses of resistance by the women workers. Where earlier I might have thought that "resistance" was the hallmark of the exhibition of agency, I have since come to think of "resistance" as too simple a way of conceptualizing agency.

The anthropologist Saba Mahmood (2001, 2005) analyzes female piety movements in Egypt and inquires into how to understand agency when the subjects of research are not enacting what appears to the researcher to be obvious "resistance." She asks: What if we think of agency not as a synonym for resistance to domination, but as "a capacity for action that historically specific relations of subordination enable and create" (2001, 203)? We would then see agency not only in acts that result in progressive change but also in those that aim for continuity and stability. Mahmood's work, combined with other theoretical work that moves beyond a dichotomous understanding of structure and agency (cf. Asad 1993; Kabeer 2000; Ortner 1996), has challenged a particular configuration of agency in the discipline of anthropology.

Processes of subject production may involve constructing social worlds and enacting behaviors that are disturbing to the political commitments of others (such as the researcher). When they went to the funeral, Kumari and the others were negotiating how to live a feminine ideal in a complex social world. This was a world structured in part by "traditional" social obligations and in part by the global marketplace. These women thought of their own lives as located at the interstices of the traditional and the modern. As such they worked to make sense of their experiences in the face of various, and often contradictory, forms of power. One particular form of power these women encountered had to do with their work of subject production in the face of the Juki-girl stigma. In a society in which sexual propriety is the index of morality for women, they were engaged in a constant struggle to be considered "good" Sri Lankan women, their position as factory workers notwithstanding. Attending the funeral was one demonstration of their good moral standing.

To appreciate the nuances of what the funeral attendees were doing, it is crucial to note that Kumari and the others engaged in this complicated project of subject production had physically demanding factory jobs, and that there were certain aspects of factory work that many women certainly were not fond of. These included the inability to rest when tired, the allotment of lunch breaks that were felt to be too short, dirty bathrooms, and the myriad regulations that governed things as mundane as the range of personal effects one could bring to the factory. Such affronts came on top of the stigma that these jobs brought with them. Even so, these women truly enjoyed other aspects of factory employment. These included the opportunity to get out of their houses without having to work in the fields, the access to consumer culture that their wages enabled, the close friendships that working and whispering side by side for many hours each day facilitated, and the pride they felt from participating in a national development program for their nation. They also appreciated having access to these new people, places, and things without having to migrate to Colombo, a city that they considered expensive, lonely, dangerous, and morally degrading.

Kumari and the others organized the funeral trip in light of these contradictory experiences and conscious struggles. The funeral trip was one way of affirming to their managers, to the other villagers, and to themselves that they were good women, concerned about maintaining "tradition" as much as the next villager. These women did what other villagers would have done, but their positionality in doing it as female garment factory workers gave it a different meaning from the same action as performed by men or by non–garment factory workers. It was in the face of all the social strictures and moral evaluations surrounding questions of being "good" or "bad" that these women organized the funeral trip. Months later, in an interview with Samarakoon Sir, I received an indication of the success of their efforts. He noted to me that Colombo women would not have organized a funeral trip for their manager's father. This, he said, confirmed to him that those village girls from Shirtex were "good."

The funeral event constituted one example of the work of self-fashioning taking place among Sri Lankan women garment workers engaged with global capitalism. Conflicting social narratives brought these women to Samarakoon Sir's father's funeral. One can begin to appreciate the complex texture of these women's efforts only when this event is framed within a nuanced understanding of gender, the localization of global production, and notions of agency. While I initially assumed these women were experiencing their new lives as oppressive, in truth the encounter was far more complicated. They had an investment in the nation and in the kinds of social expectations placed on women. But at the same time they realized that their personal lives were filled with suffering. Through their involvement in the 200 GFP these women struggled to define themselves as Good girls who were also garment workers; to make sense of their own feelings of love, pleasure, and hardship; and to reconcile their pride in the work they did with the stigma attached to it.

Mahmood (2001) argues that it is only when we are attentive to people's motivations, desires, and goals that we can see beyond a simple understanding of agency as resistance to domination. We can see the agency of these Sri Lankan garment workers in the two different kinds of work in which they engaged—the work of producing garments and the work of producing identities. Their identity construction also had two different features. It entailed creatively fashioning a niche in which they thrived within a new social milieu and enjoyed respect, and it involved responding to globalization by fashioning themselves as modern subjects in a nation-state in which they held deep commitments. This is certainly agency, though not any simple kind of "resistance."

Producing Meaning and Identities

Recall for a moment the comments of Mala, whose plea for respect opened this chapter: "A lot of people in society think garment factories are places without any culture or civilization. . . . Can a person's character be concluded from a job?" Mala and her coworkers struggled to be considered Good girls and not Juki girls. These women's concerns about how others perceived them were intricately related to personal struggles over how to reconcile their own experiences and desires with societal expectations for women's behavior. In subsequent chapters, I contextualize their personal struggles in terms of the wider changes in the organization of social inequality that arose with economic liberalization.

Some of these struggles were played out within the factories, and some in their lives outside of work. The work was ongoing—the women did not simply take on new subject positions the moment they started their garment factory jobs. Rather, their new identities emerged in part in the continued practice of learning the technical and social "skills" involved in being garment workers; it was there that these women learned the quotidian elements of how to be garment workers who are Good girls—not Juki girls. But this process

JUKI GIRLS, GOOD GIRLS

did not reach a discernable fixed endpoint. Because there were constantly new workers (with their own ideas and priorities) in training at the factories, and because of the relative novelty of this type of work in Sri Lanka and especially within villages, the new identities were continually being produced and debated in and around the factories. I turn now to describe in broad strokes how the women learned to be Good girls in the practice of learning their jobs. I examine these processes of identity formation in terms of "learning" rather than "doing," because the learning model directs attention to the transformation and creation of meaning in the learners as well as in the world around them. It thus casts people as creative agents responding to and changing the world.

The process of producing meaning and identities begins as soon as someone starts to learn a job, for the learning involved in work results in new understandings of the world. Learning is not simply the acquisition of a static corpus of knowledge. It is rather a social activity and practice through which participants, who are equipped with locally situated understandings of the world, invent and reinvent what constitutes knowledge about that world. In their research on situated learning and identity formation, the anthropologist Jean Lave and the theorist Etienne Wenger (1991) move away from an understanding of knowledge as something "out there," static, and ready to be apprehended. They reconceptualize knowledge as cultural and social products and learning as a matter of how people "participate in changing ways in a changing world" (Lave 1993, 5). This perspective on "changing participation and understanding in practice" (Lave 1993, 6) allows one to see how learning occurs within systems of social relations and involves relations of power, areas of conflict, and various degrees of participation. Seen in this light, learning entails the construction of identities within these social relations.

Lave and Wenger (1991, 76) argue that the learning that occurs in a master-apprentice relationship involves the movement of apprentices from "legitimate peripheral participants" to "legitimate full participants" in a community of practice that is engaged in its own reproduction and transformation. They argue that being a member of a community of practice implies "participation in an activity system about which participants share understandings concerning what they are doing and what that means in their lives and for their communities" (Lave and Wenger 1991, 98). In an effective apprenticeship, learning takes place not because the novice replicates or acquires knowledge from the master, but rather because she or he is given access to a community of practice and participates in the production of meaning regarding the activity. A "legitimate full participant" identifies himself or herself as a member of the community. He or she has *become* a midwife, tailor, or butcher (to use Lave and Wenger's examples [1991, 111]).

Shirtex and Serendib women workers went through a similar process to become garment workers. They gained access to the community of practice of garment workers when they were hired; they brought their own identities and understandings to factory work (which affected what this work meant to them); and they eventually *became* garment workers. Becoming a garment worker, like becoming a midwife or tailor, involved the transformation of identity through learning. This process was truly a matter of changing understanding in practice. The understanding that garment workers had of themselves and what they were doing changed through the everyday practice of work.

If we narrow our vision of agency to obvious forms of resistance to domination, we are blinded to how people might act in ways that aim for continuity and stability. Furthermore, some acts are better conceived not as "resistance to domination" but as positive acts that allow participation in a community of practice—that allow people to make sense of the world around them. To avoid the kinds of conceptual problems raised by discussing behavior in terms of resistance, I conceive of learning as sanctioned and unsanctioned *from the perspective of management*. That which management "sanctioned" was also good, disciplined, and often consistent with "traditional" expectations for women. That which was "unsanctioned" did not always map onto the moral opposite of good. It was not "bad." But it was new and different from what managers expected. At times we might consider it *modern*, but it is best to consider it simply creative and agentive. By examining Shirtex and Serendib women's efforts and actions in these terms we can see their daily struggles to be garment workers who are Good girls. Yet we can also begin to see that theirs was a new kind of Good girl identity that did not completely reproduce older categories, stereotypes, and expectations.

Accordingly, whereas from the managers' perspectives sanctioned learning may have been sufficient for garments to be produced, from the workers' perspectives it was insufficient for the women's full participation in an aspirational community of practice—that made up of garment workers who were Good girls, not Juki girls. Indeed, producing garments does not by itself enable women to be members of a meaningful community. This point was made quite clearly by Geeta, an author of one of the short essays reproduced in this book. Geeta once complained to me that specialization within the factory meant that many machine operators were unable to sew a complete garment at home (she might know only how to attach a cuff to a sleeve). To come to grips with the process of garment factory learning, I offer an analytic scheme composed of four categories: (1) sanctioned technical learning, (2) sanctioned social learning, (3) unsanctioned technical learning, and (4) unsanctioned social learning.

From the workers' own perspectives, there were social and technical practices they had to learn to be full participants in the community of Good girl workers. Some of these practices were unsanctioned by management but essential to the women's own efforts at making sense of their new lives. Discussing these social processes in terms of sanctioned and unsanctioned learning allows me to evaluate the expectations of differently situated people against the record of how, in practice, the women did some things that violated social expectations and other things that fulfilled them. I turn now to describe these four aspects of garment factory learning, introducing each with a vignette that I have written from my own analytical perspective, with quotation marks indicating information told to me in recorded interviews.

Sanctioned Technical Learning

Many of the women who worked at Shirtex and Serendib had never been in a factory before starting to work there. In an interview Kumari explained to me how she felt the first time she saw the inside of the factory. On the day when President Premadasa opened the factory and made the auspicious ceremonial first cut of fabric in the Shirtex cutting room, villagers were invited in for the festivities. "I just felt like this was a big heaven [*maha divya lōkayak*]. I got spooked [*holman unā*] thinking, 'What is done with this stuff?' I watched open-mouthed at what Mr. Premadasa cut. I was thinking, 'Why is this? Why is so much fabric hung? Are these to sew? Who hung these? Do they sew with these machines?' I was just spooked after going inside."

When Kumari first viewed the inside of Shirtex, months before she joined the workforce, the newness of the factory brought on a barrage of questions in her mind, articulated in terms of heaven and ghosts. Kumari found many things inside the factory frighteningly unfamiliar. From the machines to the

Figure 1. Large fabric bolts were among the many new things workers encountered when they came to the factories, which prompted Kumari to say she was "spooked" the first time she entered Shirtex. Photo by Seamus Walsh, printed with permission.

fabric quantities and placement, she was facing a new world. She described her reaction using an expression that I translate as "spooked," which is based on the noun *holman*, a term for "ghost."[5] Kumari was calling attention to the otherworldliness of this foreign manufacturing process.

The sanctioned technical learning in the factory started with basic questions like Kumari's and extended to the participation in the complicated learning required for producing garments. From the cutting room to the packing area, workers had to learn new technical skills. On the production floor, for instance, the machine operators had a vast list of skills to master: sewing straight, curved, or angled seams; sewing on a normal, flatlock, or overlock machine; sewing thick fabric that needs to be coaxed through the needle or thin, slippery fabric that seems to run away. In addition to basic sewing skills there were skills required to be an efficient worker within a production line. A machine operator had to learn the quickest and least physically painful way (back problems were common among machine operators) to turn to the bin behind her, grab the next batch of garments, turn back to her machine and sew, then deposit the garments into the bin in front, either for the next operator to take up (at Serendib) or for the helper to inspect and then deliver to the

JUKI GIRLS, GOOD GIRLS

next section (at Shirtex). If her arm started to hurt, what could she do to relieve it without losing rhythm and falling behind the target rate? How and when was she to enter figures into the target book (noting how many pieces were sewn per hour) that the supervisors and managers checked intermittently throughout the day? What was the proper procedure when mistakes were made? Workers in nonsewing sections had their own kind of technical learning: For women who spent their days pinning the shirts in the final stage before packing, how to cope with newly forming calluses on the fingers? For the ironers who sweated over the hot steam irons all day, how to avoid ironing sweat into the garments? And again, what was the best posture to avoid backache?

There was also sanctioned technical learning of a more bureaucratic kind: how to punch-in on the mechanical (Shirtex) or computerized (Serendib) time clock; how to understand the pay-sheet figures; how to calculate allotted days of leave and how to get them. If a worker should fall sick, would it be acceptable simply not to show up to work, or should a message be sent through coworkers or, failing that, a telegram? (The answer: Send a message, by all means.) What amount of talking was permitted? (Talking to sort out production issues, such as how to use a new pattern or fix a thread tension problem, was permitted, but socializing was not.)

Yet another kind of sanctioned technical learning concerned discipline.[6] Managerial modes of discipline included the following: a worker should know the meaning of the first bell at the end of the lunch break and what will happen if she returns to her work station after the second bell rings; a worker caught laughing or talking when not on break will receive a warning but might eventually be sent home for two weeks without pay; a worker sewing below target might be told to punch out her time card and work without pay. Managers assured me that this last disciplinary technique was meant to scare the workers into submission. But many workers and managers insisted to me that the workers were paid in the end; the manager calls the payroll department in Colombo to make sure the hours are included. (I was unable to confirm if this really happens.) The technique was effective, though, because few workers knew that it might be a ruse.

Finally, there was learning English, which very few workers could speak, and some could read and write at a basic level. With the exception of the pay sheets that were given to workers on payday, all the paperwork at the factories was in English. Managers said the paperwork was deliberately done in English so that the workers would gain experience in, as one put it, "the global language of industry and commerce." Because it was used for all paperwork, women with some training in English reading and writing were preferred for the more clerical jobs. English classes have been given at these factories for such women. During my field research period, I taught English at Shirtex and an American friend of mine taught at Serendib; the Shirtex personnel manager had given lessons at his factory before I arrived.

Managers limited the required technical learning to these types of operational skills and behaviors. But they also sanctioned certain forms of social learning as they tried to create a disciplined, productive, and content workforce.

Sanctioned Social Learning

Following the death of Samarakoon Sir's father, the Shirtex workers lobbied management to allow the entire workforce to take a Saturday off from work and rent four buses to attend the funeral in a Colombo suburb. Later Samarakoon Sir told me that this demonstrated that they were Good girls. Furthermore, he argued, they were Good girls because they were villagers. He said that when village girls migrated to Colombo for work they went bad and got caught up in fashion (*vilāsitāwa*), whereas villagers paid more attention to customs. Samarakoon Sir asserted that the workers went to his father's funeral because they had not forgotten old traditions even though the surroundings (*piṭisara*) had changed. According to him, garment workers in Colombo would not go like that to a funeral. He said that he did not blame the girls; that was just how society had become. He cited a further example of such societal transformations when he noted that people in Colombo 7 (the city's wealthiest neighborhood) thought only about themselves—they did not even know what happened next door.

Sanctioned social learning involved integrating what was considered traditional social behavior with factory discipline. This type of integration was valued by the managers and workers alike and was symbolized in the term *Good girls*, which both workers and managers used on a daily basis. To Samarakoon Sir, this funeral event demonstrated that the workers were able to integrate factory life with local customs and social responsibilities. As I have noted, attending funerals is an important social activity and obligation among Sinhalas, and a large attendance is a point of pride and a marker of status for the family of the deceased. This underlies women's frequent lamentations to me that they were not able to attend funerals anymore due to work obligations. In this case, a number of workers explained to me that they wanted to attend the funeral to show their respect (*gauravaya*) for Samarakoon Sir. Though Samarakoon Sir was quite strict in the factory and scolded workers often, many excused him for this and attributed this behavior to him simply doing his job well. They noted that like them, he also had to demonstrate to superiors that he was fulfilling his job duties. A minority of the workers stayed behind. Some said they did not attend because they were unable to reconcile factory discipline with social custom. They told me that their respect for Samarakoon Sir did not outweigh their dislike of him for scolding them. Others told me they did not attend because they could not afford the contribution required for the bus rental, and others because their husbands would not allow them to go.

Asanka Sir, the owner of Shirtex, told me he allowed the workers to take leave that day because "it was a reasonable request"—he said they offered to make up lost work time the following Saturday by working a full day—and because funerals were very important to villagers. Condoning this social activity is consistent with a number of other social activities the management sanctioned for at least three reasons: because they indicated to the wider society that the workers were Good girls, because they indicated to outsiders that management was concerned with maintaining traditional social customs (thus warding off possible concerns about modern factories and modern forms of labor abuse), and because management believed that Good girls were good workers. Such sanctioned social activities included a Buddhist almsgiving at the factory on the anniversary of its establishment, a festival on Sinhala and Tamil New Year, and collections to defray funeral expenses when a worker's relative died. By condoning these activities, the factory was seen as a place where traditional values are maintained and not a corrupt locale where parents would be wary of sending their daughters. From the perspective of management, encouraging activities that did not challenge women's traditional roles yielded a labor pool of highly disciplined women. This was one way in which the work of localizing production made it to the factory floor.

To return to Lave and Wenger's terms, identities are constructed during the job-learning process. If workers did not have full access to the community of practice they were joining, they could not construct identities in a meaningful way. The garment workers' community of practice was constructed out of more than what management sanctioned; it was also constructed out of unsanctioned technical and social learning—unsanctioned from the perspective of management but sanctioned and essential from the workers' perspectives.

Unsanctioned Technical Learning

By the end of my field research period I could not walk in the town of Kandy without encountering a factory worker. On factory holidays I ran into groups of workers every twenty feet on the main street in town. But even on workdays I saw workers in town, shopping with friends and family, walking around Kandy Lake, or heading to a park with their boyfriends or family members. They would have sent a message to work with a coworker, falsely notifying the manager that they had to take a sick day in order to go to the doctor. They would claim to be sick, or more often, attribute illness to a child, sibling, or parent.

Unsanctioned technical learning included learning how to work with or around sanctioned technical skills and rules. For example, how long after the break bell could one return to work without getting in trouble? How did one get slightly damaged (but easier and quicker to sew) garments past the checking department? Workers learned how much talking and laughing they could get away with, and how subtly to signal the arrival of a manager or supervisor to their coworker who was in the middle of relating a story. They knew that managers were sometimes more lenient about talking—for example, around the time of the New Year's festival, as workers excitedly planned their fancy dress contest costumes. They also learned that talking could be disguised as work-related conversation, and that it was easier to get away with talking than laughing.

One might expect the examples of unsanctioned technical learning to be numerous and striking because this would be the area where the power dynamics of a factory were exposed through worker resistance to factory discipline. There were certainly examples of resistance to the skills and rules required by management, as I have just indicated. But the areas I find most noteworthy perhaps are not properly labeled "resistance." They are better understood as an aspect of the production of meaning. That is, workers acted on their new world in ways that made sense to them. The labor process here had strikingly similar features to capitalist labor in other times and places through-

JUKI GIRLS, GOOD GIRLS

out the world. The forms of discipline used by management were also similar—for instance, preventing workers from talking, using targets and incentives systems, or instituting forced overtime. Yet the meanings that the workers made of the work process and discipline, and their reactions to it, were locally formed. But this is not to deny the creative use of agency as well.

The creative deployment of a Good-girl identity was a type of unsanctioned technical learning management would certainly not have condoned. While learning to be a Good girl fell under the realm of sanctioned social learning—in other words, management encouraged workers to be Good girls—management did not sanction learning to use this identity to gain advantages within the factory. As I described in discussing sanctioned technical learning, workers quickly learned the factory leave policies. But the vignette with which I began this subsection shows that they also learned how to get around them. Because managers believed the family responsibilities for villagers were numerous, they would promptly give leave for sick family members to be taken to the doctor. In particular, women whom managers considered Good girls were constantly granted leave to take care of family obligations because Good girls were assumed to be naturally oriented toward family. Village women were thus able to use the idea that they are traditional, docile, and controlled to their advantage within the work environment. In some cases, they were self-conscious about doing this. For instance, I had a number of conversations with women about getting leave to go on day trips with their soldier boyfriends who were on leave from the army. In those cases, because the women were sure managers would not let them take leave to meet a boyfriend (although managers told me they would, if the women in question were Good girls), they would consistently choose to tell managers that they needed to take a family member to the doctor. These women were using traditional expectations in response to capitalist discipline. This conscious and at times not-so-conscious mobilization of tradition resonates with Jane Collier's (1997) and Richard Maddox's (1993) discussions of the politics of tradition in rural Spain. They both argue that tradition has remained vibrant in modern Spain because it provides "an effective tool for modern people to resist the increasingly 'secular, instrumental and objectified . . . techniques of management and control' exercised by 'modern bureaucracies, large scale capitalist corporations, and the nation-state'" (Collier 1997, 213, quoting Maddox 1993, 263).

In an interview, a worker named Chandra explained to me that when some women first came to work at Serendib they did not wash properly and they smelled of sweat. "But then when they get a month's wage or two . . . they come looking beautiful the next month wearing perfume and powder. . . . Then they have fallen into society. Before that they lived with dirt dripping from their clothes. There are a lot of workers in our factory like that who have become stylish. People who came here in a rural [*goḍē*] manner."

Factory women participated in unsanctioned social learning in many ways. For instance, they learned how to apply caste rules to the factory; why it was important to know the political party to which your coworkers belong; how to wear lipstick to a wedding party without a husband or father finding out; and what television programs were popular and why. They also learned practical information for everyday living, like how to save money to build a house, where to buy the cheapest silk sari in town, and which shortcuts were not inundated with mud for the walk home on a rainy night. Although these examples are not shocking transgressions, management did not expressly sanction them because management considered them irrelevant to factory work. Some were in fact prohibited: for instance, some managers told me that they would intervene whenever they overheard politics or caste being discussed in the factories, or if they heard of people following caste rules. Nevertheless, they were crucial to workers' full participation in factory life and to their ability to become members of the community of practice of garment workers.

One of the most often discussed matters of this sort was appearance and fashion. Although I frequently heard and participated in conversations on these topics with factory women, managers and owners assumed that village women would not be concerned with them. In Chandra's evocative comment, she described the formation of a new identity as women became members of the garment workers' community of practice. The women Chandra described, herself included, did not want to be considered *goḍē*, a term that connotes rural naïveté (like the English term *country bumpkins*). Yet, although they wanted to be considered modern, they did not want to be thought of as loose Juki girls. Chandra was describing the formation of a new kind of Good-girl identity—as we will see in later chapters, she and her coworkers strove to be Good girls who were not the precise opposite of Juki girls.

Contrary to what management would hope for, the community produced through the sanctioned and unsanctioned learning at Shirtex and Serendib was not a wholly traditional and disciplined community of Good girls. The workers learned a number of behaviors that the managers would have frowned upon. However, the new kind of Good-girl identity was not one that completely opposed factory discipline—hence these women's endorsements of some of the sanctioned social learning. When we take into account all four dimensions of factory learning, we can see these subjects creatively responding to the world around them. Their self-fashioning came in response to complicated contexts, and they creatively fashioned a niche in which most seemed genuinely to thrive. It was a new social milieu where many had fun and enjoyed respect. But at the same time they were deeply committed to their place in the nation and in their villages and families. They wanted to be considered Good girls: good for themselves, their villages, the factory, and the Sinhala Buddhist nation.

The significance of the Shirtex and Serendib women's efforts to be considered Good girls and not Juki girls will become more apparent when they are situated in the context of the 200 GFP. I now turn to focus on this rural industrialization program from the perspectives of the president who established it and the state representatives, journalists, and investors who supported or critiqued it. In the following discussion, the emphasis is on the program and the way in which politicians constructed it. The struggles of people like Kumari and Mala form an important backdrop to these national political discourses. Behind the complicated and heroic rhetoric articulated by President Premadasa and his supporters, ultimately they were speaking about women who were daily sweating, laughing, crying, concentrating, and daydreaming at their sewing machines or other work stations.

CHINTA

Chinta was a twenty-four-year-old sewing-machine operator who quit her job at Serendib during my field research period in order to get married. Chinta had several older employed brothers and her father worked in a shop in Kandy. She did not use her wage for the family but instead purchased items such as gold jewelry, clothing, a cassette deck, a sewing machine, and an almāriya (wardrobe). These were all goods she felt she could not ask her parents to buy for her. She saved some money in a bank account, but by the time she married she had spent it all on items for herself and for her dowry. Her brothers also contributed to her dowry.

In an interview, Chinta discussed the effect of young women's acquisition of purchasing power on social change. She explained what happens when women get money, citing the example of clothing purchases: "There are different goods in shops. [Before we started to work,] even though there are these goods, we didn't have money to buy them. We couldn't tell our parents to buy them. . . . But when we have money, we can buy them. Then, when girls wear them, they change. They will change a little from how they were raised at home." Chinta said that some of her coworkers wore fancy (vicurana) clothes to work. In addition to changes in the clothes they wore, Chinta observed that some changed their hairstyles or wore a lot of gold jewelry.

On marrying, many women stopped working at the factories at the insistence of their new husbands. Chinta said that her husband had been concerned about how the difficult working conditions would affect her: "I will work hard, I might get sick. A lot of people say they're sick. So he dislikes [me working]." A short while later in the interview, Chinta discussed why women should not work outside the home. When I asked her if she would have liked to continue working, she said that she would have, but she saw that she was privileged not to have to work because her husband earned enough money to support the family. She also said that she had always imagined that she would not work after she got married. I asked her why so many Shirtex and Serendib women preferred to stay at home after marrying.

> Chinta: *There is the husband's work to be done. If we go to work, the things we're supposed to do at home are neglected. Then I won't get his love [*ādaraya*]. The love we have will lessen. There is no need to decrease the love because of a job. If we have a lot of needs, then it's okay to do a job. But, without so many needs, it's not good to go to a job like that to our heart's liking [without the husband's consent] and break hearts.*
> Caitrin: *Why would the husband's love lessen?*
> Chinta: *Let's say I have to go to work at seven a.m. But my husband gets up at seven. Right? . . . If I go to work, I won't bring him his tea. Then he thinks, "Even after bringing a woman home and marrying her [I cannot get her to serve me]." . . . Really, so, he marries to get some freedom [from household chores]. I must do work for him.*

When I interviewed Chinta in her husband's natal home shortly after she married, she was alone with her mother-in-law, with whom she and her husband lived. Barely out of earshot, Chinta whispered to me that her mother-in-law was strict, and that she was bored (kammäli) in her new daily routine. She missed her factory friends, and although the work at Serendib had been difficult, the days had passed quickly and were punctuated by the enjoyment of joking and having friends around her. She also referred to the benefits of repetitive factory work, where one performed the same operations on shirt after shirt, day after day. In this light, she favorably compared factory work to unpredictable housework. "At the garment factory the same work is done. So it's a little easy. This is extra, extra work. So it's a little harder, more difficult than at the factory." In a letter some months after I returned to Chicago, she wrote that she still missed the freedom that working in the factory enabled.

Chinta missed earning money to spend on her own. She also missed going on outings with her friends and having her friends to talk to and learn from. She said she learned various things in the factory that had helped her in her new role as a housewife. That included the importance of spending money wisely, since now she knew how hard it was to earn it. She also said that through listening to the problems married women faced in balancing work and housework, and especially the problems of women whose husbands hit them for neglecting the housework, she had learned about how unfair men could be and also about how to behave once she married. She elaborated:

> Chinta: When we worked we associated with a lot of married people too. Our friends, oh, their grief. Some people, if they have a job, they are weak when they do housework. Because housework is neglected, their husbands hit, hurt them. I met a lot of people with those experiences. . . .
> Caitrin: What do you think of men hitting their wives?
> Chinta: I wonder why the husbands should hit. They don't know how much we toil. We toil. We haven't stayed idle. So, they hurt us like that. We don't have to go for a job. Because they could, they should be able to, they must also provide us with food. That's what I think.

Here Chinta argued that a man has an obligation ("could, should, must") to support his wife. If he cannot, then he certainly should not physically abuse her for problems that arise due to her employment.

2. LOCALIZING PRODUCTION

Whenever locals gave directions to Shirtex, Serendib, or any of the small villages in the area, they would invariably mention the clock tower at the main junction to Udakande. On every workday morning and afternoon, the road that led from the clock tower to the factories was so thick with hundreds of women (and far fewer men) walking to and from the factories that passing vehicles had to weave slowly through the crowd. Along one side of this road ran the train tracks that took rail commuters from these and other outlying villages into Kandy. The far side of the tracks was lined with verdant paddy fields. Two-story concrete homes with lush gardens bordered the other side of the road. When the factories were built in 1992, electricity was extended down this route. The road was also widened and paved to accommodate the container trucks that transported raw materials and finished garments to and from the factories.

Inscribed in Sinhala, Tamil, and English, a plaque on the clock tower announced that it had been erected by the owners of Shirtex and Serendib to mark the founding of the factories under President Premadasa's 200 GFP. Participation in the 200 GFP required adherence to numerous policies and rules, and one mandated the construction of a clock tower at the main junction closest to each factory. All Sri Lankan cities and larger towns contain colonial-era clock towers that still keep perfect time. But in rural Sri Lanka, as of 1992, the presence of a clock tower indicates the more than likely proximity of a garment factory.

Sometimes the presence of a garment factory stands in sharp contrast to the surrounding environs. In the center of an intersection just fifty yards from and within view of the sacred Bodhi tree in the ancient city of Anuradhapura, there is a clock tower with stylized red letters beneath the faces that read, "Candy Garments," the name of a nearby 200 GFP factory that was opened in October 1992.[1] Sinhala Buddhists believe that the tree in Anuradhapura is a sapling from the tree under which the Buddha reached enlightenment in Bodh Gaya, India. Contemporary lay Buddhists attempt to emulate in small measures the intense physical and moral discipline that enabled the Buddha to attain enlightenment. When I last saw this Candy Garments tower in 1996, it was marking time while worshipers came and went from the Bodhi tree. The sight of the factory clock tower alongside the sacred tree presented a stark juxtaposition of the two notions of discipline that Premadasa so adroitly brought together in the 200 GFP. The clock tower is a modern symbol of industrial discipline and global capital. The tree is a symbol of the Buddha's much older discipline and much earlier, Buddhist-centered global flows of people and ideas. This kind of juxtaposition between modernity and tradition is common in contemporary Sri Lanka, where citizens expend considerable energy to reconcile economic development with cultural preservation. Such juxtapositions are the sites for the localization of global production.

When the 200 GFP brought export-oriented industrial garment factories into what both rural and urban Sri Lankans generally imagined to be pristine and traditional villages, this effort was accompanied by grand promises and explanations on the part of the nation's elite about the significance of such an enterprise. Those who tried to make the program meaningful to others cast it in terms of development, progress, and modernity. But they also emphasized how the program would celebrate, preserve, or resurrect the nation's esteemed Sinhala Buddhist traditions. In this chapter I demonstrate that President Premadasa was quite careful to cast the program as not just an economic panacea but as a resolution to perceived contradictions between economic development and cultural traditions. Sri Lanka is one of many countries that have, since the 1970s, welcomed foreign investment and developed programs for exporting goods and services. Ever since, Sri Lankans have been concerned that economic liberalization was bringing with it not only economic exploitation by the West but also cultural imperialism and homogenization (Richardson 2004, 48).

This chapter analyzes the uneasy relationship between the state's goals of protecting the nation from cultural and political disintegration while also opening it to foreign investment. It examines these concerns in their wider social, political, economic, and cultural contexts, presenting an extended analysis of the localization of global production via a case study of the 200 GFP. The second half of this chapter includes a detailed analysis of the politics of discipline, for Premadasa mobilized the Sinhala Buddhist concept of discipline in his attempts to appeal to Sinhala anxieties about economic liberalization and cultural preservation.

The 200 GFP: Policies, Aims, and Context

Shirtex and Serendib produced garments for export under contract to buyers in the United States and Europe. Ever since the economy was liberalized in 1977, Sri Lanka's economic growth has depended on such production for export. Sri Lanka is like many other Third World countries that embarked on paths of economic liberalization as they took up the International Monetary Fund's recommendations for growth. During the first decade and a half of the liberalized economy, much of the export-oriented industrialization occurred in the urban areas surrounding the Sri Lankan capital and main port of Colombo (Richardson 2004). Before the 200 GFP was inaugurated in 1992, there were a few factories outside the Colombo area (including a smaller precursor to Serendib that had been located in another rural area), but those were decided exceptions to local patterns of economic development.

The 200 GFP launched a major government push to industrialize rural areas. Investors in privately owned garment-manufacturing firms received massive financial incentives (including tax breaks, access to importation of duty-free vehicles, and priority on quotas for exporting to the United States) from the state to open factories in the countryside and to employ workers from the immediate area.[2] These new factories were built far from the country's urban industrial Free Trade Zones, sometimes in areas so remote that roads had to be widened and paved and electricity lines and water pipes had to be installed before production could begin. The goal (which was nearly attained) was to establish one factory in each of the country's two hundred administrative units.[3] Investors included Sri Lankans and foreigners; some projects were joint investments. Sri Lankan investors included Sinhala Buddhists and members of minority groups such as Tamils, Muslims, Sindhis, and Gujaratis.[4] Foreign investors included U.S., German, and Hong Kong firms. The 200 GFP was to provide both direct employment in factories for one hundred thousand youth and indirect employment (in related jobs in transportation, shops, and food service) for many others.

Newspapers and television stations covered the opening of each 200 GFP factory with great fanfare. In the latter half of 1992, openings were frequent; by December, factories were opening almost daily. These ceremonies were media spectacles, and they attracted vast audiences of sometimes more than fifty thousand people. Until his death in 2003, Premadasa attended opening ceremonies for each factory. The extent of media coverage of the openings and the program in general was massive, and this in a country with a large news-paper readership (literacy rates in 1990 were 93 percent for adult males and 85 for adult females) and intensely popular radio and television broadcast-ing—many people without electricity go so far as to power their televisions with car batteries.[5] There were remarkable similarities in the official discourse about the program and what most investors, managers, and workers said to me about it several years after its inception. Thus it appears that the media coverage wielded considerable influence over how people interpreted the so-cial objectives and effects of the program. This does not indicate that these people were duped, but rather that Premadasa and his supporters were adroit at explaining the program in terms that were meaningful to the citizenry.

Premadasa officially announced the 200 GFP at an inaugural 18 February 1992 meeting for potential investors, many of whom had already begun the process of setting up factories under the scheme (Fernando 1992a; *Special Correspondent* 1992a). At this meeting, Premadasa outlined the program's policies and aims, which included workforce size, minimum salary require-ments, and prescribed methods for recruiting workers.

Premadasa's 200 GFP had important economic aims: providing jobs to the rural poor, earning foreign exchange, and increasing the country's gross na-tional product (Shastri 1997, 494–95). But rather than highlight such materi-alist concerns, Premadasa's inaugural speech and numerous other statements (as well as those by his supporters) focused on two related concerns that pre-occupied many Sri Lankans at the time: the then-recent youth revolt and the Westernization of Sri Lankan society. It is conceivable that Premadasa simply used both lines of argument to sell the program to the nation and that these is-sues had little to do with his true motivations. However, the late president's true motivations—which, after all, we cannot know—are of less interest to me than his rhetoric and actions.

The state and its supporters cast the 200 GFP as a program for bolstering the nation's defenses against revolution through global economic involvement. Premadasa and his supporters argued that the program would bring "discipline" to the nation's rural heartland, which had been the main source of revolutionaries. They explained to investors and the public that, by bringing jobs to villages, the 200 GFP aimed to address the perception that recent political instability in the country—especially the youth revolt, but also marginally the LTTE separatist movement—was caused by rural, vernacular-educated, and unemployed (or underemployed) youth who felt that the benefits of economic liberalization policies reached only the urban, English-educated elite. These notions were described in the findings of the Presidential Commission on Youth, which was established at the height of the youth revolt in October 1989 to determine the causes of and possible solutions to youth unrest (*Sessional Paper I* 1990; cf. Hettige 2004). Premadasa implemented the 200 GFP in direct response to the commission's report. Among the commission's many recommendations, he was particularly motivated by the need to industrialize villages to compensate for disparities in economic opportunity between urban and rural areas.

There were at least two other commission recommendations that Premadasa also addressed through the 200 GFP. One had to do with the English language and the other with farming.[6] According to investors I interviewed, a portion of 200 GFP workers were to be given English lessons at the factories, implementing the commission recommendation that English be made accessible to more rural people. The absence of English language abilities prevents many rural people from accessing employment opportunities they desire and for which they are otherwise qualified. The English language is known in Sinhala as the *kaḍuwa*, which literally means "sword." This term is used by non-English speakers to refer to the oppressive use of the English language by the elite. The metaphor reflects the view that the elite cut down vernacular speakers with this sword (Lloyd 1998; Perera 1995; Rajasingham-Senanayake 1997). In regard to farming, the 200 GFP was to be accompanied by a program for the storage of agricultural produce to address the widespread problem of produce decomposing before reaching local markets or being processed for export. This accompanying agricultural program, abandoned due to Premadasa's May 2003 assassination, was in line with another commission recommendation that youth be given incentives to "return to agriculture." In the program's emphasis on industrialization and English-language training (both considered modern) with a return to agriculture (prized as the traditional Sinhala occupation), the 200 GFP was designed to modernize both rural areas and rural citizens, but with certain qualifications. In short, this was to be a program of modernization with tradition.

Development, Tradition, and Liberalization

When questions of culture become national conversations in Sri Lanka, as in the wake of the 1977 economic reforms, the "culture" in question is sometimes referred to as "Sri Lankan," but it most often implicitly refers to Sinhala Buddhist culture. There is a widespread sense on the part of the Sinhala Buddhist majority that its culture and traditions are the norm; anything else— Christian, Muslim, Tamil—is inherently "foreign." This is so even if, as in the case of Tamils, the "foreigners" might have arrived in Sri Lanka thousands of years ago. In fact, many Sinhala Buddhists argue that they have the right to political domination of the island because they believe that the Buddha designated Sri Lanka to be the *dhammadīpa* (literally, the island of the *dhamma* [the Buddha's teachings]), the island that exemplifies and preserves the Buddha's teachings.[7]

Although the ongoing war between the government and the LTTE is not a religious war, Sinhala Buddhists often bring religious concepts such as *dhammadīpa* into their arguments against dividing the country. The war, however, has its roots in postcolonial cultural politics and language policies. Following the 1956 election of S. W. R. D. Bandaranaike's Sri Lanka Freedom Party (SLFP) on a platform of Sinhala Buddhist ethnic revivalism, and subsequent legislation that made Sinhala the national language to the exclusion of Tamil and English, the contemporary Sri Lankan state has increasingly become Sinhala Buddhist. Ethnic minorities have become alienated by state policies on language, government hiring, and university admissions and by the Buddhist symbolism and linguistic references that pervade electoral politics (Rogers, Spencer, and Uyangoda 1998).

From 1956 to 1977 the Sri Lankan economy was characterized by state accumulation through nationalization and regulation of private enterprise alongside a complementary policy of import substitution. The SLFP ruled the country through most of this period, with the United National Party (UNP) ruling intermittently. Following an economic crisis in the 1970s attributable to the SLFP's import-substitution policies, in 1977 the newly elected UNP government initiated its "Open Economy" program of export-led industrialization, privatization of industry, and decreasing state regulations and welfare expenditures. Key features of liberalization strategies include removing state controls on imports and attracting foreign investment. A centerpiece of this program was the establishment in 1978 of the first of three free trade zones, the Katunayake FTZ, in an urban area on the outskirts of Colombo (Richardson 2004).[8] The garment industry is the nation's largest source of foreign exchange at present.[9]

The sociologist Newton Gunasinghe (1984) argues that the import-substitution regime of 1956–77 gave rise to a patronage system that favored Sinhala entrepreneurs when it came to acquiring permits and concessions from the state. With the relaxation of state regulation in the late 1970s, ethnic minorities began to prosper economically while some small-scale Sinhala entrepreneurs suffered; Gunasinghe draws a connection between this shift and a rise in ethnic hostilities in the country (Winslow and Woost 2004). Calls for an independent state by various Tamil groups intensified in the early 1980s with the LTTE waging a full-blown war in the north and east of the country, where Tamils form the majority. An official ceasefire signed in February 2002 effectively ended in mid-2006 with a resumption of hostilities.

The two major political parties that have dominated Sri Lankan politics since independence have engaged questions of post-liberalization development and cultural preservation. Although both the UNP and the SLFP seem to have favored Sinhala Buddhist interests over minority interests since independence, because the English-educated elite supported the UNP and because the UNP was the first political party to promote capitalist development, many Sri Lankans considered it Westernized, materialistic, and indifferent to Sinhala Buddhist traditions. The same people would consider the SLFP to be more loyal to Sinhala Buddhism because its supporters consist of members of groups concerned with equality and the redistribution of wealth—ideals identified by many with traditional Sinhala Buddhist values. These groups include the Sinhala-educated village intelligentsia (shopkeepers, small landowners, teachers), traditional elites (such as monks and Ayurvedic doctors), and urban entrepreneurs (Gombrich and Obeyesekere 1988, 212; Ivan 1989; Sheeran 1997).

When it was in power from 1977 to 1994, the UNP attempted an image change: party members worked to associate the UNP with Sinhala traditions. To do so, they promoted a policy of economic development with attention to morality by arguing that there had to be economic progress and development to bring the country into the twenty-first century, but that such development was not to forsake what many consider a glorious Sinhala Buddhist past.

In the early 1990s both parties cultivated this image of striving for development with attention to morality. Below, I quote a Premadasa factory speech where he argues that his party wants "an open economy with a human face." At the time of the 200 GFP's launch, the opposition consisted of the SLFP. When the People's Alliance (PA), a coalition of parties led by the SLFP, came into power in 1994 it portrayed its policies with the same slogan of "open economy with a human face" (Stokke 1995, 124).[10] These discussions of the human side of economic liberalization are consistent with a long tradition of advocating modernization without Westernization in Sri Lanka. The anthropologist Steven Kemper (2001, 1) begins his ethnographic study of Sri Lankan advertising and consumers by noting that "between the allure of the foreign and sentiments that derive from more proximate forms of community, postcolonial societies find their way." As studies of globalization throughout the world have shown, postcolonial societies are not unique in struggling between attachment to the foreign and ties to the local. However, this struggle does seem to be especially pronounced in former colonies. One legacy of colonialism in countries such as Sri Lanka and its neighbor India is a complicated perspective on the foreign when it comes to economic development and modernization. While the foreign is in some sense admired, it is also despised and feared. The same can sometimes be said for certain aspects of the local, or what is constructed as "tradition" in contrast to modernity.

In Sri Lanka, this struggle between attachment to the local and attraction to the foreign has been a central feature of nationalist thought and policies since the late nineteenth century, from the period of anticolonial nationalism through independence in 1948 to the postcolonial ethnonationalism of today. The moral contrasts drawn between the UNP and the SLFP can be understood in this context, with the SLFP in particular accusing the UNP of an orientation too far toward the foreign at the expense of national traditions. Distinctions between rural and urban Sri Lanka have been key to the Sinhala Buddhist nationalist imagination, and even here there has been no easy resolution to the struggle Kemper describes.[11]

In contemporary Sri Lanka villages are generally associated with discipline, tradition, and morality. All these characteristics are said to be absent from cities (especially Colombo—by far the largest city—and its surrounding urban areas) because of the presence of foreign influences in urban areas. Even

JUKI GIRLS, GOOD GIRLS

though nationalists generally consider the urban to be corrupt, some of them also value it positively for its modernity. These urban-rural contrasts are reminiscent of a familiar narrative from other times and places that associates the city with the modern and corrupt and the countryside with tradition, culture, and moral order. For instance, the historian Raymond Williams (1973) has famously examined the role of the country and city dichotomy in the English moral imagination. Likewise, the historian Herman Lebovics (1992) has written about the role of the pastoral in the French tradition. Unlike the situations described by Williams and Lebovics, though, it is not only urban Sri Lankans who think about these dichotomies: rural people are equally invested in thinking about their world in rural-urban contrasts—contrasts that nevertheless are continually complicated in everyday social practices.

Even the social reforms of the Buddhist reformer Anagarika Dharmapala, the most influential Sri Lankan anticolonial ideologue, were situated within these contradictions. Importantly, Dharmapala's anticolonial nationalism was a specifically Sinhala-inflected nationalism, which was formulated at the expense of other ethnic groups. It was Dharmapala who coined the term *Sinhala Buddhist* in the early twentieth century (Gunawardana 1990, 76). Dharmapala's Buddhist revivalism equated Sinhalas with Buddhism and inaugurated the concept of Sri Lanka as the *dhammadīpa*. In the late nineteenth and early twentieth centuries, he formulated a new social ethic that was widely adopted in Sri Lanka, especially among the Sinhala-educated petite bourgeoisie. Over the past century, all Sinhala status groups have gradually adopted this new ethic, but to varying degrees; moreover, its views of the foreign and the local are contradictory. The anthropologist Gananath Obeyesekere (1970) has termed this new social ethic "Protestant Buddhism" for two reasons: because some of the values were modeled on Protestant codes of morality, and because it was a protest against the degradation of Sinhala Buddhist culture attributed to the British and especially the Christian missionaries.

Dharmapala selectively integrated aspects of Westernization into his vision for Sri Lanka's future. For example, he extolled the Japanese example of modernizing the economy with Western technology while preserving the traditional social order (Jayawardena 1985, 9; cf. Bond 1988, 54; Seneviratne 1999). This balance of East and West continues to be important in contemporary Sri Lanka. The anthropologist Serena Tennekoon (1988) argues that for development projects to be socially accepted in Sri Lanka they must symbolically resolve the popular dichotomy between the spiritual East and the material West that many Sri Lankans espouse. A similar formulation was made by nationalists in India, a subject explored by Partha Chatterjee (1986, 1993), and it has been present in anticolonial movements throughout the world. Although associated with the spiritually lacking West, development and progress are seen as necessary to Sri Lankan national survival. Nevertheless they must be balanced with what are considered essentially Sri Lankan spiritual and moral values. Key questions for Sri Lankans after 1977 were: If economic liberalization is the suitable path for development, how can everyone in society benefit from it? How can the economy be liberalized but traditional moral values be maintained?

If such debates about culture and economic development supplied the wider context for the formulation of the 200 GFP, the most pressing immediate context was, without question, the recent youth revolt. As a matter of policy, President Premadasa offered the 200 GFP in response to some of the social and economic problems that the Presidential Commission on Youth identified. I turn now to examine the revolt in more detail.

The JVP Challenge

In the late 1980s the UNP government under President Premadasa faced a strong challenge from within the Sinhala ethnic group with the violent uprising of the Janatha Vimukthi Peramuna (JVP, People's Liberation Front). Formed in 1965, the JVP staged a short-lived but significant revolt in 1971. From 1971 to 1987 the group's public fortunes shuttled between proscription (with many members jailed or undergoing "rehabilitation") and official recognition as a political party. But from 1987 to 1990 the JVP launched another violent revolt, aimed at overthrowing Premadasa's government. This second revolt was so widespread and aggressive that it nearly captured state control. Most of the country that was not already controlled by the LTTE was deeply affected by this second JVP revolt. The deaths and disappearances that occurred at the hands of the JVP and as a result of the brutal government crackdown number an estimated forty to fifty thousand. Estimates vary as to how many were the responsibility of which group, although there seems to be agreement that the bulk are attributable to the government.[12] This period was characterized by extreme repression and violence; indeed it is remembered in Sri Lanka as the "period of terror" (*biṣna kālaya*). On 13 November 1989 the state killed JVP leader Rohana Wijeweera. With the remaining top leaders then killed or arrested, the revolt soon ended. In the end, thousands of sus-

JUKI GIRLS, GOOD GIRLS

pected JVP youth were dead or located in rehabilitation camps, or had simply disappeared. The villages around Shirtex and Serendib were especially hard-hit by the JVP and the government response. Immediate family members of at least a dozen garment workers disappeared or were killed during this time, and I return to some of their stories in a later chapter.

The late 1980s' JVP ideology combined a critique of foreign economic forces with Sinhala chauvinism. The JVP's concerns were both economic and social: it was critical of the uneven economic benefits of liberalization and of the accompanying deterioration of cultural traditions.[13] Scholars have argued about whether or not the JVP revolts were primarily concerned with "socialism through class struggle" or "national liberation through patriotic struggle" (de Silva 1998, 190; cf. Jayawardena 1985, 84–90, Uyangoda 1992). Nationalism and class struggle are both evident in the series of lessons for potential or new members that have been the organ of JVP philosophy throughout the organization's history (Gunaratna 1990, 61–62).

In regard to economics, the lectures included discussion of economic problems resulting from colonial and neocolonial policies—in particular, they argued that despite political independence the country did not have economic independence from foreign rule. Class inequality, unemployment, underemployment, inflation, and the related problems of rural-urban inequalities were topics that the JVP raised throughout the second revolt (Ivan 1989, *Sessional Paper I* 1990). In regard to nationalism, one important topic was the fear of Indian expansionism. The JVP was concerned that Indian capitalists were attempting to take over the country; and in fact, the event that pushed the group into revolt was the Indo-Lanka Peace Accord that Premadasa's predecessor, J. R. Jayewardene, signed with the Indian government in mid-1987. This accord allowed the Indian army (as the Indian Peace Keeping Force, IPKF) to come to Sri Lanka to disarm the LTTE. There was considerable opposition to this accord by many Sinhalas who believed it was the first step in a long-feared Indian encroachment, which the JVP had been warning of since the 1960s.

The political scientist Mick Moore (1993, 613) argues that in 1982 and 1983 the JVP had taken a chauvinist turn, which intensified in 1987 when the IPKF entered Sri Lanka. At this time, he writes, "Sinhalese Buddhist nationalism was turned from a largely tacit theme in the JVP's programme into its centrepiece" (618). The JVP contended that the UNP was selling out to foreigners, was not patriotic enough, and was too pro-American (614 n. 55)—this despite the UNP's efforts since 1977 to fashion itself as a champion of Sinhala

Buddhist interests. By the time of the second revolt, the JVP had declared itself, and was widely recognized as, the nation's primary guardian of patriotism and the Sinhala Buddhist moral order.

The popular interpretation in Sri Lanka is that the revolt was centrally focused on perceived disparities between rural and urban Sri Lanka.[14] Enter the 200 GFP, which was offered as "insurance" for democracy in rural areas in order to prevent the resurgence of the JVP. For Premadasa, the JVP revolt was a problem that stemmed from the "frustrated" aspirations of rural youth. As I show in the next section, his 200 GFP was designed to fulfill those aspirations by providing economic opportunity to those very youth. Most JVP members had been the educated unemployed; and thus, if we can believe Premadasa's rhetoric, the program always rested on an apparent contradiction: its offer of factory jobs was targeted at a well-educated populace who aspired for better jobs than those they could get in garment factories.

The Prevention of Revolution and Alleviation of Poverty

In his inaugural 200 GFP speech Premadasa explicitly focused on the JVP and discussed how his program would alleviate poverty among potential rebels. Comments by Premadasa and his supporters revealed a utilitarian rationale for the program: if rural youth have jobs, they will feel a commitment to the stability of the state and there will not be another youth revolt. Furthermore, if villagers learn capitalist discipline (which 200 GFP promoters associated with village-appropriate, moral behavior), they will be less inclined to join the JVP in the future. These themes of preventing revolution and alleviating poverty were apparent from the program's beginning. In his very first 200 GFP speech, Premadasa explained that the 200 GFP "is part of my plan to prevent another reign of terror in the country" (Fernando 1992a, 14). After he introduced the related program in which garment factory investors would be given financial concessions for building produce storage facilities, he said, "In this way we hope to decentralise industrial activity to the rural sector. In this way democracy would be meaningful to the rural people. They will also respect and honour the people who invest, realising that it is because of them that they are earning a livelihood" (Special Correspondent 1992a). In short, Premadasa argued that the conditions for a future social revolution would be eliminated if rural people felt that they were benefiting from the nation's development, and if they felt that the wealthy urban investor class had taken an interest in them.

Analysis of Premadasa's speeches at factory opening ceremonies reveals that the program had the explicit goal of solving the nation's recent problems of "unrest" through poverty alleviation. Premadasa often repeated that the only qualification for employment in these factories was "abject poverty," and that ethnicity, caste, religion, education, and political affiliation were irrelevant. As he once said at an opening ceremony speech, "Poverty is the only criteria [*sic*] for recruitment. Hunger is a universal feeling which recognizes no race, religion, or caste" (Sri Lanka News Bulletin 1993b). Referring to the Sri Lankan system (based on the British educational system) of Ordinary Level (O/L) and Advanced Level (A/L) examinations, at another speech he said, "The only qualification is, not an O/L or A/L, but P/L—poverty level" (Sri Lanka News Bulletin 1993a, 4).

To ensure that all 200 GFP workers came from the poor, all potential workers for the original hiring cycle were to be selected by managers from a pool of recipients of Premadasa's Janasaviya Program, a poverty alleviation program begun in 1989 (Stokke 1995). Once an individual received a 200 GFP job, his or her family's Janasaviya benefits were discontinued. Consistent with the emphasis on poverty alleviation, Premadasa often insisted that the program was pluralistic and nondiscriminatory in terms of who was to be employed; indeed, there were even factories established in primarily Tamil or Muslim areas, and in areas close to LTTE-controlled territory. (At a factory I visited in the north, managers told me that workers had on several occasions slept in the factories because they had been advised not to return to their homes in nearby villages due to the threat of an LTTE attack.)

History, Culture, and the 200 GFP

While Premadasa frequently gestured toward inclusiveness and described the program as simply a nonpartisan and nonsectarian poverty-alleviation program, he also invoked particular events, concepts, and people in Sri Lankan history and culture that would have been especially meaningful to Sinhala Buddhists. Yet as a shrewd politician, he was careful to include other communities within Sri Lanka. His adeptness and intentions in this regard have led the anthropologist H. L. Seneviratne (1999, 233) to refer to his "shallow ecumenism." In this section I examine how Premadasa skillfully constructed the 200 GFP in a manner that would appeal to Sinhala Buddhist nationalist sentiment but would also address a wider constituency. By examining these discursive strategies for localizing global production, we see how Premadasa negotiated the relationship between his goals of protecting the nation from cultural and political disintegration and opening it to foreign investment.

Premadasa promoted a variety of capitalism that was consistent with what are considered traditional Sinhala Buddhist values—specifically those of respect, honor, love, discipline, and hard work. For instance, he argued that an important element in the relationship between investors and workers was love. Under the 200 GFP his government was aiming to "bind the employer and the employee, the poor and the rich in a bond of love. This is the new orientation we are giving to the open economy. We want an open economy with a human face" (Fernando 1992d, 15). He urged investors to implement worker-friendly practices because of "the rule of love" rather than the dictates of the "rule of law." Premadasa stated, "The rule of love is a stage where the mighty concede what is due to the weak not because of the requirement of the law, but out of sheer love and compassion, fellow-feeling and respect of human dignity" (Fernando 1992d, 15).

Premadasa understood there to be a direct relationship between living standards and political stability. He anticipated the production of a new type of citizen through industrializing villages and enabling villagers to participate in the nation's future by engaging in productive work. The notion that work, industriousness, and discipline were the key to the future of the nation has a long history in Sri Lanka. A disciplined life and a strong work ethic were central to Dharmapala's teachings. When he discussed the ways in which employment would prevent revolution, Premadasa often reasoned that when people were allowed to work they became more committed to the social order. In the speech that I quoted in the introduction, he took the argument one step further by arguing—in a manner reminiscent of Dharmapala—that the hard work and skills required for garment work were "latent" in villagers. To ensure that villagers would not join the JVP in the future, the president appealed to their valuation of moral and physical discipline for the nation.

The 200 GFP relied on and reinforced nationalist notions that the nation's villages are the center of Sinhala Buddhist culture. In the nationalist imagination, Sri Lanka's glory would be restored through the revitalization of its once harmonious and self-sufficient Sinhala Buddhist villages. However historically dubious, this romantic idealization of Sri Lanka's precolonial villages has been

JUKI GIRLS, GOOD GIRLS

an important element in the Sinhala nationalism of the postcolonial period. For instance, a major point of Tamil-Sinhala contention has been the state-sponsored Mahaweli Development Project, a scheme to settle Sinhalas in remote areas that have a majority Tamil population, based on the claim that in the precolonial period thriving Sinhala villages were located there (Moore 1985; Richardson 2004, 49; Smith 1979).

The 200 GFP's Sinhala Buddhist significance was cultivated in part through this invocation of glorious village traditions. Premadasa modeled himself after precolonial Buddhist kings, and one of his slogans was *gama hadā raṭa hadamu*—literally, "having built the village, let's build the nation." The apparent irony of recuperating the past glory of villages through *industrialization* did not seem to be a problem in this formulation, which is likely because of Premadasa's success at localizing global production.

Such aspects of the program fall on the more subtly nationalistic side. Sometimes Premadasa's speeches were quite explicitly Sinhala Buddhist nationalist. In one speech he invoked *dhammadīpa*, the notion that the Buddha designated Sri Lanka to be a Buddhist land: Premadasa noted that due to the establishment of rural factories" . . . I can see good omens pointing to our country regaining its lost title of 'Dhammadeepa'" (Fernando and Dissanayake 1992, n.p.). In the following excerpt there is an obvious convergence of nationalist ideology and the realities of wage labor capitalism. Premadasa explained that the twelfth-century king Parakramabahu, who built a kingdom around an elaborate irrigation system in the country's dry zone, had said that not a single drop of rainwater should go to the sea without being used. Premadasa's invocation of Parakramabahu would have appealed to Sinhala Buddhist nationalists who revere this king for uniting the island against invaders (which today connotes Tamils) and for protecting Buddhism. Premadasa paralleled that preciousness of water to sweat: "When I went round the country during the presidential election campaign, I told the people that my aim was to see that every drop of sweat of [*sic*] our people shed was given the value it deserved. . . . That was why the 200 garment factories program was launched." Now, with export orders being filled, Premadasa declared, "The sweat that the factory girls shed has received the value it deserves—they have not shed their sweat in vain. Aren't these factory workers earning valuable foreign exchange? Is this not the way to recover something of the vast wealth that went into foreign hands when we were under colonial masters for 450 years?" (Fernando 1992b, 15).

In this speech, Premadasa attributed a positive valence to women's sweat (unlike the negative imagery of "sweat" in the term "sweatshops") and rhetorically used sweat to justify Sri Lanka's involvement in global capitalism. As Dharmapala argued, so, too, did Premadasa: working hard enough to produce sweat is a good thing; industriousness is good for the nation. But at the same time Premadasa appealed to Sinhala Buddhist nationalist sentiments in his veiled reference to the Tamil fight for independence (through his invocation of Parakramabahu) and to European colonialism.

It is important to consider the diversity of audiences for Premadasa's speeches. These might include not only villagers of various ethnic and religious groups (although most would be Sinhala Buddhists) but also foreign and Sri Lankan investors. Many investors were members of the island's minority ethnic groups. Although the participation of non–Sinhala Buddhist investors in the program complicated the nationalist project, an analysis of the opening ceremony speeches reveals that Premadasa was able to deploy the nationalist rhetoric to varying degrees depending on the demographics of the local area and the backgrounds of the investors. Furthermore, his comments can be read in multiple ways; and even those described in the previous paragraph could appeal to non–Sinhala Buddhists, since his reference to 450 years of colonialism was a deployment of a non-ethnically partisan nationalism.

This more broadly anticolonial argument about recovering wealth through generating foreign exchange was important to Premadasa and figured in the trilingual motto for the decade of exports, "Exports bring prosperity to you and the nation." This slogan was likely intended to make every Sri Lankan feel part of the development process. In an opening ceremony for a factory where some employees were sisters of LTTE fighters, Premadasa emphasized the anticolonial nationalism of the program. He read a verse of Sinhala poetry from a book he wrote in 1976:

> Foreign food we need not, to satisfy our hunger;
> Foreign cloth we need not, to cover our bodies;
> Foreign eyes we need not, to see our well being;
> Foreign brains we need not, to resolve our problems.
> (*Observer* 1993, n.p.)

He presented this poem at the opening ceremony for a factory that may have been funded by foreign investment and most certainly relied on foreign buyers for its success. Clearly Premadasa chose to appeal to antiforeign nationalist

JUKI GIRLS, GOOD GIRLS

sentiments in this formerly LTTE-controlled area where the residents were Tamil and Muslim.

In addition to tailoring his speeches to the audience, he would invariably speak about how implementation of the program would prevent the resurgence of the JVP. This line of argument had mass appeal, since the JVP violence affected many differently positioned members of Sri Lankan society, and since political instability was widely considered inimical to economic investment. Even so, here he was criticizing foreignness while establishing export-oriented factories, sometimes financed by foreign capital, in rural areas of the country that were celebrated for their pristine traditionalism. I did not locate—whether through interviews, informal conversations, or mass-media archives—many Sri Lankans who identified this as ironic or contradictory, and I take this as another indication of Premadasa's aptitude for the work of localizing global production.

The president's discursive strategies were sometimes subtle. At the program's inaugural speech, when he spoke of it as "insurance" against revolution, he also invoked the theme of neoimperialism. In reference to the poor people who were to become a part of the country's growth through this program he noted, "Otherwise they will tend to look upon growth as tied to the well being of a few. They will see foreign investment as a perpetuation of foreign exploitation. They will look upon exports as production for the foreigners" (*Daily News* 1992a, 15). Here Premadasa was clearly trying to woo the population into the development process: to be sure, the poor would be producing for foreigners, but the focus was to be on the benefits to the nation's poor. Given the centrality of debates about the foreign and the local to the JVP revolt, these strategies for recasting exports so soon after the revolt were especially significant. While the evidence of the JVP theme in this inaugural speech and subsequent 200 GFP media coverage and publicity was stark, the more subtle message concerning neoimperialism and its attendant economic and cultural issues requires closer analysis.

Discipline

Premadasa promised that the 200 GFP would bring with it certain social changes that would alleviate widespread concerns about the decline of discipline in villages. Factory work requires discipline in and of itself, as historians of the Industrial Revolution have demonstrated.[15] However, Premadasa and his supporters mobilized a specifically Sinhala Buddhist concept of discipline, which would have resonated with particular Sinhala anxieties about economic liberalization and cultural preservation. Premadasa not only envisioned that global production would be a means toward village-based social change but proposed a vision for the future of the Sinhala Buddhist nation. In studying these state discourses about discipline, we can thus gain key insight into how Sri Lankans tried to make sense of the changing world around them—what it meant to be Sri Lankan or a good person, what positions they considered valuable and indicative of progress.

Clock towers are a valuable window into understanding the politics of discipline and the complicated work Premadasa engaged in as he brought factories to villages throughout Sri Lanka. Anthropologists and historians have done comparative research on conceptions of time (see Adam 1990; Hughes and Trautmann 1995; Munn 1992; Rutz 1992; Thompson 1967). Vastly different social attitudes toward time demonstrate that people culturally construct time as they make sense of the world. Differences are apparent even on the most basic level: not everyone thinks of time as "passing" in the same ways, nor do they "carve up" time into the same units. There are also different conceptions of what it means to be "on time," or prompt, and on what is past, present, or future (Evans-Pritchard 1940, chap. 3). As the anthropologist Jack Goody argued in 1968, "Although all societies have some system of time reckoning, some idea of sequence and duration, the mode of reckoning clearly varies with the economy, ecology, and technical equipment; with the ritual system; and with the political organization" (Goody 1991 [1968], 31). E. P. Thompson wrote a pathbreaking essay in 1967 on the dependence of the Industrial Revolution on a revolution in the European understanding of time. Factory workers must arrive at a uniform time for a production line to function properly, and the laborers and managers must stick to the buyers' production schedules. Thus, for factory discipline to be instilled in workers, they also must absorb a new way of understanding time.

Certainly working to the clock is central to factory labor, where workers are paid according to an hourly wage. At Shirtex and Serendib, workers punch in and out on a time clock, and bells ring to mark the start and end of the workday and breaks. The day is divided into hourly periods for assessing target rates, so every day managers can be seen timing the machine operators with a stopwatch (following Taylorist time and motion techniques). To commence

JUKI GIRLS, GOOD GIRLS

this clock-regimented day, the workers must get to work on time; hence at one Colombo factory I visited, the workers had requested alarm clocks as their year-end gift from management (or so said the owner in an interview with me). Consequently, some explanations I heard for the clock towers referred to modern capitalist practices for institutionalizing dominant time and the time discipline required for factory work (cf. Rutz 1992; Thompson 1967). In this reading, the towers were simply designed to enable the workers to know the time.

But an American general manager of a 200 GFP factory provided a different explanation. He joined others who considered the clock towers to function as a sign of the times, symbolizing the social changes that accompany rural industrial development. He argued that it was meant to be "a symbol to the community that they have arrived. They have an industry. It would let the world know." Some investors provided both a symbolic and a disciplinary reading and explained the towers as symbols of the new industrial time discipline. One manager in a remote factory in the north of the country explained to me that they were meant to be a symbol of the town's development. Furthermore, he noted that few factory workers had watches when they first started to work because they were too expensive. Instead, the new recruits could get to the factory on time because of the chime of the clock. Like the monastery bells in medieval Europe that rang throughout the day as "goads to effective, productive labor" for monks and lay people alike (Landes 1983, 68–69, quoted in Wu 1997, 342), this chime of the clock would also be heard by people other than factory workers, thus possibly spreading time discipline throughout the area. According to one investor, "It was to show the people of the village that now time means something. Earlier you see the sun rise and you go out. Or if you see the crows flying, you will start tilling the field or something like that. [Premadasa] said instead of that, now you work to a clock."[16] This investor seemed to be arguing that factory laborers required more discipline than the fluctuations of nature dictated. He also implied here that notions of time based on natural processes were not meaningful.

In describing the transformations that have taken place because of the establishment of factories in villages, numerous investors and managers told me that workers would buy watches with their first wages. Indeed, many of the women at Shirtex and Serendib confirmed that they had done so. Many Sri Lankans wear watches, but often they do not keep time. On crowded and bumpy bus rides, I frequently surveyed the wrists of people grasping for something with which to steady themselves. Most wrists had watches, and they all displayed widely different times—some moving and others completely stopped. But although the watches didn't "work" according to the timekeeping function, they "worked" in another way. They worked as symbols of modernity: they were commodities that symbolized a new style and a new conception of time.[17]

Though they were both timepieces invoked in discussions about the 200 GFP, watches and clock towers were quite different objects in this social and political context. While both were understood as symbols of modernity, the towers were also interpreted as a tool for the legitimization of political power through the control of time (cf. Rutz 1992; Bowen 1992). As such, they were the butt of considerable criticism and jokes. According to one joke, some years back when Premadasa was visiting England he lamented to Margaret Thatcher that the electorate wasn't completely happy with him. Thatcher responded by saying, "Give them time." The literal-minded Premadasa built clocks throughout the country. The four faces of the garment factory clocks often kept different times or did not move at all, and numerous people made critical comments to me about the broken clock towers that dotted the countryside. In these and other critical comments, the clock towers were dismissed as a mere symbolic gesture designed to get votes when there was a more immediate need for economic restructuring and social justice in the country. Critics may have seized on the towers because they were the most visible symbol of the 200 GFP and its promised transformation of the countryside. They also may have focused on them because the lack of discipline symbolized by a broken clock tower was a significant contradiction to the centrality of discipline in Premadasa's vision of the program, as well as in his personal and political life.

The Politics of Discipline

During Premadasa's 1988 presidential campaign, his government's main political challenge came from the JVP revolt. Peace, discipline, and poverty were issues that were unavoidably associated with the JVP. Hence, the UNP's platform centered on restoring peace, enforcing discipline, and alleviating poverty (Department of Government Printing 1988). In the materials published in English, *discipline* is alternately a translation of the Sinhala nouns *vinaya* and *sanwara*. Both words mean "discipline," although *vinaya* also refers

Figure 2. A 200 Garment Factories Program clock tower in Akkaraipattu, eastern Sri Lanka. Note the clock faces that tell different times, the posters of President Premadasa that adorn the tower's legs, and the Buddhist stupa that tops off the peak (a conspicuous style in this Tamil- and Muslim-dominated area of the island). Photo by Dennis McGilvray, printed with permission.

to the Buddhist monastic discipline, or rules that the monks must follow. As Obeyesekere (1970, 55) notes, the monastic *vinaya* emphasizes personal decorum and good manners. *Saṇwara* can also refer to monks, in which context it connotes being serene, calm, and at peace. In reference to others it connotes not acting up or not being flashy, showy, or demonstrative. A *saṇwara* woman does not call attention to herself. This term is often used in reference to respectable women to refer to decency and self-control. In sum, good monks and good women should inhabit their bodies in a contained and controlled manner.

Discipline was a concept that Premadasa used in reference to his own behavior and the behavior of politicians and ordinary people. He often said that he wanted himself, parliamentarians, and other leaders to become more disciplined in order to set a good example for the citizenry, for "example is better than precept. Discipline must begin with self-discipline" (Department of Government Printing 1989, 2). Furthermore, "No country can make progress unless its people are dedicated and disciplined. These qualities must be built up in the home and in the school before one goes out into the world. A high standard of discipline will be enforced by imposing rules and regulations. It will also be done through motivation and by example set by Ministers and Senior Officials downwards" (Department of Government Printing 1990a, 8). Premadasa did not exempt himself from this requirement. People of widely varying social backgrounds often told me that Premadasa was a hard worker, a nondrinker, a nonsmoker, an exquisite orator, and a neat dresser who needed little sleep. Regarding his own discipline he said: "I keep a schedule of 16 hours a day myself. I want to instil [*sic*] into everyone that if we are to pull this country round, we have to put in more than the statutory 8 hours a day, or 5 days a week" (Presidential Secretariat n.d., n.p.).

Certainly Premadasa was an astute politician who knew how to emphasize nonpartisan values for the future of the country, and obviously "discipline" can be a secular concept. In fact, one of his close associates told me that Premadasa admired Peter Senge's 1990 book *The Fifth Discipline*, a manual for building globally competitive businesses—clearly not a book that builds on Sinhala Buddhist concepts.[18] But Premadasa's emphasis on discipline was also an attempt to foster a specifically Sinhala Buddhist moral code in response to the JVP revolt. It is telling that Premadasa's emphasis on discipline accompanied a program for restoring *dhamma*, the Buddha's teachings. It will also prove illuminating to consider the move to frame discipline as a traditional

Sinhala virtue in the context of its historical antecedents in Dharmapala's Protestant Buddhism.

Dhamma and Discipline

According to Premadasa, discipline was not to be exercised for personal gain, but for the benefit of the country: "If we are to build our motherland, if we want a society which can give everyone a fair deal, we must learn and practice collective discipline" (2 January 1991 speech, quoted in Jayatilleka and Gunasekara 1994, 11). In her study of Premadasa's use of religious rhetoric, Josine van der Horst (1995, 58) asserts that for him discipline was "a device to bring about a shift towards first a peaceful individual and consequently a peaceful society." Premadasa seems to have assumed that discipline is required for people to live according to a code of morality.

Van der Horst (1995, 53) notes that after the defeat of the JVP, Premadasa was concerned with preventing another revolt by restoring *dhamma* and discipline to society. The concept of *dhamma* (also known as *dharma*) is nuanced. Technically *dhamma* refers to the Buddha's teachings. However, in Sinhala Buddhism it is often invoked to mean not only the teachings but also the moral code that goes along with them. Beginning in April 1990, six months after the JVP leader was killed, the government announced a program to fund *daham pāsäls* (*dhamma* schools) throughout the country. Speakers at school opening ceremonies conveyed the concept behind the renewed focus on *daham pāsäls*. For instance, Melvin J. Cooray, the minister of power and energy, said, "If *daham pasal* thrives there will be no subversion" (quoted in van der Horst 1995, 83).

Van der Horst argues that when Premadasa invoked the concepts of *dhamma* and discipline, he was not referring to exclusively Buddhist concepts. Instead, he was marshaling these terms in their nondenominational and all-encompassing senses. She contends that he sought to transform the country from a violent society to a peaceful society in the same way that Emperor Asoka had in India millennia earlier. In the third century B.C.E., Asoka made a dramatic switch from waging violent war to advocating Buddhist nonviolence centered on a nondenominational sense of *dhamma* as ethics and morality. Van der Horst argues that after the defeat of the JVP, when Premadasa spoke of *dhamma* it was not as "the Buddha's teachings," but as a general concept of "righteousness" that could appeal to people of all religions (1995, 56).

In this connection it can be noted that the cognate concept of *dharma* for Hindus in India encompasses righteousness, right way of living, and spiritual and moral order.

If van der Horst's argument about Premadasa's intention is correct, it nevertheless seems to emphasize intentionality at the expense of reception. Although some people may have understood his complicated philosophy as nondenominational and multiethnic, most Sri Lankans would associate words like *dhamma* and *dhammadīpa* with Sinhala Buddhist traditions and domination of the island. This is especially so because politicians often use these terms at ceremonies related to the restoration of Buddhist *stupas* or at events at which they would invoke heroic Sinhala Buddhist kings.[19] Likewise, discipline is associated with Dharmapala, the main figure behind the so-called Sinhala Buddhist revival. I concede that Premadasa would not want to alienate the country's minorities, and so he would speak in terms that could be interpreted broadly. His speeches at the 200 GFP openings and elsewhere reveal such multivocality tailored to the audience. Rather than understand his rhetoric as contradictory or fitting into an Asokan model, however, it is best to keep in mind that he was speaking to different constituencies at the same time—in this he was a true politician.

Dharmapala and Discipline

A second aspect of Premadasa's emphasis on discipline that demands to be seen in a specifically Sinhala Buddhist light has to do with the historical mobilization of the concept by the anticolonial nationalist Dharmapala. Dharmapala touted discipline as an indigenous Sinhala Buddhist moral disposition and as a central feature of his Protestant Buddhism. Numerous scholars have written about the new value system that stemmed from Dharmapala's teachings and from his writings on Sinhala Buddhist history and culture (for example, Bond 1988; de Alwis 1998; Gombrich and Obeyesekere 1988; Obeyesekere 1970; Seneviratne 1999). My interest lies in the genealogical connection between Dharmapala's and Premadasa's concerns with discipline.

Although there has been a disciplinary code (a *vinaya*) for Buddhist monks since the time of the Buddha, there was no formal code for lay people until Dharmapala published a pamphlet in Sinhala in 1898 called "The Daily Code for the Laity." This program—which enjoyed immense popularity for at least sixty years (Obeyesekere 1970, 56)—encouraged behavior such as "rising early, bathing daily, concentrating fully at one's workplace and interspersing one's day with religious thoughts and concerns" (de Alwis 1998, 152). Of the more than two hundred rules in the code, the largest cluster concerned women's behavior, with thirty rules under the heading "How Females Should Conduct Themselves" (Guruge 1965, 36–38; cf. de Alwis 1998, 152–56). Malathi de Alwis (1998, 153) describes Dharmapala's identification of women as the prime site for creating a new Protestant Buddhist community. Through their regulated practices of "sanitation, morality, and religiosity," women would be role models for their children and the rest of society. For Dharmapala and other nationalists of his time, women were the sites of the nation's regeneration in the context of colonialism, a nationalist strategy that reemerged with the mobilization of norms of femininity in the face of globalization.

Dharmapala believed that colonialism had eroded natural Sinhala strengths and values. For instance, he identified a widespread condition of laziness and diagnosed it to be a recent product of colonialism, which threatened the future of the Sinhala people. He argued that the nation's future depended on harnessing activity and industriousness. Dharmapala's moral code contained rules for behavior as particular as how to chew betel, how to behave while walking on the street, and how to use the lavatory (de Alwis 1998, 152). With these new behaviors he hoped to remedy problems such as colonially induced laziness. But Dharmapala did not completely shun the moral perspectives of the conquerors. Obeyesekere (1970, 56–57) notes that Protestant Buddhism was indebted not only to traditional Sinhala Buddhist norms but also to Western and Protestant norms that were "cathected and assimilated as pure or ideal Sinhalese norms." These Western-derived norms then became the basis for condemnation of Westerners—for example, for being sexually lax (Obeyesekere 1970, 47). At least in part due to Dharmapala's influence, morality in Sri Lanka today is generally thought of as Buddhist, although its basic components (i.e., do not drink alcohol, kill, lie, steal) are values found in varying forms in many religions.

Although Dharmapala advocated this-worldly asceticism and lay meditation, he often wrote about the importance of spiritual *and* material development of the nation. He considered industriousness and morality to be interconnected and both especially suited to Buddhists, for whom activity and cooperation were natural values (Guruge 1965, 515–16). In his introduction to a collection of Dharmapala's writings, Ananda Guruge (1965, LXXXIII) notes that the reformer aimed to keep the material benefits of Western civilization such as education, science, and technology but eradicate Western "abominations" such as drinking alcohol, eating meat, and seizing private land for government use. The social order he wanted to preserve was rural, agricultural, and Buddhist. At one point Dharmapala wrote, "It is the agricultural and the labouring class that form the backbone of the Sinhalese nation" (Guruge 1965, 512), and elsewhere he referred to farmers and village headmen as the backbone of the Sinhala nation (535).

H.L. Seneviratne (1999, 47) argues that Dharmapala wanted to "restore the Sinhala people to their pristine glory while bringing them into modernity." He describes Dharmapala's project as simultaneously economic and pragmatic (here the emphasis was on being modern like the West), and political and ideological (here the emphasis was on a renaissance of Sinhala tradition) (1999, 36). Indeed, at the heart of Dharmapala's work is an ambivalence about colonialism, and this ambivalence is particularly evident in his perspectives on activity and work. For instance, while he critiqued the English for rendering Sinhalas lazy, he tried to restore Sinhalas to a "traditional" state using discourses and images about the importance of industry and activity drawn from the West but also combined with Buddhist notions of discipline. Dharmapala admired the industriousness of the British, but he also characterized activity and industriousness as values inherent to Buddhism: "Buddhism teaches an energetic life, to be active in doing good work all the time. A healthy man requires only 4 hours sleep" (Guruge 1965, 669).

By 1992, when Premadasa revived Dharmapala's concepts of industry and activity, Sinhalas thought of these concepts as native to their culture—the connection to Buddhist concepts of discipline was what they emphasized. Yet Dharmapala had clearly built on Western Protestant notions of the work ethic, which Max Weber (1958) famously argued was the animating force behind the development of capitalism in modern Europe. The fact that Dharmapala's Protestant Buddhist concepts were used by Premadasa to foster the establishment of capitalist factories in villages offers a striking point of comparison to Weber's own discussion of Protestantism and European capitalism.

The influence of Dharmapala's ethical code and his other writings was widespread. Gombrich and Obeyesekere (1988, 211–12) argue that the code was diffused throughout the country by means of *daham pāsäls* and the state school system (especially following the establishment of universal free education in 1947). They argue that Sinhala village teachers were important promulgators of this new value system (1988, 212). This is relevant to the case of Shirtex and Serendib, where managers and workers alike explicitly followed a teacher-student model for their interactions and some managers assumed the wider role of the teacher as moral mentor.

According to Premadasa's biographer Bradman Weerakoon (1992, 16), Premadasa's father was an active supporter and promoter of Dharmapala's views. Premadasa identified with these views as he grew up; and his political and personal interest in discipline, morality, and a work ethic are clearly part of the Dharmapala legacy. There are numerous illustrations of this influence. Both men were known for their punctuality and both spoke of the need to sleep little in order to maximize work time. It was Dharmapala who introduced meditation to lay people, and Premadasa meditated daily and included meditation in the program for "misguided youth" in rehabilitation camps. Finally, publicity material for the 200 GFP shows that while Premadasa saw villagers as the moral core of the nation and valued the tradition of village farming, he also advocated establishing factories in villages as a way to save the country from moral, physical, and financial decay. In sum, it is clear that Premadasa followed Dharmapala in seeing an interconnection among discipline, Sinhala Buddhist morality, and national development.

Discipline and Social Change

Coverage of the 200 GFP in state-controlled newspapers generally reproduced the government's views on the program. Some reporters, however, were even more eloquent than the president about the disciplinary effects of the program, and they argued that the program offered a chance at social change through the rehabilitation of the bad habits of villagers. Take the following example, from the Sinhala daily *Dinamina*:

> In addition to getting employment in the new garment factories, the young men and women in villages will get in the habit of dressing smartly and going to work. This may alleviate the habitual laziness [*kammälikam*] of being in the rustic villages [*game godē*]. . . . The children of poor parents will teach their parents. They will learn and instruct others in, for instance, how to select clothing styles [*mōstara*]. From these various things the country will develop. Not only that, the people who used to live in a dishonorable manner in village society may even get rehabilitated in this context. Rustic [*godē*] village young men, women, and their parents will become disciplined [*saṇwara*] by learning various things about traveling, food, clothing, housing, good habits [*cāritra*], etc. These changes that will occur in the villages will not just

be confined to these families but will spread through the entire country. So this is an attempt to discipline [*saṇwara*] the country. (Hettigoda 1992, n.p.)

The use of the term *saṇwara* here is noteworthy. The word carries a connotation of control and calm—in this sense, a better translation here might be, "So this is an attempt to calm the country [in the wake of the JVP revolt]." The writer is describing an entire new habitus that will result from employment in the 200 GFP. (I use the term *habitus* following Pierre Bourdieu in his *Outline of a Theory of Practice* [1977], to mean a set of dispositions that generate practices and perceptions.) For instance, in reading the reporter's list of new disciplined behaviors, I envision the villagers learning the proper comportment for traveling to the adjacent town to fill a prescription, what and how to cook, how to dress with respectability and style, and how to keep a clean home.

There are many points in this excerpt that resonate with Dharmapala's vision. The reporter's comments on how working will alleviate laziness (*kam-mälikam*) are reminiscent of Dharmapala's prescription that activity is the remedy for laziness. This notion is pervasive in contemporary Sri Lanka. Of many possible examples, I cite the comments of Piyasena, a garment worker's father, who once told me that by learning a skill in the factories, women do a service to the country rather than living as "worthless fools."

The reporter's reference to "traveling, food, clothing, housing, good habits" resonates with Dharmapala's calls for a new sanitized and moral daily behavior among Sinhalas, which he hoped would be taught especially through the example of women's "sanitation, morality, and religiosity" (de Alwis 1997, 153). The notion of unhygienic villagers is obviously reminiscent of Dharmapala's concerns with discipline, cleanliness, and tradition. These concerns are in part the heritage of colonial concerns with hygiene and appearance among native populations (Burke 1996).

The promised social changes that were to occur under the 200 GFP were complicated because of the ambivalent relationship that Sri Lankans have had toward villages, at least since Dharmapala's time. Many Sri Lankans romantically imagine villages as the locus of Sinhala Buddhist tradition. Still, as Jonathan Spencer (1992, 384) also argues, the village is both alluring and repulsive for urban people, who will say it is the locus of the real Sri Lanka, but also that rural people are "dirty, ignorant, stupid, inarticulate and superstitious." Spencer (1992, 384) writes that villages are "at once supposedly the home of all that the townsman would want to cherish and much that he would like to deny." In the context of such ambivalent attitudes toward village life, the 200 GFP would have fulfilled the common desire to reform villages while not destroying valued traditions and practices (for instance, by bringing women out of their villages for urban employment).

Compare the reporter's description above of the anticipated effects of the program to the following selections from a list of purported *actual* changes written in English around 1995, three years after the program began. The list starts off in reference to people who work in 200 GFP factories.

> They started taking a closer look at what they were wearing and went in for smarter clothing.
> Those who did not even own a pair of slippers [sandals] started wearing slippers and shoes. . . .
> The factory owners spoke to the bakery owners in these remote villages and advised them of [*sic*, on] how to make wholesome bread, which not only benefitted the factory workers but the whole village.
> The banks started expanding their services to these areas. . . .
> The standard of living in the remote villages went up.
> The status of machine operator became recognized in society.
> Areas where there was no power supply were blessed by the opening of these factories as they got their supply of electricity as a result. . . .
> . . . telephone lines. . . .
> . . . pipe borne water. . . .
> The youth with the benefits received now wanted their kith and kin to benefit as well, this has lead to the youth seeking avenues of educating themselves of the latest developments in order that they may impart this knowledge to those around them.
> The youth now happily employed have taken an interest in sports, which is sponsored by the factories that employ them and have learned the art of gamesmanship in its true spirit. . . .
> Above all the 200 Garment Factories Project which was a concept of the late President Ranasinghe Premadasa brought about a miraculous change in the rural society and gave the youth a chance to assess themselves and to stand upto to [*sic*] their own rights in society with self respect and dignity. (Fernando n.d.)

This is an excerpt from a four-page information sheet about the program written by Anthony Fernando, the senior assistant secretary of information at the

Presidential Secretariat when the 200 GFP began. When I interviewed him in 1996, Fernando was manager coordinator at Tri Star Apparels, a company with a dozen 200 GFP factories that is the largest garment manufacturer in the country. Fernando told me he wrote the list to provide information about the 200 GFP for Tri Star's potential clients.

Although the term is not used, this list very much concerns discipline in Dharmapala's and Premadasa's sense. Fernando claims that all these things have happened in the three years since the program started: the workers have started eating and dressing well, educating themselves, saving money, working hard, and playing sports. In all these ways they have become proper, respectable, and respectful members of society. I heard about changes of this sort, especially in terms of dressing well, from numerous factory owners and managers. For instance, one factory owner said that when the factories first started the women would come to work barefoot, using a plastic bag as a pocketbook. But now they have sandals and handbags, which shows that "they have developed little by little."

Fernando's list is significant because of the profound disciplinary changes it extols, but also because of Fernando's official relationship to the 200 GFP. As senior assistant secretary of information at the Presidential Secretariat under Premadasa he played a major role in the 200 GFP, which he described to me in a 1996 interview as "to promote the program through the media."[20] He authored many articles in the *Daily News*, including two nearly full-page features (Fernando 1992g; Anthony Fernando 1993). This list, then, is also interesting because it is a retrospective semiofficial view of the program. It is likely the only retrospective view that exists, since the program ceased to be forcefully touted after Premadasa's death in 1993 and especially after the government changed in 1994. Nevertheless, these factories still exist, and many of the same values and forms of discipline are still being promoted, if not officially through the government.

If the number of newspaper articles about the program is any indication, Fernando was quite good at his job. On some days there would be more than one newspaper article, such as a straight news report about the factory opening and a feature story about the investors and/or workers. There were also other reporters who wrote frequently about the factories. For instance, in late 1992 and early 1993, R. M. R. Amararatne wrote numerous articles for the Sinhala daily *Dinamina* that were almost formulaic in content. They started with a historical description of the area, moved into a portrait of current socioeconomic conditions, described the investors and their goals in heroic

JUKI GIRLS, GOOD GIRLS

Figure 3. Workers wore sandals to and from the factory, but this sewing-machine operator was like many who preferred to go barefoot at her workstation. Photo by Seamus
Walsh, printed with permission.

terms, and then—by means of vignettes of a few workers—argued that the factories would effect a social and economic transformation. The historical description always was a positive portrayal of an area prosperous and lush in precolonial times. Contemporary conditions were described as poor and desperate. The following opening paragraph from one article is exemplary:

> The main livelihood of the people of the Kaluwaragaswewa area, which has an arid climate, is agriculture, specifically *cena* [slash and burn] cultivation. During the times of King Dutugemunu and King Maha Parakramabahu this area was fertile, but during later periods it deteriorated. Until recently we saw the symptoms of that decline. The villagers of the area are severely suffering from hereditary problems such as poverty, illiteracy, lack of health facilities, etc. In certain villages about 85 percent of the total population is depending on food stamps. (Amararatne 1992b, n.p.)

By referencing the era of two kings revered by Sinhala nationalists as Sinhala Buddhist heroes, the author implies that the 200 GFP will bring about a similar era of prosperity and pride for Sinhala Buddhists.

It was in the context of the promise and excitement about rebuilding villages and transforming village social life that the political opposition launched its most effective critique of the program, what I term the "underwear critique." Premadasa was never as explicit as Dharmapala in linking women's behavior and the future of the nation, but his 200 GFP can certainly be understood within this tradition. As a major policy initiative after the defeat of the JVP, the program was cast by Premadasa and the government-backed media as a means of enforcing discipline, obedience, and patriotism in potential revolutionaries. But the 200 GFP has served less to discipline a generic rural citizenry than to monitor and discipline a female-gendered rural citizenry whose behavior—which Sinhalas in general perceive to be central to the nation's moral fiber—became the focus of the program. As I detail in the next chapter, within months of its inauguration, the 200 GFP shifted focus from youth unrest to women's behavior. When we examine this shift from youth to women we can learn much about how globalization affects nationalist discourses and practices.

MALA

The Truth about Women Workers
at Garment Factories

It is a known fact that the garment industry's contribution toward the
Sri Lankan economy and industrial development is enormous. However, if you consider development from the correct perspective, the story is
quite different. What you see is a group of intelligent, hardworking,
and educated people who work until the last bead of sweat drops to
achieve a production target set by the management. The majority of
these workers are women.

Most of these young women come from very conservative, respectable,
ordinary families. Most of them were brought up under the guidance of
their parents preserving traditional Sinhala customs.

Though these women are well educated, intelligent, and talented,
their chances of obtaining a government job are limited. When they feel
the economic burden their parents go through, they cannot stay home
doing nothing. So a woman has to decide to leave the nest she was living
in with her parents and siblings, give away the love and security she had
under her parents' roof, and join the workforce in the garment industry
located in the city. She does this with a lot of hopes, ambitions, and de-
termination to achieve economic independence for her and her family.
Though the public opinion about women in the garment industry is not
that favorable, women who join the workforce are often surprised to realize that they are joining a set of very able, capable, efficient, and
hardworking young men and women. These workers are not a group of
stupid people as they have been labeled by the outside world. With our

young woman's fears about the garment industry fading, she willingly joins the young men and women who sweat to match the speed of the machines at which they work, in order to achieve the targets. She was determined to give her best to achieve what the others were achieving to match the production targets. The labor she does to provide the production target for one day is priceless.

Unless she meets the efficiency of the machines she is working with, it is certain that she will be subjected to bitter verbal abuse from superiors. While trying to match the production target, workers have to maintain the quality of the product. After eight hours of hard labor, most often they are forced to work extra hours. At the end of the workday, most of these women are too tired even to talk with their family or friends. She walks back toward her hut tiredly like an innocent doe coming to a heavenly abode at sunset. Some of the workers have to live in boarding houses specially put up for them by the neighbors who live around these factories. There is nobody to love them, comfort them, or to listen to them, neither at those factories nor in the boarding houses. The love, compassion, comfort, and peace of life they enjoyed while growing up with their parents and siblings are long gone.

It is very unfortunate to note that some people exploit the innocence of these girls for their sexual needs. The loneliness, frustration, and newfound freedom lead them to look for comfort in strangers and opportunistic people. Sometimes girls themselves are to blame for this as they invite trouble by inappropriate behavior. Though this is not the story of most of the women working in the garment industry, it has certainly led to tarnish the image of them in Sri Lanka. Sadly, it is a common practice in our society to blame factory workers for all the vices happening in the society. This sort of unwanted publicity helps to bring the self-confidence and morale down. The obvious result of this is that the majority of innocent girls who value ethics, moral and cultural values, dignity, and pride are also been treated as dirt. This is an added stress and a cause for depression for the girls who have undergone enough agony at work. The society has not tried to understand the real people who work behind those machines nor their natural talents.

Even though the mass media has done nothing much to change the image of "the garment girl," we have to be thankful to them for at least taking some effort to restore it.

By means of short stories, novels, dramas, songs, and essays some media are trying to establish the fact that "garment factory girls" are normal human beings like all other people who are employed in other industries.

However, the mass media should take more aggressive efforts to bring out the truth about the lives of innocent, educated, talented, hardworking garment factory girls and the value they bring to the Sri Lankan economy and to the family. If people could appreciate the women who add value to the Sri Lankan economy the same way they appreciate the money those women bring in, Sri Lanka will be a much better place for everybody. I hope one day people will treat them as equals.

The day it happens will be a dream come true.

3. THE POLITICS OF WHITE WOMEN'S UNDERWEAR

The 200 Garment Factories Program rested on an apparent contradiction: the state enlisted women workers in a program designed to prevent another revolt by the JVP, but the JVP was composed primarily of men.[1] I received one suggestion for how to overcome this contradiction from various state representatives and factory owners and managers—but only after I identified it as a contradiction and asked them for help in understanding it. They explained that the factories employ women because women are better suited than men to factory labor. Nevertheless, these same people contended, the goal of preventing unrest would be attained because brothers or husbands of female workers would be able to satisfy many of their material needs with the earnings. Moreover, many added, jobs for men would be available in support sectors due to the increased need for buses, bakeries, shops, and so forth near factories.

Of course there does not need to be logic or rationality to any of the ideological claims made about the 200 GFP. The apparent contradiction frames a development program that was conceived of by the state and experienced by the state, its supporters, factory owners, managers, workers, and their families in terms that were fundamentally contradictory, ambivalent, and uncertain. Significantly, however, several months into the 200 GFP's implementation, the fact that it employed mostly women would not have seemed like a contradiction to many people anyway. By then the 200 GFP had become redefined as a program for protecting women's morality; youth unrest had dropped out of the picture. I focus on this shift from youth to women as a key point at which ideologies of gender, nationalism, and economic liberalization came together.

A widely publicized opposition party critique of the 200 GFP was the cata-lyst for this shift from youth to women. Opposition politicians argued that in the 200 GFP factories "our innocent girls are sewing underwear for white women." Anura Bandaranaike, then a member of Parliament from the SLFP, first made this critique in a public speech in approximately October 1992. I heard about the charge from people of various social positions, from workers themselves to government officials. In a country where unemployment is an important political issue, Premadasa's 200 GFP presented a problem for the SLFP. Thousands of rural youth were receiving well-paid jobs in a program that was being widely covered in the mass media. The underwear critique was only one of several attempts by the SLFP to discredit Premadasa and the pro-gram and prevent an increase in his popularity with rural voters. Unlike the other criticisms, this one actually effected change in the program. It was par-ticularly effective because it tapped into already extant Sinhala Buddhist "moral panic" about factory women.

This chapter, an extended analysis of the meaning and context of the un-derwear critique, is organized as follows. To shed some light on the signifi-cance and efficacy of the critique, I first present a brief overview of the ger-mane cultural associations of the constructs *innocence*, *underwear*, and *white women*. Following a consideration of these terms, I zoom out to the larger context for this critique. I discuss the widespread social concern, in Sri Lanka and elsewhere, about the morality of women factory workers. I move to a gen-eral discussion of gender in the formulation of nationalist projects and then to the specifics of the Sri Lankan context. Some Sri Lankan particularities are brought to light in the example of the controversy surrounding the appear-ance and behavior of a female Olympic athlete in the 1990s. I then examine the moral panic about Juki girls and how it was manifested, created, and rein-forced in the mass media. Finally, after thus contextualizing the underwear cri-tique, I return to discuss precisely why and how Premadasa shifted the 200 GFP focus from youth to women.

Innocent Girls, Underwear, and White Women

"Our innocent girls are sewing underwear for white women" (*apē ahiṃsaka kello suddiyanṭa jangi mahanawa*). The phrase begins with the Sinhala word for "our" (*apē*), which indicates that the "girls" in question are possessions of the nation and that their moral probity is an issue of national importance.

We know from context that these innocent girls are villagers, and it would have in some ways been redundant for the critics to say "our innocent village girls." The Sinhala word *ahiṃsaka* is translated as "innocent" or "harmless," and it is also the Pali word for nonviolence. As an adjective referring to people, *ahiṃsaka* connotes simplicity, purity, and naïveté. It can also mean being straightforward, not devious, and not worldly, and in this latter sense can imply being innocent of all foreign and modern corrupting influences. *Ahiṃsaka* also connotes unmarried women's sexual purity. In regard to unmarried Sinhala Buddhist women, this concept accompanies the expectation that they are virgins and sexually ignorant. *Ahiṃsaka* is often used to describe village women, and it is another way of saying they are Good girls, the term so often used for women who act properly in terms of moral norms.[2] In the same way that they would describe each other as Good girls, women at Shirtex and Serendib would often use the term *innocent* ("she is very innocent," *eyā hari ahiṃsakay*). So by employing the term "innocent," the opposition was raising issues of sexuality but also of cultural and national purity.

This concept of innocence is an important component of a widespread practice within Sri Lanka of conceptualizing authentic Sinhalaness in terms of a rural-urban divide. As we have seen, Sinhala villages are often considered the locus of tradition and impervious to moral degradation. The gendered dimension of this romantic idea of villages is that village women are considered to be innocent and to naturally adhere to codes of morality and respectability. Village women have a critical social role as preservers of the distinctive characteristics of Sinhala tradition that many Sinhalas fear are disappearing in post-liberalized Sri Lanka. In this context, it is particularly meaningful if a woman acts in a manner perceived to be antithetical to community norms in terms of sexuality and marriage choice. A woman's disregard for the ideal of virginity at marriage and for marrying a man of the appropriate caste is often interpreted as indifference to both her family's social standing and the perpetuation of the Sinhala ethnic group. Now we can begin to understand the power of the opposition's underwear critique. The implication was that innocent girls, who should simply be associated with local traditions, were now working in global capitalist industry. Worse yet, they were sewing immoral products for white women!

Ready-made underwear (*jangi*) is the symbol of foreignness and sexual impurity in the opposition's critique. Unlike the English *underwear*, *jangi* refers to underpants only (men's and women's), not to brassieres. Many Sri Lankans, but especially those from rural areas, consider underwear both sexual and dirty—not an appropriate topic for discussion. This dual association is seen in everyday social practices, such as the following: although most rural Sri Lankans dry their laundry outdoors on rocks, grass, bushes, or clotheslines, it is common to dry underwear in a private location. Mala, whose plea for respect opened chapter 1, said in an interview that underwear was not a topic Sri Lankans speak about (she referred to it in Sinhala as "unmentionables"), and they also do not generally purchase ready-made underwear but rather sew it at home.[3]

The term *yata ändum* ("underclothes") is the more common term for underwear, with *jangi* reserved as a slang term. Anura Bandaranaike's use of the slang *jangi* in his critique would have quickly indicated crudeness to listeners, implicitly driving home his point that there was something inappropriate under discussion. In the same way that hearing about this taboo subject, invoked in slang terms, in a political argument made people uneasy, the mere fact of women sewing underwear in factories would also have made people uneasy. By sparking feelings of discomfort, the opposition suggested that if they were in power, their party would continue its tradition of paying attention to the economy *and* morality—it would not provide such morally suspect jobs—and here the SLFP was playing on the association that had long been made between the UNP and Westernization.

The underwear critique was unsettling not just because village girls would be sewing unmentionables. It was also unsettling because of whom they were sewing underwear for: white women, hypersexualized figures in Sri Lanka. The reference to white women (*suddi*) was a familiar ploy.[4] Other authors have shown how "a nation can consolidate its identity by projecting beyond its own borders the sexual practices or gender behaviors it deems abhorrent" (Parker et al. 1992, 10). I note below that Dharmapala's Protestant Buddhism involved a comparison of sexually loose Western women with chaste Sri Lankan women. This was not simply a reference to a generic category of foreigners but rather to a racially designated category of "white" Europeans. This racial "othering" of white women as sexually immoral continues in contemporary Sri Lanka. Most Sri Lankans never interact one-on-one with white women, so all they know of them are the images they see on television and in films, or the views they get from a distance in tourist areas. Pornographic films available in Sri Lanka often feature whites, and white women who frequent the country's southern beaches in skimpy bathing suits are the objects of much criticism.

Of course, most people would know that articles other than underwear were sewn in many of these factories. That did not matter: involvement with foreignness at this level was itself problematic. With the underwear critique, the opposition fed already extant nationalist concerns that associated foreignness with immorality, cultural decay, and the disintegration of village traditions. Acting on the centrality of the disciplined behavior of women to the nationalist imagination, the opposition lambasted Premadasa for subjecting the nation's moral core to an immoral type of work.

The underwear critique was asking: if good village girls are going to start behaving in new ways by working in garment factories, what will happen to the rest of Sinhala society, which is reproduced through women's normative behavior? Note that this was not just a question about women's behavior. It was also a question about what village women's presence in garment factories—and the presence of garment factories in villages—implied about how the nation has become feminized through its engagement with global capitalism. This critique about village girls sewing underwear came down to important cultural questions about the relationship between women, the nation, and moral purity.

Thus the SLFP's underwear critique employed a two-pronged strategy. It harnessed societal concern about Juki girls by sexualizing the women workers—presumably to make the jobs appear unrespectable and to make the workers (and their families) not want them. Also, by raising the specific issue of dirtiness and sexuality in reference to these *village* factories, it made the jobs appear to be low-status work for which nobody should be grateful and which was compromising the moral integrity of the nation at its authentic core. Although they did not offer alternatives, opposition politicians suggested that if they were in power, their party would not forsake morality for economic gain. (When it did come into power in 1994, the SLFP did not discontinue the 200 GFP.)

First raised sometime around October 1992, the underwear critique had political and social implications that could be felt as late as mid-1996, when I was completing my extended field research. For instance, 200 GFP women workers would sadly tell me that men who knew they worked in a garment factory teased them by asking if they were going to sew underwear. As I demonstrate below, Premadasa responded to this critique with his own angle on protecting women's morality. From this point on, the government touted the program as being centrally concerned with women's behavior. It became a program intended to protect women's morality by eliminating the necessity for women's urban migration. The underwear critique and the government's response reveal that economic liberalization raises anxieties for everyone—

politicians and factory owners, women workers and the men who tease them. This is a gendered version of the struggle between attachment to the local and attraction to the foreign that has characterized the Sri Lankan postcolonial experience.

Factory Women and Moral Policing

A number of studies of different times and places have examined the prevalence of social discourses and practices regarding the morality of women factory workers. To cite just a few examples, historians and anthropologists have examined this issue in studies of nineteenth-century New York City, Paris, and Lowell, Massachusetts; mid-twentieth-century Latin America; and late-twentieth-century Malaysia, Thailand, Korea, and Mexico.[5] The migration of rural women to cities has been a significant feature of these concerns about the behavior of factory women. For instance, in the early nineteenth century, factories were started in the then-rural town of Lowell, Massachusetts. In the face of widely noted concerns about the immorality of women in English mill cities like Manchester, Lowell investors started their factories with dual objectives. They not only wanted to earn profits, they also wanted to create a profitable industrial system that could protect the morality of women workers and in so doing cultivate American republican values (Dalzell 1993; Dublin 1979). Likewise, anthropologist Aihwa Ong (1987, 179–93) describes how in the late 1970s and early 1980s similar crises of morality surfaced regarding rural-urban migration and specifically the problem of Free Trade Zone workers in Malaysia.

These Lowell and Malaysian cases are just two of many examples. At issue is a widespread concern with the sexual behavior of young, usually unmarried, female factory workers who leave their families to seek employment in cities. In all these cases, women are portrayed as central to the defense of national or ethnic traditions, and women's separation from their families is considered a cause of the erosion of these traditions. The fear, or fact, of women workers developing new sexual habits becomes a cause of particular unease for patriotically minded managers, parents, and other observers.

In Sri Lanka, too, there is great social attention to the position of female factory workers. Although Mala worked in a factory located in a village, Sinhala Buddhist nationalist concerns about women's migration to urban areas for employment were the wider context for the plea for social recognition that

Mala squeezed onto her questionnaire response reproduced in chapter 1. In later chapters I focus on some of the ways in which Mala and her coworkers were affected by these nationalist concerns about the sexuality of garment workers. But here I consider how to make sense of the empirical reality of such concerns across time and space. One may be tempted to see in this conjuncture a tendency for capitalism to cause universal effects. I do not consider capitalism to be the *cause* of this moral discourse and related social controls, but it is an important factor.

There are two reasons that I hesitate to identify capitalism as the sole cause. First, looking to "capitalism" itself for the answers might not be the most fruitful mode of inquiry. In my own analysis, I start from the following simple question: "What does sex have to do with factory labor?" Instead of focusing exclusively on capitalism, I consider sexuality as a socially embedded phenomenon. The historian Ellen Ross and the anthropologist Rayna Rapp discuss the embeddedness of sexuality by reference to the structure of an onion. They explain that as in peeling an onion, so also in approaching sexuality: "as we peel off each layer (economies, politics, families, etc.), we may think that we are approaching the kernel, but we eventually discover that the whole is the only 'essence' there is. Sexuality cannot be abstracted from its surrounding social layers" (Ross and Rapp 1997 [1981], 155). The Sri Lankan association between sex and factory labor is embedded in such disparate aspects of society as economic liberalization, caste and class relations, postcolonial cultural politics, and national politics and the politics of gender, as well as family arrangements.

The second reason is that, despite this larger conjuncture of a concern with the sexuality of female factory workers across time and space, there are locally mediated effects of economic change on the lives of local subjects. A search for universals obscures the importance of local meanings and histories. To ascertain the Sri Lankan specificity to this concern, I consider the following broad questions, among others: What does this discourse about the sexuality of factory workers look like in the Sri Lankan case? How, why, and when did it emerge in Sri Lanka? What does it mean for the workers inside and outside the factories?

Gender in the Construction of the Nation

To contextualize the specific Sri Lankan mobilizations of gender in the construction of the nation, in this section I examine more generally the linkages between gender and nation in various societies. Gender has proved an especially useful lens for analyzing questions of modernity and tradition in nationalist contexts.[6] There is a vast literature on how gendered distinctions and meanings have been mobilized in nationalist movements at different times throughout the world. For instance, women have been celebrated as fighters in nationalist struggles, reproducers of patriotic citizens, and as mothers who teach national culture to their children (McClintock 1995, 355; Yuval-Davis and Anthias 1989, 7). Discrete programs of mobilization will be marked by characteristics specific to their time and place. Nevertheless, the parallels exhibited by such movements in different societies are not to be ignored. In particular, postcolonial countries such as Sri Lanka and India show similarities because of the impact of Western ideas and technologies from a common source on their nationalist movements (Chatterjee 1993).

Deniz Kandiyoti (1991) analyzes the varied ways in which questions of modernity have affected nationalists' normative constructions of women. Nationalist movements often cast what they identify as indigenous values and traditions as more "authentic" than the prevailing state of affairs—and in so doing imply that the concepts *indigenous* and *tradition* are stable and in the past. In many cases, women have been required and allowed to be modern only up to a certain extent. In other cases, women have been sequestered from modernity. In regard to India, for example, Partha Chatterjee (1989) asks why it is that during the anticolonial nationalist movement in India in the late nineteenth century reformers focused less on women's rights than they had in the previous decades. Whereas previously Indian politicians had quite actively worked on various women's rights and social reform issues, these causes became less prominent when the political struggle for independence became more intense. Chatterjee argues that this change resulted not because the political struggle became more pressing, but because questions of women's status, rights, and position in society were redefined.

In the Indian anticolonial nationalist discourse, women became associated with a domain confined to *culture*. Culture was defined by national traditions and encompassed the realms of spiritual activity, inner contemplation, and domestic life. By contrast, men were assigned an "outer," worldly domain that was associated with Western civilization and its power to colonize the East. Chatterjee (1989, 238) writes, "It follows that as long as we take care to retain the spiritual distinctiveness of our culture, we could make all the compromises and adjustments necessary to adapt ourselves to the requirements of a modern material world without losing our true identity." Thus men could work to modernize the economy and system of government (and could, for instance, wear Western clothes and train in science and technology) as long as women participated in what was considered traditional ways of living. Chatterjee (1989, 240) argues further that modernity was not automatically assumed to be anathema to the nationalist project because modernity was limited to the men's sphere and the women's domain was kept separate from the nationalist struggle. In terms of what this formulation means for everyday social practices, he asserts, "There would have to be a marked *difference* in the degree and manner of westernization of women, as distinct from men, in the modern world of the nation" (1989, 243, Chatterjee's emphasis). Although Chatterjee has been criticized for ignoring women's agentive responses to these constructions, his argument is important for drawing attention to how central normative models of gender were to the anticolonial struggle in India.

Scholars have examined women's sexuality as an area of particular concern for nationalists and strictures on women's sexuality as a means of furthering nationalist aims. The historian George Mosse argues that in nineteenth-century Europe (particularly Germany), control over sexuality became vital to the concept of respectability and that respectability came to mark members of a nation. He defines respectability as "'decent and correct' manners and morals, as well as the proper attitude toward sexuality" (Mosse 1985, 1). Mosse's work has inspired other scholars to examine the intertwining histories and practices of nationalism and sexuality in diverse locales throughout the world (see Parker et al. 1992; Tambiah 2005). In her analysis of sexuality and militarized Tamil nationalism, the legal scholar Yasmin Tambiah (2005, 248, 253) discusses the importance of Tamil women's sexual chastity in the LTTE's nationalist struggle. In the LTTE's nationalist project, women's behavior is monitored for cultural appropriateness, "culture is made coterminous with female sexual chastity," and "a woman's morality is scripted as equivalent to her sexual behavior." Indeed, this correlation among culture, morality, and sexuality is widespread in South Asian societies. In the Sinhala Buddhist case, the dominant formulation since the colonial period has been that the ideal Sinhala Buddhist woman is a chaste woman.

Gender and National Identity: Two Historical Periods in Sri Lanka

Economic and cultural transformations accompanying capitalism have contributed to changing social relations and changing understandings of their meanings. At two distinct times in Sri Lanka's history the demarcation of women's appropriate behavior was central to how people made sense of these changes. During both periods, the strength of the national project relied on how closely real women followed the feminine ideal.

The first period took place during the anticolonial movement in the late nineteenth and early twentieth centuries, when there was great importance attached to differences between Sri Lankan and Western traditions, technologies, and practices. The other period began in the late 1970s and continues to this day.[7] This is the era of economic liberalization, when the economy was opened to foreign investment and there was a massive increase in industrialization. The contemporary period has been characterized by intense debate about how much foreign and Western influence is suitable for the country, and how women are situated within these changing social relations. At both of the times in question, the meanings of modernity, tradition, and gender in the construction of the nation were at the forefront of societal concern. The latter period coincided with the escalation of ethnic conflict into a separatist civil war, beginning in 1983. The assumed moral perils of economic liberalization and globalization have thus been interpreted against the specter of the nation's disintegration.

Beginning in the sixteenth century, Sri Lanka became successively a colony of the Portuguese, the Dutch, and the British. In the decades prior to independence in 1948, a specifically Sinhala Buddhist national identity was created and consolidated, with the effect of directly excluding members of the island's minority ethnic groups. The efforts of the nationalist reformer Anagarika Dharmapala were central to the creation of this Sinhala Buddhist identity. Gender has been key to the Sinhala Buddhist nationalist imagination over the past one hundred years—from the period of anticolonial nationalism, through independence in 1948, to the postcolonial ethnonationalism of today.

During the anticolonial campaign, questions of how to define the modern Sinhala Buddhist woman became salient. Bourgeois women were the main object of concern here, for Sinhala nationalist ideologues were focused on the creation of a class of indigenous elites who could bring the country forward to independence by embodying the correct mix of tradition and modernity. The theater and gender studies scholar Neloufer de Mel argues that in the early twentieth century the ideal Sinhala woman was to be modern, but only as far as was necessary to be a good mate for the ideal new man, who was English-educated and cosmopolitan. De Mel (2001, 59) writes: "Women were disallowed the cosmopolitanness permitted to men, and their duty to nurture future generations in Sinhala culture, language and the Buddhist religion was reiterated with greater vigour."

The twinned concerns about nationalism and sexuality were at the heart of Dharmapala's project, which elaborated specific rules for a new kind of moral behavior for respectable, bourgeois Sinhala Buddhist women (whom he often contrasted with immoral European women). Under Dharmapala's new social ethic, regulation of women's morality and sexuality became important for the nation's future. As Malathi de Alwis (1996, 106) has written in regard to Dharmapala's characterizations, "While the 'western' woman was portrayed as being sexually free, the Sri Lankan woman epitomised submission, chastity and restraint." This was in part an attempt at ensuring cultural purity through policing genetic purity. Kumari Jayawardena (1992, 162) has argued that the gender roles developed under Dharmapala's Sinhala Buddhist revivalism were consistent with the results in many Asian countries where an interest in women's sexual purity was directed at ensuring that women "reproduce the ethnic group and socialize children into their ethnic roles." Contemporary Sri Lankans value sexual chastity and virginity at marriage as Sinhala Buddhist norms, when these are in fact derived from Victorian norms, for precolonial Sinhalas did not have such restrictions on women's sexuality.[8]

During the anticolonial period, bourgeois women—not the urban or rural poor—were the foci of nationalist concern. Dharmapala's "Daily Code for the Laity" enumerated rules for ideal bourgeois behavior, though women of other classes subsequently adopted his new social ethic. By contrast with the anticolonial project, since the advent of economic liberalization it is working-class women rather than bourgeois women who have become the focus of nationalist discourses about women's morality. These days Juki girls are the particular targets of concern.

Women's labor has been the basis of two leading sources of foreign exchange in the liberalized Sri Lankan economy: women's factory employment within Sri Lanka and women's employment as housemaids or factory laborers abroad (especially in the Middle East).[9] With large numbers of village women migrating to Colombo and abroad for employment since the late 1970s, the morality of female migrant laborers has emerged as a primary target of nationalist discourse about the moral integrity of the nation (de Alwis 1998, 197–98; Gamburd 2000). As in the anticolonial movement, in this period of economic liberalization women's behavior has been the locus of considerable anxiety about how much foreign influence is detrimental to the nation. A salient characteristic of this anxiety stems from the historical convergence of social and economic changes with the escalation of the LTTE campaign for independence. In the context of today's civil war, the image of the chaste mother of the nation has taken on new importance. Nationalist discourses call on women to mother the nation. In turn, great importance is attached to preserving women's chastity: "The chastity of a woman, like the so-called purity of language, becomes a code for the nation's honour in nationalist discourse" (de Mel 2001, 214).

This intense concern with women's moral behavior today forms one half of the ideologies of male heroism and female moral purity that pervade war-torn Sri Lanka. While men are encouraged to be aggressive and fight for the country, women are valorized both as mothers who heroically sacrifice their sons for the nation without complaint and as traditional women who maintain ethnic purity through their heightened morality even as the nation around them falls into disarray.[10] Consider, for example, the following image: "A poster promoting breastfeeding . . . was issued by the Ministry of Women's Affairs. The poster, which was displayed during the height of one of the first major government offensives against the Tamil militants in the north, in 1986–87, depicted a woman dressed in cloth and jacket—a marker of Sinhalaness—breastfeeding her baby while dreaming of a man in army fatigues. The Sinhala caption below exhorted: 'Give your bloodmilk [breast milk] (*lē kiri*) to nourish our future soldiers.'" (de Alwis 1998, 206).

This notion of women's responsibility to produce future soldiers can be traced to Dharmapala's intense concern with women's chaste behavior. However, his rules for women's behavior were not just about sexuality. They included prescriptions regarding quotidian practices such as clothing and hairstyles, alcohol use, and other visible markers of cultural authenticity (Jayawardena 1992; de Alwis 1998, 110–12). Even at the turn of the century there were intense accusations that Westernized and Burgher (denoting descendants of the Dutch, Portuguese, or British) women had betrayed their culture. It was in this context that Dharmapala advocated the sari as modest clothing for Sinhala women in opposition to Western dresses. Although they were introduced from India, saris are today considered traditional Sinhala clothing. Even today, women who have short hair, wear skimpy clothing, or use alcohol are assumed to be sexually loose (Gunasekera 1996, 10).

In this context of the moral policing of women's appearance and behavior, imagine how people might read the presence of thousands of factory women on the outskirts of Colombo, living in boarding houses without their families.

Since the 1977 economic reforms, Juki girls have been key targets for anxieties related to modernization. Below I demonstrate how national politics, economic critiques, and cultural concerns all converge in the figure of the Juki girl. But before turning to Juki girls, I focus on one prominent village woman who was the target of moral censure in the 1990s and early 2000s. The parallels to the experiences of Juki girls are instructive.

Gender, Culture, and an Olympic Runner

In September 2000 Susanthika Jayasinghe won a bronze medal in the 200-meter sprint at the Sydney Olympics, thus becoming Sri Lanka's second Olympic medalist ever. At the news conference following the win, in the presence of the gold and silver medalists, Susanthika (she is popularly known by her first name) pleaded to the numerous reporters in attendance to "find me another country." This comment came soon after the following, delivered in hesitant English and quoted in newspapers throughout the world: "It was trouble for me, including doping and sexual harassment. After I won the world championships in 1997, the minister (she identified him) . . . the big guy . . . He wants sex with me. But I refused. I have a husband" (*Sunday Times* 2000, 1; parenthetical in original).

These pleas and accusations were the latest episode in a long and complicated story that illustrates the problems that may be faced by village women who lead lives that diverge from conventional gender roles. In 1996, Susanthika was celebrated in the national media as "our sprint queen." Journalists often noted that this Sri Lankan sprinting sensation was from a poor village family. Media coverage of Susanthika increased the same year when she was accused of taking performance-enhancing drugs. Her response was that she was a village girl and would never have done such a thing. The implication, which Sri Lankans would understand right away, was that, being from a village, she was inherently a Good girl and thus would not have and could not possibly have cheated by taking drugs. Her fans largely agreed, and she pulled through this scandal, still "our sprint queen" in the national media.

But in April 1997 Susanthika's reputation suffered as a result of her involvement in another scandal. It was widely reported in the press that she had been drinking alcohol at a party in Colombo. She was subjected to disciplinary action by the minister of sports, and her fan club was outraged at her behavior.

The feminist Cat's Eye column in the *Island* newspaper described the response, "When Susanthika, the much-lauded 'village lass,' was accused of drinking beer and partying, the vultures swept down; Susanthika has 'betrayed village values,' she has eaten 'forbidden fruit.' 'Who does she think she is?' they cried. She was even punished with a 6 months ban on sporting activity, but the ban was lifted after women's groups and many others protested" (Cat's Eye 1997, n.p.). In an open letter to Susanthika, Janaka Biyanwala, a Sri Lankan Olympic athlete and political scientist, read the controversy as an urban versus rural morality play, in which the good village girl had gone bad by tasting the forbidden fruit (in this case, drink) of the city. (One Sinhala-language newspaper article was entitled "Susanthika Tastes the Forbidden Fruit.") Biyanwala (1997, 25) wrote, "The bitterness of the city and the eternal sweetness of the village, you know the usual, village is pristine, and our women are only corrupted by the city or foreigners." He argued that the outrage arose because drinking alcohol is not considered appropriate for respectable women who should fit into the restrictive models of women as only wives, mothers, or Good girls.

A few months later, in August 1997, when she was only twenty years old, Susanthika won the silver medal in the 200–meter sprint at the World Athletics Championships in Greece. The first Sri Lankan international medalist since 1948, she was welcomed back to the country with a greeting by thousands of fans, a meeting with the president, and a gift of one million rupees.[11] This grand welcome temporarily masked the intense criticism that was being directed toward her by various voices in the media. For now she had gone unequivocally beyond being a good village girl. She did this by cutting her hair short and wearing a revealing runner's outfit in the competition. "Colombo Calling," a left-oriented media watchdog, critiqued the general media coverage:

> Susanthika Jayasinghe, a rural peasant woman from Kegalle, recently cut her hair short, and dispelled any attempts at myth-making about herself as a symbol of traditional Sinhalese womanhood. Wearing a skimpy swimsuit-like athletics costume, she won the silver medal in the two-hundred meter run at the world athletics meet in Athens. But no Sunday newspaper in Colombo found her picture or story worthy of front page coverage. So, glory in winning a global medal in athletics by a woman,

wearing modern sports attire, is not news enough—or nationalist enough—for the print media. (Colombo Calling 1997, n.p.)

This report then contrasted Susanthika's situation to that of the village men of the nation's cricket team who had also recently attained a historic win (they won the 1996 cricket world championship) and whose faces were all over the newspapers and television.

Until she drank alcohol, cut her hair, and wore an objectionable outfit, Susanthika had been a worthy national symbol of a traditional Sinhala Buddhist woman. But now she had finally exceeded the limits of acceptable appearance and behavior for an innocent woman or a Good girl. Women who violate these strictures are assumed to be sexually loose. Indeed, Susanthika's sexuality became an issue after her appearance and behavior were read to signal that she was not a respectable woman. In October 1997 Susanthika accused sports ministry officials of sexual harassment. The next year she accused a ministry official of "spiking her urine with banned steroids after she refused his sexual advances" (thus her comments at the 2000 Olympic news conference).[12] In response a lawmaker in parliament referred to her as looking like a "black American man" (Cat's Eye 1997, n.p). Since black skin is associated with Tamils and is considered ugly for its racial impurity, this was a deep double insult: Susanthika was stripped of her femininity and of her authentic Sinhala ethnic purity.[13] Being neither a woman nor a pure Sinhala, she was not worthy of respect.

The story of Susanthika's rise and fall is familiar in Sri Lanka. Like actresses, athletes, and female politicians in the United States, Susanthika's public social role created space for the possibility of moral criticism. But the Sri Lankan story is different from the American story because it was not just due to her public visibility that she risked social censure. The problem arose also because Susanthika was a village girl who attempted to cross the symbolic rural-urban divide by becoming a modern, cosmopolitan athlete. Had she been from Colombo, it is likely that there would not have been concern about Susanthika's appearance and behavior. She would have had no chance of becoming a symbol of national purity in the first place. As the earlier quotes from Cat's Eye and Biyanwala indicate, her critics frequently invoked her village origins. Juki girls are similarly situated in Sri Lanka. Susanthika and Juki girls face criticism both because of their public mobility and also because they are "inno-

Figure 4. A woman sewing at a Juki machine. Named after a Japanese industrial sewing machine brand, the term *Juki girl* is a derogatory nickname for female garment workers. Photo by Seamus Walsh, printed with permission.

cent" village women who are now associated with the city and the moral degradation that the city connotes.

Juki Girls

The centerpiece of the government's original economic liberalization package was the establishment in 1978 of the Katunayake Free Trade Zone (FTZ) in an urban area on the outskirts of Colombo. Situated near the international airport, the Katunayake FTZ is by far the largest of Sri Lanka's eight FTZs today. Initially the workforce consisted primarily of women migrants from villages, most of them unmarried and Sinhala Buddhist. Soon after its establishment, there emerged considerable moral panic about good village girls going bad in Katunayake. The moral campaign against FTZ women has focused on reports of the following issues: prostitution, premarital sex, rape, sexually transmitted disease, abortion, and sexual harassment. Given the concentration of women in the area, and given that the women in question had acquired a reputation for inappropriate sexual behavior, several nicknames emerged for the town and the FTZ: *istiripura*, *vēsakalāpaya*, and *premakalāpaya*. *Istiripura* literally means "women's city," but it has "the subtle undertone of a city of easy women or easy virtue." *Vēsakalāpaya* means "the zone of prostitutes," and it is a play on the real name *nidahas velenda kalāpaya*, literally the zone of free trade. *Premakalāpaya* is the "zone of love."[14]

The social category *Juki girls* is a key symbol of national anxieties about fading traditions. Colombo is perceived by many Sri Lankans to be a corrupt, morally degrading space, and this perception is symbolized by the position of Juki girls. Of the thousands of factory workers in Colombo, by far the most work in the garment industry. These women generally have migrated from their villages, and so they live in boarding houses away from their parents. They are frequently seen walking in the streets, going to movie theaters and shopping, and socializing with men.

The Juki nickname had emerged at least by 1979, the year after Katunayake opened.[15] It is part of common parlance today, and women and men of various backgrounds throughout the island use the term. When used by people other than urban factory workers, the term unequivocally connotes sexual promiscuity. I often heard rural factory women use it to disparage urban garment workers. However, I have heard anecdotal evidence that urban garment workers have recently begun to construct a positive identity around the term, using the term "Juki" with pride, as a way of asserting their difference from other women.[16] In illustration of the usage and negative connotation of the word, when prospective grooms advertise for spouses in Sinhala newspaper marriage proposals, they sometimes disqualify garment factory workers with the phrase "no garment girls" or "no Juki girls" (Tambiah 1997). Other types of women's employment do not present these extreme social problems for the workers (nursing, teaching, domestic service, and even work in a porcelain, biscuit, or match factory). An examination of the Juki stigma allows us to examine why garment factory work has a special place as a particularly disrespectable job.

In terms of the social history of the Juki nickname, there are two interrelated issues to consider: Why did this nickname emerge so soon after the economy was opened to foreign investment? Why did it disparage working women in sexual terms? The UNP government was elected in 1977 and immediately liberalized the economy. Critics of the UNP—the SLFP and the JVP—were quick to construct and draw attention to what they saw as certain alarming moral issues surrounding this new economic strategy. The behavior of FTZ women was one such issue, for soon after Katunayake was opened, there were reports of inappropriate sexual behavior between area men and female workers. For instance, in the period just after the FTZ opened, rumors circulated about men being brought in by the vanload to attend industry-sponsored nighttime music shows at which there would be vast numbers of unaccompanied women in the audience.[17] The fact that these women were unaccompanied was significant, for it meant that they were away from those who normally monitor women's behavior: parents, brothers, husbands, boyfriends, relatives, or other villagers.

Clearly, identifying women with sewing machines dehumanizes the women who feel that they are already treated like machines in the workplace (see Geeta's essay, where she writes that in these factories "people have become just like machines"). The Juki nickname seems to have emerged as part of a political strategy by critics of the government to draw attention to the dehumanization inherent in global capitalism. The foreignness of the Juki brand is likely significant, because critics would have been keen to highlight the problematic moral nature of a *foreign* economic and social process. Juki does not simply identify women with machines (which would be significant enough), but with a foreign machine brand. As far as I know there is no Sri Lankan industrial sewing-machine brand. But if there were, a nickname based on an indigenous product would not have been as effective as the Juki moniker. By highlighting the foreignness of the machine and of the production process, the name implies the prostitution of the Sri Lankan state to foreign investors through the metaphor of the prostitution of Sri Lankan women.

The Juki stigma thus seems to have emerged from political concern with issues regarding the nation, inequality, and global economic strategies. Yet, rather than focus directly on class inequality, this approach criticized women in sexual terms. Why sex? With women's respectability indexed to their sexual behavior, Sri Lankans intensely want to ensure that women remain the guardians of traditions. Any suspected violations of these cultural norms thus become problematic.

Other researchers have argued that the attitudes, such as jealousy, of the people who live in the town of Katunayake have been largely responsible for perpetuating the negative Juki girl stereotype (Voice of Women 1983; Weerasinghe 1989). While I concede that the jealousy of unemployed men or the parents of local girls who are eclipsed for jobs by out-of-towners may play a role, the stereotype is not simply a local problem. The Juki-girl stigma has

JUKI GIRLS, GOOD GIRLS

held firm for three interrelated reasons. Underlying all three are concerns about the agency being exhibited by young women in their encounters with economic globalization.

First, critics seem to read the public visibility of these women as indicative of their lack of adherence to what are understood as traditional roles for village women. These roles involve a seamless transition from daughter to wife and, soon thereafter, mother (Bandarage 1988). Within the traditional expectations, someone must always be controlling women (first the parents, then the husband; brothers can substitute for either). There is no stage of life at which it is considered appropriate for single, unmarried women to live away from their parents and communities. (One obvious exception would be university residence halls, but the "wardens" who run these single-sex halls act very much as parental figures.) Meanwhile, most of the garment workers in Katunayake live in boarding houses away from their parents, so they enjoy more freedom in their social lives than other single women of their age. For instance, they usually walk home from work in groups or with boyfriends, and some go with men to films or to watch airplanes at the nearby airport. Criticisms of these women often articulate a concern that young women who are not controlled by parents will not be controllable at work: they will not behave correctly in their expected roles in a disciplined industrial labor force.

Second, there is an important class dimension to the Juki stigma, a point also noted by the sociologist S. T. Hettige (2000, 190–91). Class mobility exhibited by poor village women (as manifested in their new fashions, consumption patterns, and ways of speaking, and their participation in various forms of entertainment) is perceived as a threat to the status quo by middle- and upper-class Sri Lankans, in the cities as well as the villages. In this regard, middle-class Sri Lankans in Kandy and Colombo sometimes told me that they could not distinguish between factory workers and office workers on their commute. They also told me they could no longer find good domestic servants because garment factories now employed many people who would have previously become servants.

Third, there may also be present an element of male anxiety about female employment, especially given the fact of widespread male unemployment. Masculinity in Sri Lanka is measured in part by men's abilities to take care of women—their mothers, sisters, wives, and daughters. For this reason, men in all classes of Sri Lankan society are generally expected to tell their wives to quit their jobs as soon as they marry. Because the garment industry employs only a small percentage of men, many unemployed men have seen women receive jobs that they wish were open to them. The sociologist Asoka Bandarage (1988, 69, 72) argues that these women, like Sri Lankan women who work as domestic servants in the Middle East, are condemned because they are away from the patriarchal control of husbands or fathers, and their economic and social independence threatens male authority.

Taken together, these three points reveal that, in short, these urban women garment workers are violating social norms that hold urban poor and rural women "as the sole upholders of the manners, customs and traditions of a glorious Sinhala past" (de Alwis 1998, 193–94). Despite an expansion of women's involvement in paid work since the economy was liberalized in 1977, the Juki stigma has held on with remarkable tenacity and reached beyond the urban areas. Despite their location in villages, the Juki-girl stigma affected women even in 200 GFP factories such as Shirtex and Serendib. These women fought this stigma daily to demonstrate that they were good village girls who also happened to work in garment factories.

Good Girls and Bad Girls in the Media

Women at Shirtex and Serendib knew about Juki girls through negative rumors that circulated in their villages about women who migrated to Colombo and through mass-media coverage of urban factory women. Juki girls were frequently featured in mass-media forms that the workers consumed, such as television, radio, magazines, and newspapers. The focus of these features (which continue to appear to this day) was only sometimes the exploitative work conditions in the factories. More often it was the outside-of-work social conditions in which the "unchecked freedom" of these women was said to lead to "bad behavior." For example, a 1996 Sinhala newspaper article contended that young village girls who come to work in the FTZ are forced into drinking alcohol and engaging in sex (Wijebandara 1996, 14). The author describes the women who fall into this trap of "bad behavior" as "innocent" when they arrive at Katunayake from their villages. But, the author continues, they are soon introduced to their new surroundings. Old-timers at the FTZ— many of village origin themselves—tell the rookies, " 'This is not the village. If you are living here, you must adjust yourselves to the ways of this place.' The people who drink arrack [a hard palm liquor] preach to the others saying that beer is what females drink and you do not get drunk on it. This is also preached to the drinkers of Coca-Cola. . . . Young girls who are drunk are used for sexual activities and pictures of them naked are also taken." As in the story of "our sprint queen" Susanthika who drank the forbidden fruit of the city and lost her chance at being a respectable village role model for women, here, too, alcohol is the symbol of the fall from rural grace. As the anthropologist Sandya Hewamanne (2002, 272–73) notes, the women in these stories are typically cast as victims of men (usually police and military men) rather than as sexually desirous agents. In contrast, Hewamanne argues that their engagement with new forms of sexuality is an intentional challenge of middle-class sexual norms.

At the time of my field research, the role of teledramas (serialized nighttime television programs) was especially important for the development of the Juki-girl stigma. More recently, Sinhala films about garment workers have become an important medium for debates about morality, culture, and national identity. Between 2001 and 2003 alone, four popular Sinhala-language feature films focused on women garment workers—all in regard to their relationships with army men (Abeysekera 2005). The 1997 film *Pura Handa Kaluwara* (Death on a Full Moon Day) was one of the first films to tackle this theme. With the intensification of the government's war with the LTTE in the mid- to late 1990s, the parallel processes of militarization and globalization have increasingly become the foci for gendered debates about the nation's future.

Popular Sinhala films and teledramas idealize the moral purity of rural life and contribute to the moral panic about urban factory workers (cf. Tambiah 1992, 110). These visual media often focus on women's sexuality through a dichotomy of city and village represented by stark good versus bad conflicts (Abeysekera 1997, 5; 2005). In her analysis of Sinhala film from 1947 to 1989, Laleen Jayamanne (1992, 71, 68) has argued that "the 'good girls' of Sri Lankan cinema" were narratively located in the village. She also notes the following simple binary oppositions that structure generic Sinhala cinema's mythical narratives: rich versus poor, city versus village, bad versus good, and Westernized versus traditional values (57).

These filmic themes have continued during the era of economic liberalization, with women's roles in the Open Economy an especially important site for filmmakers to represent cultural anxieties about liberalization. Sunila Abeysekera (1989, 52) has indicated that for women in genre films the good versus bad dichotomy is defined purely in terms of sexuality, whereas for men it is not. A man can be deemed bad in many respects, but improper sexuality is the defining characteristic for women. Abeysekera describes the representations of good and bad women:

The typical "good" woman . . . is imbued with virtues of passivity: patience, self-sacrifice, willing submission to suffering, obedience to patriarchal authority. Visually, too, she dresses in a "simple" manner, is unostentatious, full of gentle smiles and downcast eyes, non-aggressive to the core. . . . The "good" woman almost always affects traditional modes of dress such as the Kandyan saree (the osari) or the cloth and jacket. . . .

The "bad" woman . . . is most often Westernised, would even wear dresses or trousers, have short hair, smoke, and behave aggressively towards men and be of "loose moral character." At the same time, she is loud-mouthed, shrewish, and thoroughly unlikeable. (Abeysekera 1989, 52–53)

These narratives are a cinematic expression and reinforcement of a general cultural theme about morality that supplies the context for how women at Shirtex and Serendib experience their new social roles as garment workers. Women at these factories invoked many of these same characteristics when they discussed how they differed from urban factory women. They would use terms like "decent" (*saṇwara*) or "simple" (*cam*) to describe the appearance and behavior of their coworkers. Wearing trousers and short hair, smoking, and looking managers in the eye were all described to me as negatively valued behaviors. The Good girls of Shirtex and Serendib were working within the Good-girl model described by Abeysekera and depicted in Sinhala film. However, it will soon become clear that they were also attempting to expand the definition of Good girlness to fit their new lives as village factory women.

Two popular Sinhala-language teledramas about urban garment workers also fit squarely in this dichotomizing mode. Airing around the time of my field research, these two shows about the plight of village women who migrate to Colombo to work in garment factories fueled the Juki-girl reputation. Airing for a limited period—from several months to years—such serials can be immensely popular and are often watched together by entire families. From January to March 1996 I watched the full run of *Ira Handa Yata* (Under the Sun and Moon) in my neighbors' house with parents, children, and other neighbors, male and female. In this teledrama, the main character, Dhammi, is involved in a relationship with a man she meets at a bus stop. Romantic walks on the beach ensue, but the crucial scene is when the couple has sex in a beachside hotel. The filming of this scene renders ambiguous the question of whether Dhammi willingly participated in the sexual encounter. Some time later Dhammi awakens in the hotel to find that the man has disappeared—

along with her gold necklace. The fact that he stole her gold necklace is particularly poignant because it is widely said in Sri Lanka that the first thing garment workers buy with their first wage is a gold chain—which doubles as a fashion statement and as savings for dowry. When Dhammi tries to find the man, she learns that he had given her a false name. After discovering she is pregnant, Dhammi searches and finally finds the man, who apologizes and promises to get a good job and stop being a crook. The couple reunites, marries, and presumably lives happily ever after.

In a 1994 teledrama called *Grahanaya* (Entangled), the main character, Felicia, engages in a romantic relationship with a man while she lives in Colombo and is subsequently shamed by her village. She is then forced into a long-term sexual relationship with her factory owner by a female supervisor. Felicia receives financial rewards in exchange, but in the end she has a child, is ostracized by her family, and tries to murder the owner. By the end of the teledrama, Felicia has financially prospered from her relationship with the boss and now runs her own sewing shop where she can keep watch over her child while working. But such an ending with the woman living independently cannot suffice. The final scene has Felicia attempting to stab her boss and then being taken away by the police. Such a tragic ending is familiar in Sinhala film: independent women or women who flout the male social order usually end up repentant, dead, insane, or living as Buddhist nuns, for—as Abeysekera (1997, 6–7) puts it—once a woman falls, she is fallen forever. In Sinhala cinema, a good woman cannot lead an independent life (Abeysekera 1989, 52–53; Abeysekera 2005; Caprio 1997, 6).

In both teledramas it is clear that the suitable role for Good girls is as wives and mothers. This is a general cultural theme, but by tapping into the moral panic about urban garment workers the teledramas' creators have given their shows even more import. The fact that two such shows were on the air between 1994 and 1996 is evidence of the extent of the moral panic at that time, and the concerns have increased in subsequent years.

Moral Panic

Societal alarm about the bad character of Juki girls resembles Stanley Cohen's formulation of moral panic: "A condition, episode, person or group of persons emerges to become defined as a threat to societal values and interests" (Cohen 1972: 9; cf. Carby 1997; Goode and Ben-Yehuda 1994;

Thompson 1998). Juki girls and Susanthika pose such a threat in contemporary Sri Lanka: to people in various social positions there is something about these women that signals the disintegration of revered cultural traditions.

If we consider Juki girls as yet another social context for the potency of the underwear critique, Cohen's notion of moral panic and Erving Goffman's formulation of stigma further illuminate the social context for the underwear critique and the state's subsequent refocusing of the 200 GFP on the issue of women's morality. Cohen (1972, 198) describes how a group that is "highly visible and structurally weak" can become an easy object of attack for moral panics orchestrated by more powerful members of society because of conflicts of interests and power differentials—the more powerful members of society want to maintain the status quo and find the new groups' visibility a threat to the social order. Cohen argues that representatives of the mass media can create moral panic by reporting on deviant behavior in order to delineate behavior that is "right" or "wrong." Furthermore, the media and the public create the panic by using emotive symbols, such as the terms hooligans, thugs, and wild ones, in Cohen's 1960s British examples (1972, 55–57). The term *Juki girl* has become one such "emotive symbol" in contemporary Sri Lanka.

Cohen helps us understand that moral panics are a form of social control that create and reinforce a moral dichotomy of right and wrong. This framework focuses attention on the role of moral panic in the maintenance of values and interests. But as we can see from the situation of Juki girls, moral dichotomies of right and wrong are not only *reinforced* when moral panics take hold. Sometimes these moral panics indicate the presence of (and facilitate) a process in which there emerge new understandings of right and wrong and of what is good and bad. Furthermore, the situation I am describing is more pervasive than the top-down movement implied by Cohen. In the Sri Lankan case, it is not simply people in power who desire to maintain certain values— these desires are more hegemonic and self-disciplining. This point relates to my comments earlier that villagers are just as invested as urbanites in thinking about their world in stark and value-laden rural-urban contrasts. It is also evidenced by some village garment workers' critiques of urban Juki girls. The relationship between village garment workers and Juki girls is complex, and it was precisely this issue that Mala raised when she wrote in her questionnaire response that "when we come to work amidst society we are subjected to the insults of young people just like us."

Goffman (1963) focuses on the "management of stigma" by stigmatized people and demonstrates that even people on the deviant end of a moral panic may have quite complicated identities since, as members of society, they have internalized the normative categories. For both Cohen and Goffman, "passing" as a person of a different social class or as a nonstigmatized person is a significant moment in the construction of normativity. When people see members of their stigmatized group acting in stereotypical ways, those of the group who pass as "normals" can be both repelled and ashamed, just as Shirtex and Serendib women would be repelled by Juki girls in Colombo.

The anthropologist Susan Seizer (2000, 2005) has examined the "stigma of public mobility" experienced by women actresses in India whose occupation puts them in a stigmatized position, and who love their jobs but will not admit it because they are embarrassed. Seizer beautifully describes the negotiations women make to overcome this stigma of public mobility when they move between different public spaces and the performances of femininity they deploy in these different spaces. Juki girls are likewise positioned as stigmatized objects of moral panic, and the unusual extent of their public mobility certainly plays a role in their stigmatization. The public visibility of these women, which is so often noted in representations of Juki girls, has meant that they are the most visible symbol of cultural change (cf. de Alwis 1995). In similar vein, Yasmin Tambiah (2005, 251) discusses the burden of public mobility on LTTE women fighters who circulate in a male world. The women must make up for this movement in the men's sphere by proving their virtue. Tambiah argues that for these women "sexual chastity becomes overburdened as the marker of their virtue." Likewise for Juki girls: these women's public mobility has placed on them an extra burden to be sexually chaste. The struggles the women at Shirtex and Serendib engage in to be considered good Sinhala Buddhist girls despite being garment workers run ironically parallel to the efforts of female LTTE fighters to be considered virtuous Tamil women.

The moral panic about Susanthika and Juki girls is only in part attributable to the stigma generated by public mobility. Also important is the extent to which they are perceived to violate nationalist ideals of femininity when they cross the urban-rural divide. The main "emotive symbol" that is used to describe garment workers is the term *Juki girl*, and many garment workers inside and outside FTZs are at pains to pass as non–Juki girls. Many Shirtex and Serendib women tried to "pass" by enacting certain sartorial and social practices. For instance, most would be sure to brush their clothes and hair of cotton dust and thread before leaving the factory gates, and many would choose to commute alone rather than among packs of women who could be clearly marked as garment workers.

These women tried to manage the Juki stigma by deploying new kinds of Good girl identities, but they also participated in some ways in the very moral panic through which they were stigmatized. Many women frequently drew stark contrasts between urban and rural garment factory workers, and some even used the term *Juki girls* in a negative manner to refer to the urban workers. In doing so, they perpetuated certain repressive gender constructions. Their attitudes resemble those of the Malaysian electronics workers observed by Aihwa Ong (1987, 191) whose "positive attempts at constructing their own gender identity depended on a cult of purity and self-sacrifice." These women's complex understandings of their social position were in large part complicated by the nationalist discourse on Juki girls and factory labor. The underwear critique had brought these issues to the level of national political conversations. With this context in mind, I now return to discuss precisely why and how Premadasa shifted the 200 GFP focus from youth to women.

Shifting to Women's Morality

The 200 GFP began in February 1992 and in the early months it was consistently cast as a program for preventing youth unrest. Analysis of newspaper and parliamentary reports on the program shows that criticism of the 200 GFP intensified in October 1992, when the frequency of factory openings peaked, with factories opening almost daily. The first published reference to the underwear critique that I found comes from this time period. Premadasa responded to the critique in two ways: he dismissed it as a political ploy by the opposition and he countered by initiating a discussion about morality and social class. For instance, the president argued in one factory speech that the opposition politicians' interest in the underwear of foreign women revealed that it was the politicians who were morally compromised, not the factory workers. Referring here to his party as "we," he drew stark contrasts with the opposition politicians, whom he called "they": "The garment sector is expanding rapidly, though the opposition is criticising this. They say rural women are sewing panties for foreign women. This is how they humiliate the rural masses. We also go abroad, but during our visits we gather something useful and fruitful. They go overseas to look at panties of foreign women!" (Mohamed 1992b, n.p.). With this shift in argument, Premadasa turned the tables on the opposition by latching on to the fact that the critique was not just about the actual articles that were made but about the moral status of the women workers.

Engagement with the critique's insinuations about class and morality was also seen in a theme that Premadasa raised in a number of speeches starting that October. He argued that the opposition's critiques of the 200 GFP were an attempt to discredit a program that was providing good jobs for the rural poor. He claimed that the opposition was critical because their party consisted of the aristocracy, who wanted to maintain a poor class of servants for their homes (de Silva 1992a, 1992b, 1993). In some speeches Premadasa accused the opposition of simply wanting to keep down the poor. Although I have not found a written reference to this, numerous people told me that on several occasions Premadasa made the morality connection here as well by adding that when poor women become servants "all they come home with is something in their stomachs from the rich man." Perhaps this allusion to pregnancy was just a bit too unsavory to report in the newspapers, and perhaps this was what one reporter meant when he wrote that Premadasa "recalled how poor rural children and youths were employed as servants in aristocratic homes and subjected to untold hardships" (de Silva 1993, n.p.).

Also alluding to this issue of servants and morality was a 200 GFP television advertisement. In this advertisement—which I never saw but heard about from various people—a couple in a luxury car arrive at a poor villager's house and tell the mother that they will hire the daughter as a servant in their home. The mother refuses the offer by responding with pride that her daughter works in a garment factory. Later the girl is shown after she receives her first paycheck, bringing home a sari for her mother and a sarong for her father. Numerous people I spoke to said that the motif of the girl bringing home gifts for her parents was another reference to Premadasa's claim that if she were a servant, rather than clothing she would have brought home an illegitimate grandchild. Likewise, because saris and sarongs are considered traditional Sinhala Buddhist clothing, Premadasa was also making a connection here among morality, social class, and tradition.

I have found only one instance prior to the underwear critique in which the president linked the 200 GFP and women's morality—in marked contrast with the frequency of the linkages in the period following the critique. In a June 1992 opening ceremony speech, he referred to the "nefarious activities" into which some FTZ girls had been forced because very little of their salaries remained for their families back home once they paid for room and board.

Readers would have understood this to be a clear reference to rumors that urban FTZ women were engaging in prostitution to supplement their meager factory incomes. The president pledged that with jobs in villages, these "nefarious activities" would be avoided (Mohamed 1992a).

But even before the moral accusations became common, press coverage of the 200 GFP in the government-controlled newspapers often pointed out the moral benefits of the program. An unabashedly supportive newspaper reporter described the anticipated social transformation as follows: "The factory workers, many of whom are young women, will continue to live in their homes and contribute to family welfare, thus preventing the breakdown of traditional values and family life which often occurs when workers move to the cities in search of employment" (Special Correspondent 1992b, n.p.). This quotation is just one of many examples of how journalists emphasized issues of gender, morality, and changing social values to argue that the program would solve many of the nation's modern problems with a modern solution: involvement in the global economy. Following on the underwear critique, the argument that the program prevented immorality by preventing women's migration to Colombo became even more widespread and was voiced by the president himself. In short, the claim was that keeping women in their villages would keep women — and the nation — from going bad.

This argument about morality and class had an enduring social effect, resulting in the long-term transformation of the 200 GFP from a program for preventing youth unrest to a program for protecting women's morality. Premadasa's supporters began to emphasize the protection of women's morality as the program's most important feature. This is what was remembered during my field research period in 1995–96. Most people recalled a vague connection to the recent youth revolt only when I pressed them. In the end, the opposition and the government concurred on the importance of women's behavior to national development.

Sexuality, Morality, and Sinhala Buddhist Nationalism

Another important context in which to place the underwear critique was the government's ongoing war with the LTTE. The opposition may have also believed that the proper role for the nation's innocent girls was as citizen mothers who reproduced disciplined male soldiers. But if (according to this line of thought) they were busy producing immoral garments, what kind of undisciplined army would protect the Sinhala Buddhist nation?

The 1997 film *Pura Handa Kaluwara* (Death on a Full Moon Day), set in Anuradhapura, takes on issues of gender, globalization, and militarization. When the military delivers a sealed army coffin containing his son's body, a blind but insightful father refuses to believe that his soldier son was killed and declines the government compensation for surviving family members. To make up for the abrupt end to the brother's army salary, his sister secretly finds employment at a garment factory to help support her family. When her inquisitive boyfriend follows her to the factory, he finds soldiers waiting for garment women at the end of the day. The boyfriend rushes home to tell the mourning father, "You are thinking about your son, and your daughter is going into prostitution." In an interview, the director, Prasanna Vithanage, discussed the social context for this scene. He mentioned the 200 GFP and continued:

When I made the film in July 1997, prostitution was just beginning in Anuradhapura. Now, after Colombo, the highest prostitution rate in Sri Lanka is in Anuradhapura, the sacred city. Soldiers who come from the north spend two days in this city and a whole prostitution industry has developed. The wages in the garment factories are very low and so some of the girls go to massage clinics and from there they are pushed into prostitution. I heard of one incident involving a young soldier who went to a brothel and was shown all the girls available. He saw his sister amongst these girls and became so angry that he attempted to kill the brothel-keeper and his sister. The brothel-keeper took him to another room, calmed him down and got him another girl. You see how the war has eroded basic human values and the conception of Sri Lanka as some great Buddhist civilisation. (Phillips 2000, n.p.)[18]

This film vignette disrupts the easy dichotomies of rural-urban and pure-impure that pervade Sri Lanka and underlie the underwear critique. In highlighting the conjuncture of two socioeconomic factors—the presence in the area of soldiers on leave from the nearby front and the presence of underpaid garment workers in rural 200 GFP factories—the film engages questions of economy, sexuality, morality, and Sinhala Buddhist nationalism in a time of ethnic conflict. The sociologist Newton Gunasinghe (1984) correlated the rise in ethnic hostilities in Sri Lanka with economic liberalization. Given the visible role of women in the new economy, one might then pose the following questions along the lines of Gunasinghe's thesis. How has the moral panic about the behavior of female factory workers been associated with the ethnic hostilities? And what kinds of connections have been made between factory women's morality and concerns about the dissolution of the Sinhala Buddhist nation?

The dichotomy between villages and the city, already much discussed in these pages, glosses a politically charged landscape in which village Sri Lanka is claimed for Sinhala Buddhists—and, to a certain extent, other Sinhalas— and not minorities, particularly not Tamils. By providing rural industrial jobs, the 200 GFP promised the restoration of the nation's moral and political order at a time when the LTTE was threatening secession and when the country was recovering from the JVP revolt. The strategy of placing nontraditional, global capitalist industry in villages to prevent the disintegration of tradition might seem to pivot on a contradiction; and in fact, it was precisely this contradiction that the underwear critique addressed, upping the stakes by framing it in explicitly sexualized terms. In response, the government played up the identification of the nation's villages as sites of authentic Sinhala Buddhist tradition. In this formulation, keeping women in villages would be a means to protect the Sinhala Buddhist nation's moral order.

So did this in fact occur? Did Shirtex and Serendib workers' location in villages somehow keep them innocent, pure, and traditional? Perhaps not surprisingly, I demonstrate in the following chapters that this heroic picture of the purifying power of villages becomes much more complicated when we look at how the women at Shirtex and Serendib actually experienced their work and new lives, attempting to devise ways of embodying Good girls despite being garment workers. We now turn to those real lives, experiences, and struggles.

GEETA

Geeta was an unmarried twenty-four-year-old sewing machine operator at Serendib. She is the author of an essay that is included in this book. With an external bachelor's degree (earned by taking part-time evening and night courses as a commuter student—an important alternative for Sri Lankans, whose university system has too few places for qualified students) in sociology, Geeta complained to me that before becoming a garment worker she used to frequent the library and read nonfiction books and newspapers. She described herself and her coworkers as each "like a frog living in a well," unaware of anything happening outside its small world. She offered the following explanation of the simile:

There is no time to look at a paper. Really we're enclosed here [in the factory]. We've all come to the same mental state. The next day early in the morning at 5 a.m. we come to work here again. So, what happens in society? [We don't know.] Now, for example, a Tiger [LTTE] threat. We don't even know if there is a thing like that. We don't know what has happened outside the institution. And, in an emergency. Even if one's mother dies, it is really very difficult to get leave like that. Even in that case one must report back for duty again after two or three days pass. . . . I went to the library frequently before coming to work here. It's been four months now since I came for work and I have not yet had the

*chance to go to the library. So I've come to a great decline in terms
of mentality. There's no freedom. A worker here doesn't have any
understanding about society.*

Here she explained that workers were distanced from society because they
kept such long hours, didn't have time to read newspapers, and couldn't
even go to funerals (an important social obligation among Sinhala
Buddhists).

The first time I met her, Geeta had only been working at Serendib a
few months. On our first meeting, we had a conversation about her job
and my research as she sewed. Her first question for me was what I
thought of Marx and Spencer. At first I misunderstood, assuming she
was referring to Marks & Spencer, the UK department-store chain
that imports clothes from Sri Lankan factories. But when she told me a
moment later that she has a bachelor's degree in sociology I realized she
was referring to Karl Marx and Herbert Spencer.

When I formally interviewed her a few months later, she brought up
the Marxian notion of the division of labor. She said that on account of
the division of labor within factories, workers could not get the leave they
needed because there were not enough other people at the factory with the
required skills to cover their work. She and others told me that many
workers were unhappy knowing that although they had been sewing at a
factory for three years (this was in 1995, three years after the 200 GFP
began), they could not produce a garment on their own at home. First,
they might know only how to do a single operation, such as attaching the
front and back of a shoulder, and nothing else: "She can't produce an
item of clothing by herself. She can only do one part." Second, they would
know how to sew on electric machines but not the manual kind they
might have at home. Geeta explained:

I don't know whether it is because I am studying sociology. I discuss this with everybody. I ask, "Can you do something like this at
home alone?" They can't. They can't operate a machine at home.
That means, here we have Juki machines [electric machines].
They can't operate a [pedal-powered] machine like a Singer at
home. Like that, we have to leave work in the end with empty
hands. We gain no experience here and we don't ever work hap-

pily either. I come to work with a lot of distaste. All the girls come in a state like that. Really, the people have become just like machines. These girls must do the work that is done by machines. If we think about a machine, its production is very high. The girls have had to become like machines.

4. JUKI GIRLS, GOOD GIRLS, AND THE
VILLAGE CONTEXT

I argue in the previous chapter that the opposition party's underwear critique and the Juki stigma were both centrally concerned with women's sexual chastity. When the opposition decried that "our innocent girls are sewing underwear for white women," the "innocent girls" were village women assumed to be naturally ignorant about sexual impropriety and other "foreign" and nontraditional behaviors and influences. As compared to FTZ women, Shirtex and Serendib women were able to reap certain benefits (inside and outside the workplace) because they still lived in their villages. Workers, managers, and investors all made assumptions about these and other 200 GFP women because of their village locatedness.[1]

In this chapter, I examine why and how living in their villages was important to Shirtex and Serendib women's daily struggles to be considered Good girls, not Juki girls. To do so, I first describe the area where these factories were established and the linkages that developed between the factories and the surrounding villages. I then move on to examine an important related issue cited by diverse people: the moral protection that being in their villages provided factory women. After discussing this recurring theme, I go on to profile one Shirtex woman for whom the village location was supremely important. I then turn to examine how the two teledramas about garment workers informed the dichotomous understandings of village and urban garment workers expressed by people in and around Shirtex and Serendib. The chapter provides an overview of the ways in which these particular factories and the people in them are connected to these particular villages, but also of how Sri

Lankans more generally make sense of village locatedness in a world of rapid social change.

This chapter contains numerous examples of stark contrasts that Sri Lankans make between villages and cities, and between what is good and what is bad. I have noted that Good girls are women who behave according to cultural expectations for female respectability, and that Shirtex and Serendib women were new kinds of Good girls. They were not the precise opposite of Juki girls or bad girls, but neither were they engaged in straightforwardly traditional Good-girl behavior; yet since they adhered to its core features—in particular, virginity—if not all the details, they were still considered good by themselves and the community. For Shirtex and Serendib women, being perceived as good by those around them was of great importance. The threat of the Juki stigma was especially troubling to these women because their fellow villagers shared their intense concern with women's reputations, respectability, and traditional norms. The texture of this new Good-girl identity will become clear in the remaining chapters of this book.

Villages, Identity, and Change

The Shirtex and Serendib women's Good-girl identities appear to be in marked contrast with the identities constructed by women workers in the Katunayake FTZ, as described by Sandya Hewamanne (2002, 2003). Hewamanne found that Katunayake women easily embraced and reveled in their oppositional identities and, in fact, took pleasure in challenging middle-class Sinhala Buddhist norms of femininity. These challenges were manifested in their clothes, hairstyles, musical tastes, manners of speech, bodily comportment, and leisure-time activities. Hewamanne provides vivid descriptions of women flirting with and exchanging addresses with men on trains and at beaches, reading and discussing women's magazines that middle-class people consider vulgar for their sexual content, and drinking beer at factory-sponsored events. The picture she draws is one of women creating new identities that challenge old norms. She refers to hints of concern about what villagers back home would think, but these concerns only affected the women when it came to their outward behavior in their own villages: "When FTZ workers visited their villages they performed 'good girl' routines in public while making fun of their own performances within the privacy of their room" (2002, 362). By stark contrast, village garment workers have to "perform" the Good-girl role constantly.

Shirtex and Serendib women workers' concerns about how others perceived them were intricately related to personal struggles over how to reconcile their own experiences and desires with societal expectations for women's behavior. The previous chapter identifies particular ways in which Sri Lankans have invested women's behavior with special significance during the era of economic liberalization. However, all Sri Lankans, regardless of gender, have worked to make sense of economic liberalization in their lives. In the face of the social changes brought by liberalization, many have wrestled with how to reconcile their concern for duty, obligation, tradition, and social convention with their desires to experience and enjoy new opportunities and the accompanying new ways of thinking about and acting in the world. The Shirtex and Serendib women's struggles, which took place inside and outside work, were specific articulations of these larger social processes.

In her ethnography called *From Duty to Desire*, Jane Collier (1997) analyzes changing social relations in rural Spain between the 1960s and the 1980s. She investigates how Spanish villagers explained that there had been a shift during this time from people acting according to duty to acting out of desire. Collier examines these shifts in understandings of social action in relation to the changes in social inequality that have accompanied industrialization. She links "the development of 'modern' subjectivity to changes in how people enacted and experienced unequal social relations" (1997, 18). Collier argues that when the agricultural economy crashed in rural Spain in 1964, opportunities for employment in capitalist industry increased. Whereas earlier social status was inherited, an important change took effect with involvement in the national labor force. Now that there was a growing link between work and social status, families could achieve high status through work, and educational opportunity became an important route to lucrative employment. People were uncertain about how to account for differences in wealth because their old hierarchies and meanings were no longer useful (1997, 66). Collier's book thus examines how people experienced and made sense of the uncertainties wrought by the transition to capitalist industry, and she pays particular attention to "the self-concepts that villagers used for monitoring, interpreting, and managing their own and others' actions" (1997, 27).

As with Sri Lankan villagers, the Spanish villagers not only examined and made sense of their own experiences, but they were keen observers of what others were doing. In both situations, villagers took a great interest in observing, monitoring, and responding to their own actions and those of others around them. In this way, the village is like the panopticon discussed by Michel Foucault. In the eighteenth century, the English Utilitarian philosopher Jeremy Bentham proposed the notion of a prison in which detention cells would be arranged around a central viewing area, such that prisoners can be observed at all times. In his book *Discipline and Punish*, Foucault (1977) argues that because prisoners in this prison-panopticon do not know whether or not they are being watched (since the guards could be looking anywhere) but assume they must be, they end up monitoring themselves. We will see below how people at Shirtex and Serendib discuss the significance of being seen by their fellow villagers. If we consider the village to be like a prison-panopticon, where everyone is her own surveyor, we can better understand some of the ways in which village garment workers made sense of the world around them, monitored their own behavior, criticized Juki girls, and explained Juki girls' presumed aberrant behavior. This village panopticon helped produce Good girls who were not only good for the nation and the village but also for the factory.

Foucault uses the panopticon as a metaphor for how people in modern society are governed by others but also govern themselves. Foucault refers to the monitoring of others through domination and coercion as "techniques of domination" and he refers to self-monitoring or self-regulation as "techniques of the self." He argues that societies are governed both through domination and self-regulation. Both techniques are present in modern society: individuals are monitored by others (your school's honor board can expel you for plagiarism), and they monitor themselves (you don't plagiarize anyway because you've been taught that it's wrong). This dual mode helps us understand the ways in which the people I discuss were making decisions and acting on the world because of what was expected of them, but also because of what they expected of themselves.

Foucault's analysis of external and internal monitoring as well as Collier's study of changes in wealth and status illuminate many of the shifts that Sri Lankans have experienced since the economy was liberalized in 1977. A transition from inherited status to status achieved through occupation marks recent experiences for many Sri Lankans who try to access the benefits of economic liberalization policies. When the women at Shirtex and Serendib worked to forge identities as Good girls, they did so in the context of their

JUKI GIRLS, GOOD GIRLS

and other Sri Lankans' efforts to make sense of and respond to the inequalities of globalization.

Sri Lankans in the 1990s scrambled to deal with the social inequality that emerged following the 1977 economic reforms (Hettige 2004). This inequality was evident in various social relations within Shirtex and Serendib. For instance, the differences in wage levels of managers and workers allowed managers to travel to work in private air-conditioned vehicles while the workers sweated in crowded buses. The managers had cleaner (and Western-style) toilets and dining halls and higher-quality tea during breaks. Social relations in the wider social world were also steeped in inequality. While the wealth of many urban English-educated Sri Lankans has increased with the new economic opportunities, many other Sri Lankans are impoverished. Subsistence farming, important to generations of Sri Lankans, has become unviable for most rural people due to the decline in agricultural markets that accompanied the state's focus on export-oriented industrialization and widespread landlessness caused by population growth. People who had been engaged in farming for generations must now seek employment in cities, abroad, or in the military. However, in ways that are not uniform, some rural Sri Lankans have benefited from economic liberalization policies. Some previously poor rural people have managed to get lucrative jobs in the new economy, perhaps through engagement in local business or tourism or by migrating to work in the Middle East. Thus it is quite common to see adjacent village homes where the contrasts in size, quality, and aesthetics indicate vast differences in wealth. Sometimes even siblings live in hugely different ways. Perhaps one brother has found a route to success in the new economy, and so his children attend an elite private school and speak English at home, while the other struggles to farm the family's tiny plot and to come up with enough money to buy books for his child who attends the village school and learns English from someone who can barely speak it herself. Or maybe one sister has worked as a housemaid for the past fifteen years, sending home remittances that have allowed her husband to build a new home and send the children to private school. Meanwhile her sister, who cares for the migrant sister's children, barely survives on her own husband's meager income from farming.

For many Sri Lankans, new economic opportunities have brought changes in wealth and status that have not been easily incorporated into preexisting social categories. The intense moral debates over economic liberalization, and the Juki-girl stigma itself, are indicators of people's conflicted efforts to accommodate these profound changes. Various other markers are seen in the civil war that has been taking place since 1983; in the high levels of unemployment and underemployment of an educated populace; in the late 1980s youth revolt that nearly paralyzed the country; and in the rising suicide rate— Sri Lanka's is one of the highest in the world (Marecek 1998).

I now turn to describe the village environment around Shirtex and Serendib. These descriptions should be read against this wider context of a society in transition.

Shirtex and Serendib in Context

Two photographs that I took during my field research symbolize for me the inequality and contradictions of economic liberalization. Serendib's factory manager, Sampath Sir, came to work each day in his Mitsubishi Pajero, which he parked in the shade to the side of the driveway. On one occasion, a group of women workers posed for me in front of this Pajero. On another, a group of male managers posed in the same spot. Sri Lankans often have themselves photographed (frequently in studios) in front of objects or landscapes that are status markers. A certain prestige accrues to photos that transpose their subject within a desired world just out of reach (cf. Afterimage 1997; Appadurai 1997; Pinney 1998). While both Pajero-posing groups were participating in this Sri Lankan tradition of posed photographs, they would have owned to conflicting associations about the particular make and model of car. During the government crackdown on the second JVP revolt, many of the sixty thousand suspected JVP members who were killed or disappeared were taken away in Mistubishi Pajeros that were suspected to be official state vehicles (Amnesty International 1990, 15–16, quoted in Onderdenwijngaard 1995, 21). Thus these Japanese cars, which once symbolized the wealth and opportunity of economic liberalization policies, became symbols of state violence. While some workers had on occasion whispered to me about Sampath Sir's Pajero and the JVP, the two groups that posed in front of the Pajero clearly considered the car a desirable symbol. Yet for the managerial group, who owned or regularly traveled in Pajeros, the car would have symbolized something very different from what it meant for the workers. Such conflicting understandings of a foreign commodity are rife in economically liberalized Sri Lanka.

The image of the Pajero, which symbolizes wealth and violence, provides an apt entry into the village environment of Shirtex and Serendib because economics and violence are two symbolically dense frames of reference in which the villagers experience and evaluate the social inequalities that are transforming their lives. I discuss below in broad strokes issues related to employment, caste, education, politics, and economics in the area where these factories were located. My objective is simply to provide a glimpse of the workers, the places where they live, and the complex linkages between the villages and the factories.

The 200 GFP regulations required that workers in each factory live in that factory's Assistant Government Agent (AGA) Division. Approximately 90 percent of Shirtex and Serendib workers lived in the Kandepitiya AGA Division,[2] an administrative unit of approximately thirty surrounding villages. But because Serendib relocated and then expanded from a smaller site in another rural division, about 20 percent of Serendib workers came from the older factory and lived outside Kandepitiya. These distant Serendib workers traveled by train or bus—up to an hour-and-a-half commute in each direction. About twenty of the one thousand workers lived in even more distant areas of the country and rented rooms from villagers. The remainder lived in Kandepitiya and got to work by riding buses down bumpy village roads or walking on well-worn village paths that wound between paddy fields, houses, and home gardens. During the rainy season the walkers—some of whom traveled more than an hour—arrived with their feet and legs covered in mud. With their clothes also soaked, on such occasions the workers often caught colds that spread quickly in the poorly ventilated factories.

During my field research period a few years after the factories began, only a very small number of the total workforce lived in Udakande; most lived in surrounding villages. Prasanga, a villager who was a strong supporter of the factory, once told me that he wanted to get more Udakande residents to work at the factory "to make the factory more meaningful to the villagers." He had recently tried to help recruit a group of Udakande women for a training session at Serendib. But he said that these families were like all families in Sri Lanka: they were reluctant to send their daughters to the factories because of the Juki stigma. Prasanga explained that a bad reputation could harm a woman's future marriage prospects, and he opined that because Udakande families were generally wealthier than other Kandepitiya families, they had the luxury of choosing not to send their daughters to the factories. Indeed, many Udakande residents were white-collar workers—teachers, bank clerks, engineers, police officers, health-care workers, minor government officials—who commuted to Kandy for work.

The population of the villages and small towns in Kandepitiya was mostly Sinhala Buddhist, although there were small populations of Tamil and Sinhala Christians and Hindu Tamils. Tamils who worked at nearby tea plantations more heavily populated one area of Kandepitiya. Rambupata, a village adjacent to Udakande, was mostly Muslim.

The workers generally came from poor farming families with plots of land too tiny to cultivate for subsistence. Often the family's sole income was the garment worker's. Due to a rising population, the percentage of landless or land-poor residents of Kandepitiya has been increasing over the past fifty years, as it has with other nearby AGA divisions (Sarkar and Tambiah 1957; Tambiah 1958). Kandepitiya is situated five to ten miles outside the small city of Kandy, which is only a thirty-minute to one-hour bus or train ride away. Thus Kandy was a popular employment center for Kandepitiya residents who could not survive on the land. Family members of garment workers served in a wide range of jobs: as day laborers on other people's lands; as municipal workers building and cleaning roads; and as carpenters, masons, and shop clerks. In addition, every family seemed to know someone who worked in the Middle East—men as drivers (like the husband of Kumari from the introduction, who had been in Saudi Arabia for twelve years) and, more commonly, women as housemaids or garment workers. In many of the workers' families there was a son or husband in the army, but the other men were often unemployed and could find only occasional day labor. When not working, these men spent their days loitering in village public spaces, such as in front of *kadēs* (small shops) or on the cricket field just outside the factories' grounds.

As Premadasa predicted, various villagers who were not employed at the factories earned money through factory-related economic ventures. Some men drove groups of workers home from work in their private vans on the days overtime was required. One woman cooked lunch packets for workers and delivered them to the guardhouse shortly before the lunch break. Fifty feet outside the gate through which Sampath Sir drove his Pajero each day there was a *kadē* run by villagers where many workers would stop to buy small items like bananas and chocolate bars after work. Sandya, a tenant in a house across from the *kadē*, also earned some money from factory workers. At the factory gate there was a guardhouse where guards frisked exiting workers to ensure that no stolen garments or supplies (fabric, thread, buttons, pens) left the grounds. Apparently doubting the efficacy of these searches, the factories implemented a rule while I was there that prohibited the women from bringing anything into the factories besides a water bottle, an umbrella, and their handbags containing lunch, a wallet, and a comb or brush. Soon afterward, Sandya began to offer the workers a bag-checking service. For a few rupees a day, women could get a tag from Sandya to check items they brought from home—a women's tabloid magazine, a home-tailored dress to sell to a coworker, a love letter from a boyfriend in the army, photographs from the latest wedding party that a work section would have attended together.

Other local women bought leftover fabric ("cut pieces") and sewed clothes, curtains, and patchwork bedding for their own families or to sell. Serendib regularly sold stacks of fabric at a manager's nearby house for varying prices depending on the quality of material and the size of the scraps. Kumari, whom I profiled in the introduction, regularly bought these cut pieces. When I formally interviewed her, she had recently bought one kilo of fabric for 50 rupees, from which she made three skirts to sell to coworkers. At that time, fabric for one skirt would have cost at least 100 rupees in a market. Once on my bus ride home I sat next to a toddler clutching her mother and wearing a dress made out of the same knit cotton fabric as a tank top sewn for a U.S. clothing chain in the factory two weeks previously. Because workers regularly made clothes for themselves or other workers out of these scraps, and because overstocked clothing was occasionally sold to workers for lower than local prices, the Serendib management instituted a rule against wearing such clothes to the factory to prevent confusion as to whether or not the women were wearing stolen material or finished garments. The searches when they exited the factories, the rule about what could be brought to work, and the rule about what not to wear all indicate a certain level of managerial mistrust of workers; this was a point that did not escape the workers.

The educational level of the workers varied. The Sri Lankan education system is based on the British system, and most workers at these factories had completed their Ordinary Level (O-Level) exams, the rough equivalent of an American high-school education. Some workers had less education (usually eighth grade), and less than 1 percent of the workers were illiterate. These factory workers grew up in a much-criticized national educational system that produces far more students who qualify for university admittance than can be admitted. Analysts have shown that one contributing factor to the second JVP revolt was the prevalence of educated unemployed or underemployed workers (Moore 1993, *Sessional Paper I* 1990). Shirtex and Serendib employed numerous educationally well-qualified factory workers. A large number had done their Advanced Level (A-Level) exams, the rough equivalent of a college preparatory degree, and some had barely missed admittance into the university. Geeta, the essay writer, was one of several workers with a university degree. A few others were attending university part-time or were working at the factory between completing their exams and beginning university studies.[3] Certain jobs were generally reserved for the women with the highest educational qualifications, often positions involving English, among them line leader, quality inspector, and "input girl" (tasked with retrieving fabric from the cutting room for distribution to the machine operators). Nevertheless, one other woman with a bachelor's degree was a helper at Shirtex—one of the lowest-paid positions.

Caste is another factor to take into account in considering the social composition of the workforce. Despite historical changes in the particulars of caste-related behaviors and rules, it remains an important social category in contemporary Sri Lanka for Buddhists as well as Hindus.[4] Castes are inherited status groups corresponding to traditional occupations, but contemporary members are often not practitioners of that occupation. In present-day Sri Lanka, caste does not correspond with economic class; on the contrary, low-caste people can be quite wealthy and high-class. The highest and most populous caste in Kandepitiya and the country as a whole is the *govigama* (farmer) caste. The Shirtex and Serendib workforce was composed primarily of *govigamas*. But an adjacent village to Udakande consisted exclusively of members of one of the lowest castes, just above *roḍī*, the so-called outcastes. These were the *gahala-beravā*s, who were traditionally executioners. Members of this caste worked in the factories, as did employees from some more middling castes, such as washermen, potters, and drummers. According to a local government leader, the area was 75 percent *govigama*, and the remainder was a mixture of these lower castes.

My interest in the role of caste in these factories was sparked by a conversation early on in my field research with a political scientist who mentioned that she had heard that when another 200 GFP factory first opened, *govigama*s refused to work alongside *roḍī* workers. I wanted to examine to what extent older social divisions played a role in social relations within the factories because this would help me understand the relationships between "traditional" social relations and new relations fostered by industrial production. Indeed, caste did play a role in relationships among workers at Shirtex and Serendib, though it took me a while to discover this. I eventually learned the importance of caste despite the initial response from all quarters that "it was useless to try to discern someone's caste" (which meant that it was an unimportant thing to do) and that "everyone is the same." This is the standard response throughout

Sri Lanka. As a result of modern educational campaigns, people have come to see caste distinctions as something one should not recognize, so there are elaborate discourses about its absence from contemporary social life. Although many Sri Lankans do not follow caste rules, some people in all social classes still do.

When I finally realized that caste rules were followed in ways both subtle and overt at the factories, the majority of workers whom I questioned quite vocally declared themselves opposed to the practice. But there were many workers who observed caste restrictions within the factories. When I asked them about it, some of those workers denied their participation while others were quite frank in their explanations of the importance of caste hierarchies. Caste-based behaviors were evident especially in the canteens where workers normally shared food with one another. At lunchtime, women who worked in the same lines or sections would sit together. They would each open their lunches, which were wrapped in newspaper and plastic wrap, and included rice and one or more curries as well as *pol sambol*, a coconut chutney. Each woman would take a small sample of food in her right hand and reach across to her friends' opened rice packets to deposit the sample. The first few minutes of each meal consisted of this mutual food sharing. But, per traditional practices, some high-caste workers would not accept food from low-caste workers, even if they were intimate coworkers. Likewise, at teatime workers used cups provided by the factory, which they would return emptied to the canteen workers for cleaning. But some high-caste workers kept their own cups for use at teatime so as not to share dishes with low-caste workers. Caste could even affect the terms of address workers used for each other, with some high-caste workers instructing low-caste workers not to call them by the kinship terms for siblings that most workers used within the factory.

Because many of the workers' parents still maintained caste divisions, I knew of many instances when high-caste women attended wedding parties of low-caste women but did so in secret from their parents. Since the factory employed people from different villages, these kinds of transgressions were possible—parents often did not know anything about the families their daughters were visiting. But transgressions were not always the rule. Subsequent to my return to the United States, I learned that one very popular and friendly worker at Shirtex named Daya, who was from the *gahala-beravā* caste, quit her job after very few of her friends attended a party at her house. One of her close high-caste friends who did attend told me that Daya was too hurt by this obvious snub to return to the factory.

Daya's economic circumstances, in contrast, gave one indication that caste prestige did not correspond with economic class. She was from a very well-off family that owned paddy fields and a large cement home. Her house was surrounded by a lush home garden and replete with household appliances (run by car batteries—they had no electricity because they were not on the national electric grid). There were other workers whose families lived in such relatively comfortable circumstances. The degree of wealth among the workers' families varied widely. While one worker may have been from a family that lived in a nonelectrified one-room mud home on rented land, her coworker may have come from a family that owned a five-room cement home complete with electricity, a stereo system, VCR, television, and refrigerator. The last commodity would sometimes be used for a purpose other than its intended function. I often saw unplugged refrigerators being used as living room cupboards, those actually being used for refrigeration inevitably being located in the dining room, where visitors could appreciate them. Some families that owned paddy fields even hired laborers to plant and harvest. In a few rare cases, families owned a car, although motorbikes were more common.

The original five hundred workers selected to work at the two factories were supposed to be from what President Premadasa called "the poorest of the poor"—families on the rolls of the Janasaviya welfare program. Some of the workers who were obviously not so poor had come to Serendib from the previous location where there had not been a Janasaviya requirement. Technically any of the others who were not from "the poorest of the poor" should have been hired only after Premadasa's death in May 1993, when the rules were loosened. But I heard complaints (which I could never confirm), especially from SLFP party members, that at least some of the original jobs were allocated according to political favoritism.

A Serendib ironer named Chuti, whose husband had been killed by the JVP, told me that the factory employed both former JVP members (or their family members) and UNP members like her. She noted that she was working alongside people who thus were deeply implicated in her husband's death. She said that this mixture of JVP and UNP members had come about because the Provincial Council minister, a local UNP politician charged with compiling the list of potential employees, recommended poor people for factory positions regardless of their political affiliation. He simply provided a list of eligible Janasaviya recipients to the factories, and the management hired workers off that list. Chuti reported this to me with apparent ambivalence: she seemed to be proud that her party's minister was so fair but disgusted that she had to work with former JVP members.

I heard about this nonpartisan distribution of jobs from UNP members quite often; just as frequently, members of the SLFP or the People's Alliance (PA was a coalition of parties led by the SLFP that was in power from 1994 to 2001) told me the opposite. They said that UNP members enjoyed preferential employment. I was not able to confirm the role of politics in hiring practices, and I knew what seemed to be an equal number of SLFP and UNP people from the original batch. The topic of party politics arose often in the factories, consistent with Sri Lanka's reputation for a citizenry highly engaged with the political process. For instance, some workers alleged that during the 1994 presidential election, local politicians warned them that if they did not vote for the UNP they would lose their jobs. Regardless of the truth of these claims, questions about the political composition of the workers indicated that there was considerable dispute about Premadasa's declaration that "poverty is the only criteria for recruitment."

The Kandepitiya area was infamous among outsiders for the intensity of JVP activity during the late 1980s. Kandy residents to whom I mentioned my research locale would often comment that there had been a lot of violence in the area during the recent "period of terror." They would invariably mention one or more of the following incidents: that a bus driver from the area had been killed for operating his state-owned bus despite a JVP curfew against travel; that even though most people killed on either side were men, a mother and daughter had been killed by the JVP in the area (a second daughter worked at Shirtex); and that the bodies of fifteen suspected JVP members had been found burning in tires in one village, presumably killed by the army. During the revolt, villagers there and in many parts of the country would awaken in the morning to find posters throughout the village telling them to refrain from going to work during the day or turning on lights and going outside at night. After a JVP killing, letters would be sent around the village warning people not to attend the funeral. Villagers would also be instructed through posters and notices to attend JVP meetings in the area. One woman told me that she and her family had attended a meeting out of fear of what would happen if they refused. Women JVP members, dressed in black disguises from head to toe, had lectured them about the party's philosophy. During the 1988 election (which was won by Premadasa), people were warned that they would be murdered if they voted. The JVP targeted members of the

UNP, the military, the police, and their families. When the government retaliated in 1989, the army killed or abducted thousands of suspected youth. Suspicion fell most heavily on known SLFP members, who the government believed were JVP recruits.

Approximately twenty women at Shirtex and Serendib had husbands who had disappeared or been killed during that time. Many workers had lost other family members (brothers, fathers, uncles, one mother, and one sister). In an interview, a woman named Champa told me about the death of her father. This was in August 1989, when the JVP threatened police and military members and their families with death if they did not desert (Alles 1990, xxi, appendix VI). At the time, Champa's brother had been in the army and the JVP had come to her father asking for the brother's address. According to Champa, her father had refused and retorted, "I don't know, ask him yourself." Three days later the JVP came, forced her father out into the garden, and shot him.

The father of a machine operator at Shirtex named Pushpa had been killed shortly after the 1988 election in which he had voted for the reigning UNP party. Pushpa told me that one evening a group of men had knocked on the door claiming to be collecting money for a social cause. When her father went outside, he was shot. Pushpa explained to me that her father had not been involved in politics at all and seemed to have been killed only because he had voted, but possibly also because people had been jealous of their family's prosperity.

In survivors' stories I heard, as well as those documented by others, narratives commonly referred to jealousy and false accusations to explain the murder or disappearance of victims of the JVP or government alike. Jealousy (*irisāwa*) is a disposition that Sinhalas openly attribute to themselves and to others. Workers, supervisors, and managers commonly referred to jealousy as the root of conflicts in the factories and in their villages. One manager told me that if there were anything that would ever make him leave Sri Lanka it would be the problem of jealousy. The anthropologist Lindy Warrell (1990) has analyzed jealousy among Sinhalas as an emotion that emerges when there is a discrepancy between expected hierarchies and actual behavior. Although this emotion has long been present among Sinhalas, in contemporary Sri Lanka, references to jealousy are omnipresent and seem to be expressed when people try to make sense of the uneven benefits of economic liberalization. The frequent invocation of jealousy as an explanation for JVP violence is consistent with this reading.

The husband of Tamara, a machine operator at Serendib, disappeared in 1989. When I interviewed Tamara and her in-laws in 1996, they believed he had been taken by the army and was still alive in a camp where, they alleged, suspected JVP members were being secretly detained by the government.[5] Tamara explained to me that because her husband was an active SLFP member, his UNP enemies had reported him to the government as JVP. Her in-laws were devastated by the disappearance of their son, who they had believed would be the most successful of all their children. As the father said, "If he were here today, this family would be very well off." Tamara herself never went a day without crying for her husband to return. When I visited her home five years after his disappearance, she showed me a current photo of her, her two children, and the husband—an old photo of her husband had been superimposed onto the photo as if he were still present in their lives.

Few JVP members survived the retaliations of the army and police, although many of their relatives did. Factory workers would point out to me alleged former JVP members or their relatives who were living in their villages or working in the factories. But nobody would admit to such a connection themselves. As in Pushpa's case, if the family member had been killed or disappeared because of suspicion of JVP membership, the family would tell me that jealousy or anger had caused their enemies to report them falsely. This sort of "retaliative violence" was certainly rampant at the time (van der Horst 1995, 34; cf. Onderdenwijngaard 1995). The Presidential Commission on Disappearances refers to the common "personal motives" (including jealousy over university admission) that led people to cause others to disappear at the hands of the government (*Sessional Paper V* 1997). Jealousy seems to operate here as a mechanism for dealing with social inequality. The question of "personal motives" in deaths and disappearances at this time raises the issue of the darker side of the village panopticon. While we will see below that villagers often understand the ways in which neighbors watch and monitor each other as protection, such surveillance also clearly contributed to the tragic consequences of the JVP revolt and its suppression by the government.

Whether or not the people who disappeared or were murdered in the area had been falsely accused, people whose families were considered to be on the opposite sides of this violent conflict worked together at Shirtex and Serendib. That the very people who were affected by the JVP revolt worked in these factories was consistent with the 200 GFP's explicit goal prior to the underwear critique. It had aimed to prevent another revolt by providing jobs to the same constituency that might otherwise revolt against the government for not providing jobs for the rural poor. The fact that these neighbors-turned-enemies had now become factory coworkers pointed to yet another aspect of the experiences of the 200 GFP workers that was fraught with the strains and uncertainties that characterize the post-liberalization period in Sri Lanka.

The Village as Panopticon

This brief description of the village environment around Shirtex and Serendib illustrates where the factory women came from each morning and fills in some of the social, economic, and political linkages between the factories and the surrounding villages. References to caste and JVP violence show some of the ways in which problems, conflicts, and social relations from the village entered the workplace. There is another level on which village located-ness was supremely important to women workers: it offered them moral protection. Managers, investors, and workers alike invoked an idealistic image of villages as traditional, pure, and community-oriented by comparison with cities. By citing a few examples out of many, I explore the pervasive assumption that there were important differences between village garment workers and their urban counterparts. In effect, the village was a moral panopticon that disciplined village women. Managers and investors, workers and other villagers all assumed that to be a village-based garment worker was ipso facto to be a Good girl who, concomitantly, exhibited the discipline required for factory production.

Managers and owners ascribed a number of features to rural garment workers that marked them apart from their urban counterparts. Since village workers came from their homes to work they were said to be happier than urban workers, most of whom had migrated from villages to live in expensive and shabby boarding houses. One owner explained that rural women, unlike urban women, "shed industrial tension when they leave the factory." Others said that village women were more obedient, shy, respectful, or disciplined or better-mannered than urban women because they were "under parental control." Owners and managers contended that urban women abused their freedom and were spoiled and stubborn because they were away from their parents. They further noted that the cities were rife with the kind of people who would lead village girls astray, as evidenced by the reports of the illicit sexual activities of village women in Colombo. Outside-of-work behavior reflected back on work behavior: A woman who behaved improperly outside of work

JUKI GIRLS, GOOD GIRLS

was undisciplined, and it was the same lack of discipline that would be manifest in her work as well. All these differences suggested that the rural workforce would not only be more docile but more productive.

Three years after establishing a 200 GFP factory, one investor told me he was quite pleased with its success. The reasons he gave me were quite common among investors and managers I spoke with, and they all had to do with differences between the workforce in Colombo and in villages. This investor explained that there had been "initial problems" with training the new employees, people who "are not used to the industrial type of life." But after the training was done, the main benefit of the program was that this was a "fairly captive workforce." He continued,

> They have no other place to go to work, right? So, whereas here [in Colombo] there is a lot of competition among employers. So that was a plus point. Another thing was, the workers were not that corrupted by city life. So you could train them the way you wanted to. . . . You see, now, people in the city, like working in the zones, they have been to eight or nine factories. They are used to various indisciplines, unionism, all that type of thing. And say when you ask for a certain target, they will say "no we will give only half that," thinking that management will increase it tomorrow. But these folks, that way, was like a virgin situation where we could train them into the concepts that we believe were right. So that way it was an advantage.

This sense of the advantages of employing rural laborers, steeped in a "virgin situation," was something I heard quite frequently from investors and managers.

Whenever I mentioned to Shirtex and Serendib workers as well as area villagers rumors that male managers sexually abused female workers in urban factories, they would reply with, "Here that doesn't happen." To my query, "Why not?" the response would invariably be a one-word answer, *"gamē"*— "it's in the village." I also often heard this one-word explanation when managers and owners would explain to me that compared with FTZ women, village workers were easier to handle or control (the latter term would be in English, whether they were speaking English or Sinhala). As Arjuna Sir, a manager who had worked at Serendib and in a factory in Colombo, said in English, "Kandy girls are easy to handle. It's in the village, no?" A supervisor at another 200 GFP factory told me in Sinhala that the women in her factory were easier to control than Colombo workers. When I asked her why she simply said "*gamē.*"

For many people like these no further explanation was required—the difference that a village made was obvious and could go unspoken. Villages were simply assumed to be inhospitable environments for sexual abuse and naturally to furnish disciplined women workers for capitalist industry. Important to the construction is the notion that villages are places where community matters above individuality. Thus villagers care deeply about what others think and behave in ways that reproduce the prevailing norms. This is the self-disciplining that is referred to in Foucault's discussion of the panopticon and techniques of the self. I now turn to analyze these modes of self-discipline through an examination of the Sinhala Buddhist concepts of *lājja-baya* (respectability), reputation, and character.

Lājja-Baya

Self-disciplining largely takes place because of the internalization of behavioral norms. The Sinhala concept of *lājja-baya* (literally, "shame-fear") is an important concept that carries with it certain expectations; it is in their efforts to adhere to these expectations that people monitor and check their own behavior as well as the behavior of others around them.

In the series of quotations I examine below, various people discuss how location influences women's behavior. A female garment worker at Serendib mentions that factory women do not behave in ways that are considered inappropriate with men because they are afraid (*bayay*) that villagers will tell their parents about what they are doing outside of work. The brother of a woman worker at Serendib notes that village women would never start misbehaving with boys because they would be embarrassed (*lājjay*) to show their faces to their parents after that. These terms *lājjay* and *bayay* are crucial to understanding the Shirtex and Serendib women's efforts to look good to their fellow villagers.

The activist and writer Eva Ranaweera suggests that whether or not a woman is *lājja-baya* affects the woman's place in a community. She quotes in Sinhala a line from a southern Sri Lankan folk poem, which I translate as "I can't be in the village because I am ashamed" (*gamē inna bā ban maṭa lājjawē*). She says this line refers to "group enforced socialized shame" (Ranaweera 1992, 19). Indeed, I constantly heard the phrase *maṭa lājjay* (I am ashamed) from garment workers in the context of social pressures to conform. Shirtex and Serendib women, for instance, often said that if they were to be seen even just holding hands with a boyfriend, they would not be able to stay in the village because of shame.

Läjja-baya applies to men as well as women, but it is frequently invoked with special reference to women's behavior. The concept has been described in different ways in several important ethnographic studies of Sri Lanka, but all these descriptions refer to the centrality of interpersonal social relations in an individual's adoption of this disposition. According to the anthropologist Gananath Obeyesekere (1984, 504), when coupled with *läjja*, *baya* is not general fear or cowardice, but the "fear of ridicule or social disapproval." Jonathan Spencer (1990a, 171–72) argues convincingly that *läjja* should be translated as "restraint, a holding back from the gaze of others, keeping intense encounters at arm's length," to convey that it has a positive value as "a proper ingredient of all good public behaviour." Malathi de Alwis (1998, 46) translates *läjja-baya* as "respectability" and argues that it "is not only one of the key categories that is used to govern the behaviour of Sinhala women but it is also constructed as a crucial signifier of Sinhala 'culture' and 'tradition.'" The respectable woman of today is one whose public movement is circumscribed and who is demure and dressed with decorum. A woman with a sloppily tied sari exposing too much midriff can elicit comments of being *läjja-baya näti* (loose and immoral, literally without *läjja-baya*), as can a woman who moves in public too much and speaks too loudly. Rather than being contradictory, these arguments about *läjja-baya* emphasize different aspects of the same cultural code: restraint, respectability, and shame-fear are all involved in what it means to have *läjja-baya*. The concept of *läjja-baya* is closely related to *sanwara*, as a sense of discipline, control, or decency.

Reputation and Character

As with *läjja-baya*, reputation and character are important indices of what others think about men and women's conduct, but again, these are particularly weighted for women. Reputation is assessed by the *katakatā* about a person. *Katakatā* is a term for orally transmitted information about people, bizarre conduct, or events (Ratnapala 1991, 177; cf. van der Horst 1995, 189–205). Most frequently *katakatā* means "gossip about people and their character" (van der Horst 1995, 189). The content of such gossip can be good or bad, and the sum total of the *katakatā* about an individual constitutes his or her character (*caritaya*) (Ratnapala 1991, 177). Thus character and reputation are essentially the same (van der Horst 1995, 189). Character, which is clearly delineated into "good" or "bad," is an important consideration in selecting a spouse, and good character for men and women is consistently mentioned in newspaper arranged-marriage proposals (Ratnapala 1991, 177).

Character inheres in both men and women, and having good character (in the sense of "probity, decency, and sincerity") is a determinant of whether one is a good Sinhala Buddhist (Sheeran 1997, 265). We can see the ways in which men's characters were important at Shirtex and Serendib in the workers' and villagers' frequent reference to the factory managers as "good." On many occasions parents and other villagers from this area told me that they were quite pleased that key Serendib managers were brothers from Udakande—"*gamē aya*" (village people). Parents told me that they didn't mind sending their daughters to Shirtex and Serendib, since there were villagers in the management. Often simply noting that the male managers were good, they would go on to state that things were different with managers at urban factories. Clearly such people were concerned both about women's *and* men's respectability, but note that the emphasis also preserves the women's respectability. They must still be good, since they have not been exposed to anything that would mean otherwise.

Although technically character is important for men as well as women, in social practice women seem to be much more vulnerable to aspersions than men. This bias seems to be connected to the anthropologist Nur Yalman's (1963) now famous observation that a community's concerns with purity center on the purity of women, not men. As I have argued, women's sexual purity is central to Sinhala Buddhist identity. The Sinhala language has several expressions that sum up this gendered differentiation of character, for example, "A mud stain sticks to women, but not men," where "mud stain" (*maḍa pällama*) is a metaphor for social stigma. Another refers to a man's inability to gather negative strikes against his character: "A man is a ship that crosses the ocean and leaves no trace." A third example is discussed by Hewamanne (2002, 301), who is Sinhala, as follows: "There is a Sinhala saying that no matter where a male child goes or whatever he does he could return clean if he takes a bath. Growing up, we were told that girl children did not have that privilege (meaning that a woman's reputation once tarnished could not be saved)."

Although character and stigma are general terms for moral behavior and refer not simply to sexual morality, I noted a consistent conflation of character, stigma, and sexual morality in my conversations with people in and around Shirtex and Serendib. Many people told me with clear conviction that this difference in how stigma does or does not attach to someone came down to anatomy: men could do whatever they wanted because they would not get pregnant. Parents of women garment workers told me that they did not worry at all about what their sons did out of their sight. One father told me that girls were cause for worry because they did not have that much brainpower and were immature. In an interview, a worker named Chandra told me the following: "If a boy works the night shift, even if he comes home alone, whatever happens, nobody inquires that much. But for a girl, girls must be brought up like flowers, according to our culture. Otherwise, it's a big problem [*upset*]."[6]

This gendered distinction can also be understood in other terms. For a woman, any social situation that lowers her esteem in society can mark her as "unrespectable" (*läjja-baya näti*). Such a woman gets a "bad name." There is a great amount of importance placed on the preservation of a family's good name (*honda namak*) (Ryan 1953b, 149); and when a family member is involved in something untoward, the impact affects the whole family's name and hence its social standing. If a woman were found not to be a virgin at marriage, the discovery would give not only the woman and her family but also her husband's family a bad name.

Among Sinhalas, *family* is a wide category, ranging from immediate biological relations to people related through marriage whose relationship is maintained for strategic reasons. To an outsider it can be confusing that *näyo* (kin) seems to be applied to such a varying category of people. As the anthropologist James Brow (1996, 51) explains, the inclusiveness of terms such as *näyo* invokes a collective identity in contrast to members of neighboring villages. But *näyo* can also refer generally to people of the same caste, even in another village—that is, to people with whom marriage ties could be established (Tambiah 1958, 26). Because of the wide applicability of the various categories for family and because villages are often composed of a single caste—understood as the widest rubric of family—maintaining a good name as an individual is essential for the maintenance of the family name and the village name. A stark morality is at work here because a name is either good or bad—there is no in-between. Therefore, if a woman gets a bad reputation through improper premarital sexual relations, her family, and at the extreme her village, can also be considered in a negative light. A woman's bad name can also affect her marriage prospects, a problem in an environment where a sure way to preserve the family's good reputation is through the arrangement of a good marriage. Thus, for the women at Shirtex and Serendib, the significance of remaining in their villages is even weightier: they do not want to behave in a manner that will tarnish their village's name.

The Village Difference

Respectability (*läjja-baya*), reputation, and character all are concepts that become meaningful in the context of attention from other villagers. Assessments of whether or not you are respectable and have a good reputation and good character emerge from what villagers think about you and what they see you doing, saying, and wearing. I present now several examples of comments from my interlocutors about the difference village locatedness makes to village women garment workers. These observations come from people who would have different interests in discussing and monitoring garment factory women's behavior: one male manager, a female garment worker's brother, and two female garment workers. I often heard this sort of narrative from female garment workers, their parents, and managers: girls need to be under parental control to protect their character, or else they will have too much freedom and will risk getting involved in unsuitable relationships with men, either through force or volition. By virtue of being visible to villagers at every moment, village garment women would not be tricked by men into inappropriate behavior, and they would not act inappropriately with their own boyfriends. I was often reminded that since villagers tend to gossip, parents would quickly hear if a woman was seen doing something like holding hands with her boyfriend at Peradeniya Botanical Gardens (a popular spot for couples located just outside Kandy). The frequent reference to women being "tricked" by men is related to the notion that village girls are innocent: they are simple, naïve, and not worldly—they need the protection of the village.

Gamini Sir

Gamini Sir, who had grown up in a village but subsequently moved to Colombo, was a manager at Shirtex when it opened in 1992. In an interview, Gamini Sir explained to me various ways in which women learned new things and changed after they began work there. I then asked him, "Do some people think that is bad, that women are becoming less traditional?" His response was not gender-specific, and he even implicated himself in these processes.

But still they haven't gone out from their culture. Right? They are still in their villages. Still they are with their parents. While they are learning something they are still with the culture, no? They are not corrupted. That is very important. That is very important for any society, as long as they protect their culture and they are well behaved, that is very useful. Whether they earn millions and millions, if their culture is not changed, if their behavior pattern is not changed that is . . . most important. Behavior pattern, as long as it develops in a good way. Because they are always bound to somebody. Villagers. Even when we were in the village, we . . . used to listen to our parents always. What they used to guide us. But when you are living alone, we have our own ideas, right?

Sanath

A young man from Udakande described vast urban-rural contrasts in a Sinhala-language conversation with me about the Katunayake FTZ. Sanath had worked as a welder in a Katunayake factory. He told me in Sinhala that, for girls, Katunayake was like a "paradise" (he used the English word). Boys couldn't even get in a bus there, for if they do it is very unusual (*mokadde welā*, "What's happened?"). Girls tease and bother them, pulling their ears and their hair. "There are thousands of girls there," he said. Sanath told me this in order to support his contention that village girls would never start misbehaving with boys because they would be embarrassed (*läjjay*) to show their faces (*muhuna denna*) to their parents after doing so. But, he said, when village girls go to Katunayake, that was a different story: their parents and villagers could not monitor their behavior.

Teja

Teja was a twenty-six-year-old buttonhole machine operator at Shirtex. Prior to joining Shirtex, she had worked in the Katunayake FTZ. Teja drew the following contrasts between village and urban women: "Just by looking at these girls here in this factory [Shirtex] you can tell they are good, and that makes you feel happy. You can see that these girls have a good upbringing because they dress decently [*sanwaray*]. Even the way they talk is also decent. The girls in the factories at Katunayake are not decent like that. Very indecent. Some are decent, but most are not. That's because there's nobody to look after them. Their parents are not near them. Their sisters and brothers are not near them. So they are not afraid [*baya*]."

Susila

Susila was a thirty-eight-year-old mother of two teenagers who worked in the finishing section at Shirtex. Susila was glad that she could set a good example for her children by working at Shirtex, since Shirtex was a reputable factory where nothing inappropriate occurred. In my interview with her, I asked Susila if people in her village ever expressed concern about the behavior of women at these factories. She quickly said "no," and then launched into a discussion of the condition of village women in the FTZs:

> They really don't have the company of their parents or relatives outside the factory. They can do as they please. Now if [in Colombo] I say I want to go to the beach with someone, I can go because there is nobody to keep an eye on me. Even the madam at the boarding house gives permission for that. Because even they don't try to mold girls. They are just trying to give food and drink to the girls and get the monthly fee. They do not think about molding the girls. If a villager sees someone in Kandy, or in the [Peradeniya Botanical] garden, they give the message that a certain person was seen there and the parents inquire after that. "Where did the child go?" It's not like that outside the village. Because of that, I think the village children are not induced to go down the wrong path. Because of the protection of those parents and outside relatives. If they leave the village, there won't be any protection. I can do whatever I wish to do, when I go out. But you can't in the village. You have to think, "Will that person see me?" "Will that person see where I went just now?" Actually, people come and report. "I saw you in the bus. I saw you at the bus stop." Like that there are things. So, because of that, bad things don't happen in villages.

It is in the context of such typical contrasts between the close policing of the village and the amoral anonymity of city life, made by themselves and those around them, that Shirtex and Serendib women constructed identities as new kinds of Good girls. It will become evident in the next chapter that even these women enacted new behaviors that were not straightforwardly

JUKI GIRLS, GOOD GIRLS

good and traditional. It was precisely by constructing themselves as good that they were able to create a space for new behaviors.

There are striking similarities in these narratives about the importance of village locatedness offered by one manager, a brother, and two women workers. Why would there be such uniformity? On one level, it is likely that these people identified with the nationalist discourses about villages as loci of tradition and valued the related norms for women's behavior. They were articulating contrasts and concerns that have a long history and that I heard in many different places in Sri Lanka. Also, it is likely that all these people wanted me to think that the women at Shirtex and Serendib were good. I was an anthropologist writing a book about the factories. Wouldn't they want themselves and their factories to look good to me? But there is more to the story than this—they also wanted others around them to think they were good.

There would have been different motivations for painting village workers in the best light through disparaging Juki girls. Investors and managers would likely want villagers to think that theirs were factories that employed Good girls because then they would be able to continue to recruit workers. The parents, husbands, or brothers had ultimately given their women dependents permission to work at the factories. If they thought that the facilities and the women in them were good, their permission would have been justified. Managers worked hard to make sure that their workforce was good; and they did not hire, or quickly fired, anyone who was not. They also wanted good women because one of the things that *good* meant was that they would be more controllable and better workers.

For their part, women workers would likely have wanted people to think they were good because they needed to preserve their reputations. By emphasizing their respectability over that of Colombo factory workers, they could then gain the social space to do some things not normally allowed to village women. It was as if they were claiming, "Look, we're obviously good, so, please can we just . . ." (have a boyfriend, wear a little makeup, go on trips with friends). We cannot cast them as victims simply because they appear to adhere to many norms dictated for women. The contrasts between good village women and bad city women given above by Teja and Susila, as well as the various ways they and their coworkers live out those contrasts, do not necessarily indicate that they are victims of oppressive middle-class norms. Rather, they are engaging in positive acts that allow them to participate in a community of practice and in so doing to make sense of the world around them. These women wanted to be good and wanted to be considered good.

Yet the village panopticon was not something all village women took comfort in. Managers often lamented to me that they would have liked to have a wider labor pool to select workers from, but that they did not get enough applicants. They said that some women from the surrounding villages seemed still to prefer to work in Katunayake. The managers and workers sometimes invoked the constant watchfulness of villages as a factor that pushed these women away. When I asked workers why some local women preferred to work in Colombo, they offered a couple of explanations. Some plainly said that it was precisely because nobody from their village would be watching. Hewamanne describes Katunayake women who revel in the freedom away from their village; I imagine there are many women who would feel like them. Others said that if they were to go to work in a Colombo factory, their fellow villagers might not know that that was what they were doing, and so their reputation would not be automatically soiled. They could even pretend to have a job at a bank (a desired profession, as we will see in the next chapter). Here we see the other side of the village panopticon, which at its extreme resulted in killings and disappearances during the "period of terror." The converse of protection was gossip and criticism. In a conversation about the social risks of wearing tank tops, one worker (wearing a tank top when we spoke) told me that "villagers watch [*balanawa*] more than is necessary." Some people thought of the panopticon in terms of protection and care (as Susila noted in reference to boarding-house caretakers, girls in the village were nurtured and cared for, whereas girls in the city are neglected), while others thought about it in terms of suffocating nosiness about others.

A "Good Girl" at Shirtex

The experiences and struggles of Teja, who sewed buttonholes at Shirtex, illustrate well the stark contrasts many of these women draw between villages and Colombo, as well as between women who work in each locale. For Teja, the village location of the factories was supremely important. Teja had worked in the Katunayake FTZ before coming to Shirtex. She came to Shirtex as soon as it was opened near her village. I first met Teja because of a response she had penned on the questionnaire I distributed to all the workers when I first arrived. Like Mala, Teja wrote something quite moving at the end of the questionnaire, in a space underneath my last query for "additional information for me to know about you or the factory." In this space Teja wrote: "My *nangi* [younger sister] and I lost the love of our mother at our birth and have lived amidst a lot of problems. But now both of us work, and in the future we hope to look after our father and live a good life without being a problem to anybody. With every defeat [*parājaya*] in life, I will make it an experience and learn from it and try to make my life better."

I had not yet met Teja when I received her questionnaire. I found her out right away, and we ended up having many conversations inside the factory and outside. Armed with a clear image of a woman who was "not good," Teja had worked hard to be good and to be considered good by those around her. The "bad" woman who solidified her own sense of moral rectitude was her mother, who had left her family when Teja was three and her sister was one. Teja grew up with her father and aunts and uncles in her father's natal village, near Udakande. Her mother was from Colombo, where she and her father had met, fallen in love, and married. It was only when Teja was twenty-four years old that her mother returned to find her. In an interview soon after this reunion, Teja described to me her current relationship with her mother.

Teja: Now, after twenty-one years, she came to the factory looking for me. She sends me letters now. . . . Now we're big, no? So she likes to have us with her. . . . But, even if she is our mother, we don't have the feeling that she is our mother. That means, when we were small, we didn't get our mother's love. . . . Because of that we don't feel like she's our mother. We love our aunties like mothers. How she loves us, we don't love her. We love father more than mother.
Caitrin: Did she say why she had left you?
Teja: Why did she leave us? At home, our uncles and aunties say that she is not good [*honda nä*]. She's very *social* [Teja used the English word]. That means, she's very attached to outside [*bāhira*] things. She wears lipstick, nail polish. Doesn't do any work at home. Short hair. Like that. She doesn't breastfeed us, saying that she might lose weight.[7] She's a mother like that. That's what my aunties say. But now that she came, she says that father isn't good. Drank alcohol. We can't decide who is telling the truth. But we value a lot of what our aunties say. Because the villagers say the same. We have to believe what our own aunties say. That is, . . . if father was causing problems for mother, if he drinks, the thing that should be most prominent for her is the thing called love for her children. That means, she will suffer any amount. Someday, the children will get older. If she wanted to raise the children well, she would have

undergone any suffering. We don't believe what mother says. Our aunties are telling the truth.

This is a richly loaded statement on what makes a good woman. It resonates with Dharmapala's idealized image of Sinhala Buddhist women, as discussed in the previous chapter, and with the good women of Sinhala film. A woman who is not good is *social*, wears makeup, has short hair, and is "attached to outside things." The latter expression bears discussion. The term for "outside" is *bāhira*, which can also be translated as "external," "unwanted," or "extra." It refers to things that are outside of the norm, and it often implies foreign behaviors, things, and ideas. In all these translations there is an implicit value judgment: because it is foreign, we don't want it around. The implication is that these are not traditional, normal, expected behaviors, things, or ideas. Teja goes on to say quite clearly that this not-good woman is not a good mother. A good mother would stay with her children no matter what. She would put her children above her own bodily self-image (she would breastfeed), and she would suffer on their behalf.

Teja said that everyone in her village expected that she would turn out the same as her mother. "But I am totally different from my mother. She's from Colombo. So she had adjusted herself to the Colombo way. Maybe if we were with our mother we would also be like that. But we are in the village, no? So we got used to the village way." Teja grew up in her father's village, passed her O-Level exams, and then finished her schooling. She went to work in the Katunayake FTZ when she was nineteen years old. When I asked her if she had feared she would become more like a Colombo person upon moving there, Teja responded:

No. I went with my auntie's daughter. She was living at a villager's house there. Because of that, I didn't feel scared. Because I was poor, those other things didn't matter. I got accustomed to bearing those things. [The problems in her life were less important to her than dealing with her poverty.] . . . Even though I went to Colombo, if I live properly I won't adapt myself to those conditions. When villagers go to Colombo, they are not used to touching money. After they go to Colombo, when they get two or three thousand rupees in their hands, they forget the village. They get involved in doing outside things [*bāhira dewal*]. As soon as they go, they cut their hair into bangs at the front. They start to wear lipstick and nail polish. When they first go to

Katunayake it is because of their poverty. So, they send money to their family at first. To take care of them. After like six months, they forget why they came. There are lots of people who forgot and got lost [from the correct path in life]. Then, they don't use their salary to eat and drink. They don't eat much. They only eat and drink what the factory provides. Their health deteriorates. But they don't think about it. They buy necklaces, four, five, ten rings. Katunayake people's hobby is buying gold things. If they are going somewhere, their body is like jewelry [the whole body is covered with jewelry]. When you see that it is very ugly.

It is important in Teja's narrative that she stayed with a villager when she worked at Katunayake, for this shows that she would have someone watching over her. By noting this at the start of her story she sets up the ways in which she is different from the other women she will soon describe. She also mentions hair, makeup, and jewelry—all markers that are often invoked in discussions of whether or not women are respectable.

Teja left Katunayake as soon as she could get a job at the newly opened Shirtex, in large part because she wanted to be with her family. In light of the negative reputation of garment workers I asked her if she was afraid that people would think negatively about her once she started to work at Katunayake. Her response was simple: "No. The people who know me know that I'm good." It was here that she discussed the differences between women at Shirtex and at Serendib, quoted earlier. She described Shirtex women as dressing and talking decently (*saṇwaray*) and attributed the indecency of Katunayake women to the absence of relatives nearby and these women's concomitant lack of fear (*baya*).

She invoked the fear of social censure that figures in the concept of *läjja-baya*. The term *saṇwara* (decent) was frequently employed by the workers and other villagers to refer to women's appearance and behavior. *Decent* here implies being disciplined and having self-control; it can also be translated as "respectable." It is a virtue advocated by the Buddha, and so is sometimes translated as "virtuous practice": by controlling one's body and mind one is being a good, virtuous person. On numerous occasions, factory women used *saṇwara* in reference to clothing, explaining to me why women should not wear trousers but skirts, dresses, or saris. If women wore trousers, it would show that they had no self-respect or self-control; they were not behaving respectably. A *saṇwara* woman does not call attention to herself. As further examples of clothing that was not *saṇwara*, one woman offered tank tops and short skirts because they exposed too much of the arms and legs. Such clothes could also lead to a woman being called unrespectable, or *läjja-baya näti*. In essence, Teja contended that this lack of control among FTZ women stemmed from their independence from normal village social pressures and controls. Many of the workers would go a step further and agree with managers and owners that the FTZ women's lack of control impeded their factory productivity.

A bit later in the interview, I asked Teja if the telecast of *Grahanaya* led villagers to think negatively about Shirtex and Serendib.

Teja: No, they didn't think like that. They think like that about Colombo factories. "See what happens when you go to Colombo," they say. . . . But if something like that happens in a village factory, people in the village don't keep mum about it. The villagers are watching out for those things. So, the managers are scared. If the sirs try to fill unnecessary needs, because of the villagers, they're scared. They don't do that. . . .
Caitrin: Do people in the village think that the girls who work here dress like the girls in Katunayake and go with boys?
Teja: No, they don't think like that. No. This is why. These girls, even though they work here, they go to their parents in the evening. These girls are scared of their parents. That's why they don't do those things. Those girls [in Colombo], it doesn't matter what time they go home after getting off work. Nobody looks for them. That's why they get involved in those things. Here, let's say we went somewhere without telling. There are people, you know, they tell. They go to your home and tell, saying, "She said she's going to work today, but she went to such and such place." So girls are afraid of that.

Although many women at Shirtex and Serendib had boyfriends, Teja did not. She was saving money for a dowry for a marriage to be arranged by her father. At the time of the interview in December 1995, the army had suffered important defeats. Almost every day, news spread through the factories that a worker's husband, brother, or uncle in the army had disappeared or been killed or was severely injured. At that time, I began to hear many women, including Teja, saying they wanted to join the army. When I asked her why, Teja cited her "love for the country" (*ratata ādarē*) and her desire to "protect the country" (*raṭa āraksa karaganda*). Elaborating thus, she referred to her coworkers:

> Now, really, our boys die. To fill that space, even though we are girls, if we go it's good, right? Even now I would like to go. Jayanthi, Sumitra, like that, they are all interested in joining the army. But we don't have the athletic qualifications. If they took people who had passed from eighth grade, or who took their O-Level exams, then I could go. For now there are enough boys. But, if there were a situation where there weren't enough boys, if they'd take us, we'd go. More than that, I'd like to take care of disabled people. To nurse them. There is Ranaviru Sevana and all.[8] I would even like to marry a person like that. That means, without a leg, hand, blind, a person like that. I would like to marry and sacrifice my whole life serving a person from the army.

Unlike her mother, she was ready to "sacrifice her whole life" for someone. In the shadow of her mother's example, Teja hoped to chart a much different future.

How to Be a Good Girl? Teledrama Lessons

So far in this chapter I have focused on the cross-cutting connections that bind Shirtex and Serendib to their surrounding villages. Some of these intertwining relationships are quite straightforward—for example, village social distinctions cross over into the factories, and the factories employ people from area villages. Others are more complicated and involve how people make sense of the factories' presence in villages, such as the ways in which village factory women are assumed to be "good" because they are still living in their villages. Workers and managers, as well as area villagers, made sense of the presence of these factories through stereotyped images they had of Juki girls and the harmful effects of urban living on innocent village girls. They learned about Juki girls and urban life largely from the mass media, especially the teledramas I discuss in the previous chapter. What they learned confirmed the strongly dichotomous understandings they already had about the village and the city, and this in turn affected their lives both inside and outside the factories.

The two teledramas about garment workers affected women at Shirtex and Serendib in many ways. Many factory women had watched *Grahanaya* when it aired the year before my field research commenced. On Friday nights during my field research period they watched *Ira Handa Yata*. The literature scholar Janice Radway (1986, 96) wrote in her well-known 1986 study of women readers of romance novels that the content of a message is "not simply found in that message but is constructed by an audience interacting with that message." Following this now commonly accepted insight, rather than offering a textual analysis of these teledramas, I analyze them in terms of how they were received by the audience. My spectator analysis was intentionally limited to the social world of the factories—the workers, their relatives, factory managers and owners—the very people for whom the Juki reputation was of pressing importance. Their immediate contact with the world of garment factories influenced how they read and made sense of the programs.

The factory workers read the text of the teledramas in reference to their own struggles with being considered Good girls. Rather than acting as passive consumers of the medium, garment workers actively read the teledramas and did two distinct things with the representations of Juki girls: they learned a lesson from Felicia and Dhammi in how not to behave, and they distanced themselves from Felicia and Dhammi and the negative Juki-girl stereotype. Despite actively doing something with what they saw in these programs, because of the social context in which they were embedded, the appropriate code for women's behavior remained constant. In the teledramas and from people in and around Shirtex and Serendib I heard the same prescriptive narrative: a Good girl is a virgin at marriage, dependent on men, and subservient to parental authority, prepared to be a good wife and mother.

Many people (from workers to managers to parents) complained to me that the teledramas reinforced a common two-pronged perception. First, viewers began to think that all garment workers were "bad girls" who initiated relationships with strangers. Second, they also assumed that all garment factories were places where managers raped the workers or forced them into prostitution. One supervisor told me that after the teledramas aired, people looked at her oddly and that some people thought she forced girls into relationships with managers. Similarly, a sewing-machine operator told me, "When people hear that I work at a garment factory they look at me in a funny way" (*gāment āhunama amutu balāpamak tiyenawa*).

While many women blamed teledramas for the bad name given to garment workers, they also said that the shows served as a good lesson for workers not to get caught in such situations. Many said therefore that the broadcasts had both a good and a bad side: they warned village women (whom I heard described as innocent, naïve, unexposed to society) how not to behave but also provided a negative stereotype of garment workers. But a Serendib machine operator named Samarasinghe said that some people had come away from the teledramas with a positive message: that women struggled when they went from their villages to work in Colombo and support their families. As she eloquently stated in an interview, the programs "show how women truly devote their energy and time and fight to give meaning to their life. . . . It is good to show how hard this girl works daily, how she struggles with this heap of steel, devoting so much time, spending her entire day like that." More commonly, people focused on the negative. A Serendib manager told me in English that the problem depicted in *Grahanaya* was that when village girls go to Colombo they "get involved in all sorts of things" because they have "no shame"—he quickly rephrased this and said "no fear." Here he was obviously invoking the concept of *läjja-baya* (shame-fear), discussed above. Nobody ever raised objections to me about the stereotypical images of men (sex-driven, insincere, crooked) depicted in these programs. But the absence of social commentary on the men here reflects Sunila Abeysekera's contention, noted in the previous chapter, that it is women who are pigeonholed and not men: Nobody is reading the men as *only* these things, whereas they are all reading the women as entirely bad.

The negative Juki-girl reputation worried not just women who worked at the factories but also investors and managers who believed that the stigma inhibited their ability to recruit new workers. In an interview one investor mentioned that he had been considering asking others to join with him in paying for the production of a positive garment factory teledrama.[9] This businessman obviously saw a straightforward relationship between a program's plot, the spectator's reception, and social attitudes. While this may sound like a simplistic understanding of how media reception works, in this context the analysis was warranted. Everyone I spoke to about the teledramas assumed that the programs represented reality. While some lamented that the programs unfairly made everyone who worked in garment factories look bad, they all conceded that the kinds of things that happened to Dhammi and Felicia really did happen.

Susila, the mother of two teenagers, stated to me that Shirtex and Serendib were not like the places depicted in the teledramas that people thought of when they said *gäment* (garment factory). She told me that as a parent she needed to set a good example for her children—an example she was able to set through her work at Shirtex. More often than I could count I heard this from workers: the managers are very good in this respect; and because there are villagers in management, the kind of thing that happened in *Grahanaya* would never happen in these factories. Moreover, many said that since the factory was in the village, other villagers would never let such things happen.

The obvious violence perpetrated against Felicia was not the focus of my audience sample's concern or commentary regarding *Grahanaya*. Because the women at Shirtex and Serendib themselves had continually to ward off bad reputations, their focus was rather the lack of moral character that led Felicia into her sorry fate. It is conceivable that under other social circumstances *Grahanaya* could be read in terms of female empowerment for a survivor of violence or in terms of powerful men using influence to hurt dependent women. But among these village garment workers the emphasis was elsewhere. The lesson was how to sustain an identity as a Good girl. This reading enabled the women at Shirtex and Serendib to distance themselves from bad girls by emphasizing how they themselves were Good girls—especially because they were living in their villages, at home, under the protection of their parents.

These spectators' comments demonstrate that working women attempted to escape the full force of the Juki reputation by claiming the respectability offered through their presence in villages. But, as I show in the next chapter, many of these women struggled over how to comply with the social role expected for them—which they themselves wanted to fulfill—while at the same time making room in their Good-girl lives for the new desires and experiences that garment factory work enabled.

Voices from Parents

I end this chapter with the voices of the parents of Kanthi, who worked at Shirtex. Kanthi was twenty-three years old, unmarried, and living at home with her parents. The first set of comments, from the mother, allows us to see more of how the media portrayals of garment workers resonated with village parents' fears about their daughter. The second, from the father, further encapsulates many of the issues addressed in this chapter.

I interviewed the parents a few days after the *Ira Handa Yata* episode aired in which Dhammi had sex in a hotel room with her boyfriend, Sugath. Around that time, Kanthi had been lobbying to get her parents' permission to go to work in a garment factory in the Middle East. Her mother, who had watched this latest episode with her daughter, told me that it was precisely because of this kind of thing happening that she and her husband would not allow their daughter to leave the village to work. When I asked her if the program made her think about her daughter, she responded:

> *Mother*: I think she isn't like that. Those people are living outside [the village]. That is why we don't send her outside the village. Yes. That person called Sugath somehow fooled one of those girls and took her somewhere and even took her necklace, getting her in trouble [pregnant]. . . . Therefore that is why we don't send her outside the village.
> *Father*: Yes, yes. That is correct.
> *Mother*: That one [Sugath]. He is also a pickpocket. She got friendly with him. They set her up with him. Got her friendly with him. Yes. That's why we don't send her [our daughter] outside the village.

Numerous times in the interview, the father returned to the question of giving Kanthi permission to work in the Middle East, since it was a current topic in their family. In one portion of the conversation, he told me that he would not have let his daughter go to Colombo to work in a garment factory. I asked, "Why not?"

> *Father*: I wouldn't allow. The reason is, she is a girl. She doesn't understand very much about the troublesome state of things in our country. When she goes, men talk to her for love and might even harm this child by taking her. Therefore I dislike those [Colombo factories]. I agreed [to let her work at Shirtex] because this is nearby. Just last week, she said that she wants to work in a garment factory abroad. Then I said, "If you go like that, don't come home again. Go forever," I told her. "But don't come home again saying 'Father.'" I told her like that.
> *Caitrin*: And then what happened?
> *Father*: Then she was a little angry. For not allowing her to go abroad. I said, "Then don't live thinking you have me or your mother or siblings and that you have a home. Then go. There's nothing else for me to say. If you go like that, go. But don't come again. Don't hope to get any aid from me either."
> *Caitrin*: You don't like her to go abroad?
> *Father*: This is the issue: when she goes to those garment factories, we

don't know anything about the factories abroad. What sort of problems will arise for the child? This is a girl, not a boy, right? There must be protection for girls, right? Now if she works here [at Shirtex], I can even go at night. If she is late, I go. I go to see, "Why is this child not home?" We go there and ask. When she goes to a place like that [abroad], we don't know what happens. If it's a boy, it's okay.

Caitrin: What's the difference? Are you afraid of her going with boys?

Father: Yes, yes. Today there are cunning men among the males. Among young men, there are very cunning ones. They go and fool girls and destroy innocent [*ahinsaka*] girls, isn't it? We're very scared because of things like that.

SITA

A twenty-nine-year-old mother of two small children, Sita worked in the cutting room at Serendib, numbering sheets of fabric before they were cut. Many layers of fabric were laid down by women and cut through at once by the cutters, who were usually male. Because parts of the bolts could vary in color, each garment had to be made from pieces from the same layer of fabric. Sita and other cutting-room helpers numbered the layers so the proper components could be bundled together for assembly in the production section.

Sita supported her family with the help of her husband. The mother of a four-year-old son and a nine-year-old daughter, she explained that in today's society children needed more things than in the past:

> The wage my husband gets really isn't enough to live on. For chil-
> dren it's not like the old days. All the comforts have to be given.
> It's useless to try to make them understand that we don't have
> something. Saying "no" won't do. Children should be given a
> chance to live luxuriously. I am happy that I'm able to bring up
> the children well. With the money I can get clothes and cover the
> children's expenses the way we want to. I'm very happy because I
> can also look after my mother and father well.

Sita used her wage primarily to pay off a 50,000–rupee loan she and her husband took to build a house. In 1996, after three years of working at the factory, she had paid off 25,000 rupees with her own wage. But Sita was like other mothers who felt that there were personal sacrifices they had to make in order to earn those wages. She lived near the factories, but other mothers who lived far away would sometimes leave home in the morning before their children woke up and, with overtime, return late in the evening, long after the children had gone to sleep. Some of these women told me they were concerned that their children did not have enough of their mother's influence to prevent them from getting in-volved in bad things—they were particularly concerned about girls' in-appropriate relationships with boys and men. Additionally, as mothers usually help children with schoolwork, some said the education of their children was suffering. Sita intended to stop working once her daughter attained puberty. Here she referred to her own experiences, for several years before she started at Serendib she married someone through a "love marriage" rather than an arranged marriage. In reference to mother-daughter relationships Sita said:

> *There comes a time when the mother should be close to her daughter. Then she has to be with her mother like a friend. Then I will stop [working]. . . . When she becomes a little bigger, re-ally she might be urged to get involved in other things. She goes to school. She might get friendly with someone. . . . So if the mother is with the child, the child can understand a lot more about society. . . . How to live in a good society. How to be a per-son who doesn't go on the wrong path. To get friendly with a boy, he must be a good person. No need for an unsuitable person. We have to put her into a good situation where she can live a good life. Now me, because my mother brought me up properly, though I got friendly [with a boy] and she told me not to, because I got friendly with a good man she approved later. Otherwise she would have disliked. Just like that, I have to give a good up-bringing for my daughter.*

In response to my query, she said that even at her daughter's current age of nine it would have been better if she were at home spending more time with her daughter, but for financial reasons she had to work. She told me, "I'm sad about not being with her. My son is also small. I really feel sad. When I have to work at night I cry and cry and stay on work-ing. It can't be helped. I have to stay at work. But when that happens I often cry. When I am not allowed to go home I somehow manage to work—but only after weeping."

5. THE GOOD GIRLS OF SRI LANKAN MODERNITY

Shirtex and Serendib women joined their managers, parents, and politicians in drawing sharp dichotomies between innocent village girls and Juki girls who were corrupted by city life. Many Sri Lankans could easily offer the following as key characteristics of Good girls: virginity until marriage, a life under parental control, an arranged marriage to a suitable partner, observance of "traditional" customs and rites like funerals and puberty ceremonies, respect toward superiors, and conventional norms for appearance (long hair tied back in a braid, no makeup, no trousers). Virginity until marriage is the focal point; it is assumed that, if followed strictly, many of the other characteristics would ensure virginity. (If the Good girl under question were married, then the focus would be on appropriate sexual relations with her spouse, under whose control she lives.) Although they described themselves as Good girls, a close analysis of Shirtex and Serendib women's daily lives reveals that while they always maintained the centrality of virginity, they were expanding the acceptable definition of the term *Good girl*.

This chapter examines the nuances of this emergent Good-girl identity. It is evident that these women had ambivalent responses to the expectations put on them, and they worked hard to fashion identities as women who were Good girls, despite being garment workers. One echo of Sri Lankan women's ambivalence can be found in the way fast-food restaurant employees in Harlem respond to their work. The anthropologist Katherine Newman (1999, 297) argues that for the Harlem workers this stigmatized work "is both a blessing and a curse." As she notes: "Having a job of this kind keeps them afloat and gives them a modicum of freedom. But it also subjects them to the withering criticism of a society that defines low-wage service jobs as something akin to the untouchable status of the Indian low castes." In short, for these fast-food workers, the main impediment to their full satisfaction with work has to do with the status problems resulting from working in a stigmatized job.

How do people carve out meaningful lives for themselves in the context of such stigma, especially in a society where issues of reputation and social hierarchy are so important to social status? This is the work of producing meaning and identity in which Shirtex and Serendib women were engaged every day. Their ambivalent construction of a Good-girl identity may not have seemed important to (nor was it respected by) many people around them (managers, husbands, parents), but it was how they made sense of their new lives. The fact that we sense ambivalence and contradiction in what follows demonstrates how very complicated this work was for them, in that they were juggling multiple commitments and contradictory desires.

As we see in the previous chapter, many Shirtex and Serendib women, their parents, and managers expect and draw sharp contrasts between village and city garment workers. But the situation is far more complicated than these contrasts imply. Discourse and practice often do not match. Although Sri Lankans generally say that caste rules are no longer followed in Sri Lanka, if one looks closely one easily finds that caste permeates society. In a like vein, although people speak eloquently of stark contrasts between urban and rural garment workers, there are many ways in which Shirtex and Serendib women engaged in new social practices that were similar to those of the very FTZ women who were so scorned in their society.

The strength of the social values surrounding women's behavior, combined with the pervasiveness of the Juki-girl stigma, meant that the Shirtex and Serendib women generally wanted to be considered Good girls. But their experiences as factory workers in a village led many to try to create a new way of being Good girls that was not the simple moral opposite of Juki girls. President Premadasa and his supporters and critics did not envision this emergent Good-girl subject position—a position between modern and traditional, urban and rural. The politicians did not take into account the question of how rural women might actually experience and express their new social roles as factory workers.

Although they enjoyed relatively more freedom from normal village and family social roles than non–garment factory village women, they aligned

JUKI GIRLS, GOOD GIRLS

themselves with conventional norms of respectability by referring to themselves as Good girls. But they did not want to be simply Good girls whose lives were subsumed by the village. Rather, they desired certain aspects of the urban social life enjoyed by Juki girls. These women longed to go to Colombo without leaving home—they wanted to traverse the rural-urban divide without physically doing so because there were signs from everywhere that it would be socially suicidal to migrate to the city. They understood that it was impossible to be a Good girl once actually there, and that there was no in-between the rural and urban once one got to the city.

Of course, the women at these factories had complex subject positions and followed different approaches to factory life. I focus on what seemed to be the dominant social persona. Not coincidentally, it was the persona devised by the people with whom I associated. With a few significant exceptions, I spent most of my time with the factory's Good girls, and it was in my experiences with them (in their homes, on trips, in the factories) that I identified this other way of being a Good girl—a Good girl of Sri Lankan modernity.

I now examine the contours of these women's new social lives. I close with some "outsider" (parents, managers, villagers) perspectives on this Good-girl identity that demonstrate what these women are up against as they worked to create a place in the world around them.

Mala and Society's "Cross-Eyed Looks"

I began to appreciate the complexities of being garment workers from Mala, whose plea for respect opened chapter 1. Profound and moving, her comments bear repetition:

> A lot of people in society think garment factories are places without any culture [*sanskrutiya*]. . . . When we come to work amidst society we are subjected to the insults of young people just like us. It would be a great resource if there arose in the world a movement that would be able to properly direct the cross-eyed way society looks at the valuable services of valuable male and female workers. Can a person's character [*caritaya*] be concluded from a job?

Mala began by referring to the widespread fears that factories are the breeding ground of behavior that is morally unacceptable and does not fit into the purview of Sinhala Buddhist culture. She then lamented being "subjected to the insults of young people just like us." When I asked Mala to elaborate, she explained to me that when she and her coworkers boarded buses and trains on their commute, young men would make comments to them such as, "Oh, Garment got on, here comes Garment. . . . Also they say the names of unmentionable garments and ask us whether we are going to sew them." Here the young men dehumanized the women by calling them "Garment" (a term used for "garment factory")—thus labeling the workers as the site of production itself, not unlike what happens with the Juki nickname and the parallel nicknames *gāment baḍuwa* (garment pieces) and *juki käli* (Juki pieces). The reference to underwear was doubtlessly a reference to the opposition's underwear critique, but even without this political context the comment would have had sexual overtones. In Mala's experience, men were not the only people who disrespected garment workers: women on the buses and trains would not even direct toward them the courteous smiles normally expected among strangers.

I heard numerous stories about insults during the daily commute from other workers. For instance, one woman said that sometimes when she and other garment workers boarded public buses as schoolchildren were being transported to and from school, she would hear people tell the conductors in a rude manner, "Don't let them in, this is a school bus, those are garment workers." This recurring theme of comments about women as they commute supports the assertion that the public visibility of women contributed to the moral panic about them, as with the "stigma of public mobility" Seizer (2000, 2005) described for Indian actresses, and Yasmin Tambiah (2005, 258) noted for LTTE women in Sri Lanka.

Mala closed with a query, "Can a person's character [*caritaya*] be concluded from a job?" Clearly she would answer "No" to this question. I discuss the term *caritaya* in the previous chapter, especially its relation to standards of marriageability. Mala often discussed with me her own and her coworkers' hopes for good marriages. One day during *Ira Handa Yata*'s run, we talked about the teledrama while she deftly sewed together the side seams on men's dress shirts. She observed that while the teledramas did depict sorrow, they attributed all sorrow to a girl's bad character. She told me that she wanted to write the director of *Ira Handa Yata* asking him to make another program about the good character of garment factory workers.

In the face of the Juki stigma, Mala, like many workers, was trying to get another job when I knew her at Shirtex—what she described as a "good" job.

To this end she was learning English at the factory, taking courses in sewing and bridal dressing, and sitting for government teaching exams. In a letter to me in Chicago six months after I had left, Mala told me she wanted to quit her job because she couldn't bear the "mental and physical pain" of the work. Physical pain may have referred to any number of problems such as back pain, headaches and dizziness, weight loss, respiratory problems from inhaling cotton dust, or other ailments. Both factories were often stifling hot, and women often complained to me of feeling faint. On several occasions I saw small groups carrying a collapsed colleague to the first-aid room.

When Mala referred to "mental pain," it could have been in regard to at least two different issues, which we had discussed on many occasions: the lack of respect garment workers receive in their village and wider communities, and the crude manner in which some of the Shirtex managers (but especially production manager Yohan Sir) treated workers, which many workers complained to me about.

Mala told me that although managers had never scolded her harshly, she often witnessed rough treatment directed at others. One day when we ran into each other in a shop in Kandy, I had an animated conversation with Mala and a coworker. Jayanthi worked in the finishing section at Shirtex, folding shirts and inserting pins to hold them in shape before packing them. I had met Jayanthi some months earlier, on her first day on the job. Her fingers were bleeding from pinpricks, so in addition to learning what the managers expected her to learn to get the shirts done (sanctioned technical learning), she was also learning how to avoid getting blood on the new shirts (unsanctioned technical learning). But within days this problem disappeared because she had developed calluses on her fingers. That day in the shop, Jayanthi told me she found it painful to hear Yohan Sir speak to workers as if they were children, saying things to them like, "Where did you go to school? In a toilet?" When she heard that, she knew that the women in question must have felt *lājjay* (ashamed, embarrassed) to be scolded so in front of their coworkers, and especially among fellow villagers.

Mala felt the lack of respect for garment workers in many ways. In addition to being insulted on the daily commute, she was scorned in her village. Although many people in the area wanted to work at the factories, Mala told me that when she first got the job, neighbors insulted her mother by saying: "You say that your daughter got good exam results. Could she find a better job? Why did she have to go to a factory?" Indeed, Mala had done quite well in her A-Level exams and just missed getting the marks that would have gained her admittance to a university. She had been stymied in her efforts to get a government job, a rejection she attributed to her family's SLFP affiliations at a time of UNP dominance. As she wrote in the same questionnaire, "I tried very hard to get a job according to my educational qualifications. . . . As my financial problems were increasing, with a sad heart I accepted this job because I could not get any other job."

In a January 2000 letter, Mala told me she was still working as a machine operator at Shirtex—it had been seven years since she had started at Shirtex, but she could not find another job. She told me that she had recently taken quality control courses in Colombo on Sundays with the hopes of getting promoted within Shirtex to a staff quality control position. At the same time, Mala continued her self-employment courses. She had completed weekend courses in every aspect of wedding preparation—making and decorating cakes, dressing brides, styling hair, making jewelry, sewing bridal saris—and could by then be employed as a wedding coordinator. She hoped to plan weddings while she continued working in a garment factory and perhaps after she married, if her husband wanted her to stop working at the factory. I learned in a letter in 2003 that Mala had wed through an arranged marriage and stopped working altogether at the insistence of her new husband.

In her January 2000 letter, Mala told me that all the workers who had been hired when Shirtex opened in 1992 were physically exhausted after more than seven years in the factory and felt desperate to stop working. Many were agreeing to arranged marriage proposals they normally would have refused so that they could quit work but also receive the financial benefits women are entitled to if they stop working in order to marry.[1] Mala predicted that many would marry men who would hit and scold them. Because Sri Lankans often correlated domestic violence and the drinking of alcohol, Mala seems to have been saying that her coworkers were agreeing to marry men with reputations as drunks.

Looking for a "Good Job"

The majority of women I associated with valued their factory jobs for various reasons, such as the wages, the friendships, and the exposure to "society." Many also valued the access to a modern lifestyle within the comfort of their villages, as I discuss below. At the same time they conceded that although they would miss their friends and the new social opportunities offered by factory work, they would have preferred not to work in garment factories if they had not needed the money or had been in a position to find a different job—a "good job." Many women echoed Mala's reasons for wanting to quit: some concerned the actual work process—the work was exhausting, low paid, and made them ill—and some were about the status of garment workers.[2]

Scholars have examined job preferences among Sri Lankan women, and their findings are consistent with the types of jobs that Shirtex and Serendib women dreamed about. Malathi de Alwis argues that jobs considered best for women in Sri Lanka are "a continuation of domestic chores in the public domain" (de Alwis 1995, 142). The political scientist Jean Grossholtz (1984, 125) notes that women in the 1980s preferred occupations such as schoolteacher, nurse, typist, stenographer, and retail sales clerk. She argued that these jobs were considered appropriately female, since they relied on skills developed in housework (taking care of children, nurturing, waiting on others) and the flexible hours could be combined with household duties (cf. Jayawardena and Jayaweera 1986, 3). The point about combining jobs with household duties was especially relevant to garment workers; they often found it challenging to juggle employment with serving husbands and caring for families.

Even women who settled for equally gendered jobs as garment workers hoped for something better but typically female. Their job preferences were influenced by gender considerations in terms of expectations about women's household labor and of their own concerns for how their reputations would be affected by cultural norms about women's behavior. Many workers identified jobs they would prefer over garment factory work, and these often corresponded to those listed by Grossholtz. On one Saturday, a group of thirty or so women at both factories were given leave to take the government teaching exam, and letters I have received since then indicate that many have continued to pursue these jobs, although none has succeeded in finding one. Most workers had hoped for a government job (the most sought-after employment in Sri Lanka, owing to the short working hours, high pay, prestige, and pension) but came to the factories as a last resort. Some people had entered the factories with the misconception that because they had been started under the 200 GFP, they were government factories whose employment conditions would fit their idea of "government jobs." Women often told me that because they couldn't find "a job"—as opposed to "another job"—they ended up in the factories. That factory jobs were not considered "jobs" is a colonial legacy: Colonial education was oriented toward white-collar jobs, and diversely situated people considered white-collar jobs the only proper employment then and now (Ivan 1989, 78).

Many of the women who had missed the cutoff for university admission in their A-Level exam results continued to desire government jobs and pursued them through clerk and teaching exams. But advancement has been rare. One woman who studied for and re-sat her A-Level exams while I was there subsequently went to nursing school. Even more women from these factories were taking classes after work and on Sundays in sewing (knowing how to sew one hundred shirt cuffs in an hour does not mean that you know how to sew a complete garment), bridal dressing, hair styling, and flower arranging; and a smaller number of women were learning computer skills, typing, and shorthand, taking exam preparation courses for A-Level or General Arts Qualifying (GAQ) exams, or studying for external bachelor's degrees.

Garment factory work was often more lucrative than many of these jobs or the jobs further education might promise, but many of the women told me that they would opt for respectability over money. While some expressed hope that such jobs would be easier to combine with a successful home life as mothers and wives, many spoke about the social respect garnered through teaching and to a lesser extent through self-employment. But whether or not they would really opt for the lesser-paid but more respectable jobs if given the opportunity remains an open question. One worker had received training as a court clerk in Kandy but came to the garment factory because it paid more.

Many who had given up hopes for their own success dreamt of their children's. I asked all the women workers whom I interviewed formally if they would allow their daughters (real or potential) to work at their factory. All but one emphatically said, "No." Many vowed that they would not send their daughters because of the difficulty of the work. For instance, one woman explained that "I wouldn't like her to get scolded. She would have to work until nine o'clock [at night]. She would have to somehow stay awake, exhaust herself, and suffer. I wouldn't like my child to have to suffer like I do." They almost uniformly said they would educate her well and try to get her a "good job" like teaching, nursing, work in a bank, or work as a clerk. One woman explained that a bank job was good because when you went to work in the morning you knew what time you would get off. At Serendib, by contrast, "after we go inside we don't have a certain time we get off, and we don't even have our own lives." In her view, because as garment workers they could not predict what time they would be let off (required overtime was often only announced shortly before the end of the normal workday), they did not have control over their own lives. By correlating control over one's life with a respectable job, she seemed to be speaking to the prevailing societal assumption that a woman who lacks control over the circumstances of her life is a woman who has lost control over herself. As we have seen with earlier discussions of concepts such as *saṇwara* and *läjja-baya*, a lack of self-control means violating cultural norms validating women as disciplined and respectable.

Sunila, a twenty-seven-year-old married mother of two daughters, was the one woman who spoke differently. She said that she would send her daughter to the factory to work no matter how much money she had, even if her husband were the prime minister. Rather than coddling her daughter, saying how beloved she was, and "making her an idiot . . . by seating her on a chair and feeding her," Sunila would send her to the factory to learn a skill. Sunila was eager to point out that there were skills to be learned in a factory that could not be acquired elsewhere in society. I had expected more women to say things along these lines when they spoke about their aspirations for their daughters. I imagined they would talk about the value of the technical skills and the social lives their factory jobs provided. But in their statements about their hopes for their daughters they simply wanted their children to be free of such difficult and stigmatized jobs. I am not sure how to assess Sunila's very different opinion. She was an unusually gregarious and humorous person, and it may be that she was just saying what she did to impress me or to be funny. But Sunila also had a reputation, which I discuss more in the next chapter, for a lack of concern with being considered respectable and dwelling on what others think.

Even those women who so clearly said they would not send their daughters to work at the factories seemed to articulate a complicated perspective when it came to their own work. The ambivalence should become apparent in the following section, in which I turn to describe the contours of the emergent Good-girl identity among Shirtex and Serendib women.

Marriage Prospects

Despite concerns about reputation, character, and the Juki-girl stigma, many women had boyfriends or husbands whom they met after starting work. Although some met through arranged marriage proposals (and their boyfriends were thus their fiancées), many were involved in what they called "love affairs" (using the English term), to be distinguished from relationships arranged by parents with marriage as the end goal. Rather than indicating a short or illicit relationship, these women used the term *affair* to mean having a boyfriend whom they intended to go on and marry. This newly opened social space of romance became a sort of testing ground in which women workers developed their new Good-girl identities.

The Juki-girl stigma affected these village women factory workers in many ways, one of which had to do with marriage prospects. Mala once told me that a marriage proposal made to a coworker had been withdrawn when the man learned that his prospective bride was working at Shirtex. In regard to this disqualification of potential brides due to their employment in garment factories, Yasmin Tambiah (1997, 29) argues that economic freedom raises the specter of sexual promiscuity. This puts garment workers in a difficult position, since many of them are working to support their families and, in the case of unmarried workers, to collect money for their dowries. It was common for these women to enter into arranged marriages, which usually required dowries, as indeed did some "love marriages." Prior to recent economic changes, parents would have collected the money and goods that make up a dowry—the larger the dowry, the better the marriage match. But by the time of my field research in the mid-1990s, one effect of economic liberalization was that often parents simply could not collect enough to secure a desired match. Garment work paid considerably more money than the other jobs that these women may have been able to find—such as working in a paddy field, on a road construction gang, or as a salesperson in a shop. Yet, despite its relatively high pay, it carried with it very low social recognition.

Given the very real possibility that a man might withdraw his marriage proposal upon learning that the woman was a garment worker, women sometimes tried to hide their current or previous factory employment from prospective grooms. They feared that otherwise they might not be able to refuse a less than optimum marriage—that is, a marriage to a man who for some reason or other was less desirable. The desirability and appropriateness of a marriage proposal were determined by factors such as whether the couple liked each other, but also the spouse's educational level and employment status as well as the size of the requested dowry. Other, more conventional requirements were likely important though they were not cited in conversations with me. In the early 1950s Bryce Ryan (1953b, 150) wrote that the rigid requirements for a good marriage match were "membership in the same caste, the bride more youthful than the groom, a virginal bride, and close matching of horoscopes."

People often told me of the importance of a woman's reputation and character to her marriage prospects. While there were plenty of men who did not automatically consider garment work bad *kaṭakatā*, I heard numerous cases of husbands and boyfriends of garment workers who pretended that their mates did not work at a garment factory, for fear the women would be considered to have bad moral character (*naraka caritaya*), which would in turn affect the man's family's reputation. I once made a significant faux pas in terms of considerations of bad *kaṭakatā*. A worker named Thanuja told me that her husband worked at a photo studio in Kandy where I developed my film. Simply wanting to meet my friend's husband, a few days later when I was at the studio I asked for him. But since I didn't know his name, I described him as "a man whose wife works at the garment factory in Udakande." They told me there was no such person. The next day Thanuja told me that her husband had been close by when I asked this question, and though he wanted to meet me he did not come forward. She explained, quite earnestly, that this was because he had not told his coworkers that his wife worked at the factory for fear of how it would affect his reputation at work. In fact, the only people in his village who knew she worked there were her husband's parents.

This couple's concerns to maintain a good name had led them to lie about the woman's occupation to friends, colleagues, and neighbors. There were other stories like this. Aspiration to social respectability is here expressed through the idiom of female sexual morality, for they wanted to ensure that the woman was not considered a Juki girl, with the moral degradation the term implies. In the case of men who prevented their wives from working once they married (a common occurrence), these concerns led them to suffer a financial loss. This is a clear demonstration of the far-reaching and unpredictable effects that can be produced by nationalist discourses on women's normative behavior.

Some newly married men professed to me (and their wives repeated this in private conversations) that they made their wives quit their garment factory jobs as soon as they married because they did not want to worry about what others might think. Women also told me that men did not want their wives to work because they wanted women to do all the housework. Sita, whose profile appears before this chapter, spoke on this subject in an interview: "That is because there are more problems at home [when women work]. Some men don't like to help their wives with the housework. There are hard drinkers who don't like to. They only consider their freedom. They don't like to look after kids, sweep the house, wash clothes, and work in peace with their wives. Those are the ones who don't like [women to work after marriage]." She also later added that if there were no relatives (such as a woman's mother-in-law) available to watch after children, these men would definitely ask their wives to quit after they had a child. Many of these are not issues unique to poor villagers, although the housework and child-care issues are less pressing for better-off families who employ servants (a quite common practice in Sri Lanka even among people who are not rich). Many men told me that men of all classes would rather their wives did not work because they would be embarrassed to admit they did not earn enough money to support a family.

The various reasons men had for this distaste for working wives were succinctly captured in a conversation I had with Kumar, a three-wheeler taxi driver in his early twenties who occasionally drove me from the central market in Kandy to my house at the end of a long day. Kumar had a girlfriend who was still in high school and I asked him if he would let her work at a garment factory. He immediately said no, that once they married he would earn money to support her (*mama hambukaranawa eyāṭe salakanna*) and not vice versa. He also said others would assume that she worked because of his shortcomings (*maṭa mädikamak*). Also that if she worked, since girls are not so *fit* (he used the English word), she would be too sickly and tired to be able to do the housework well.

When I asked Kumar why so many men told their wives to quit working once they married he outlined three reasons in a very clear and organized fashion that implied that these were all well-known cultural tropes.

1. So that she has time for housework. If she comes home at six from work she doesn't have time for housework.
2. Because he suspects (*säka*) her. Because she comes alone at night, something could happen to her. Here he made the common move of conflating a woman becoming involved in an affair of her free will with a woman being raped.
3. Because his friends will not think well of him (*ganan ganne nä*). It is for this reason that, if the income cannot be sacrificed, many men lie and do not tell anyone that their wives or girlfriends work at a garment factory.

JUKI GIRLS, GOOD GIRLS

When I then asked Kumar what kind of women he liked, he said he liked poor girls because they had fear (*baya*). When I asked him what he meant, he explained that if he could not support her well, she would understand, whereas rich girls would not. Poor girls would not do "bad things" (*naraka dewal*), because they would fear getting in trouble at home. He offered "going with boys" as an example of "bad things." Kumar's invocation of the concept of fear among poor girls raises the issue of class position and respectability. Wealthier women are generally considered more respectable than poor women because they do not suffer the stigma of public mobility. But for Kumar, because poor women have more to lose they are more careful about what others will say; thus they have the fear of social censure that is so crucial to being a good, respectable girl.

Love Affairs

Shirtex and Serendib women were more commonly in love affairs than other women in their villages—though other villagers also did have boyfriends. Many of the ways in which Shirtex and Serendib women met their boyfriends were directly made possible by their garment factory lives. Couples met on their daily commute, on trips that they took with their factory friends, at work (there were approximately five married or dating couples in both factories), or through social connections with factory friends. Although these relationships were referred to by the English term *love affairs*, which seems to connote sexual relations, the assumption was that because these were Good girls the relationships did not involve sex. I was never able to ascertain if any of these relationships actually did involve sexual activity, and while it is certainly conceivable that some did, the interesting question such speculation raises is, What counts as sex? It might involve intercourse, but more likely involves Sri Lankan tactics for preserving virginity—noted particularly among university students—such as what is known as "interfemoral" sex and other "activities that provide sexual satisfaction but also preserve virginity" (Silva and Eisenberg 1996, 6). But it is also possible that these relationships were not sexual, and in many ways this seems more likely, for reasons that will be made apparent.

Although there are strong moral strictures against premarital sexuality, having boyfriends and girlfriends is quite common in Sri Lanka today, especially among the more Westernized, urban, and English-medium social strata. Love affairs connote "romance" more than "sex." In her research on female university students in Kerala, India, the anthropologist Ritty Lukose (2001) argues that romance signifies the ambiguity of modernity in Kerala; where earlier *love* and *marriage* were synonymous, the newer space between love and marriage is an area in which the reformulation of female sexuality is invested with cultural meaning.

In Sri Lanka, too, university students, who come from a range of backgrounds, occupy a special social space in terms of romance, sexuality, and marriage. Although social surveys and AIDS information campaigns have indicated a high incidence of sexual activity on Sri Lankan university campuses (Silva and Eisenberg 1996), when people make pronouncements about sexually immoral women, it is never campus life they are talking about. Perhaps university women escape public scrutiny because campuses are secluded social worlds and so, unlike garment workers, these women are not seen moving about in public every day. As early as the 1950s, Bryce Ryan noted the incidence of romantic love among the "trousered urban elite" in Sri Lankan universities but argued that bracketing it as a merely temporary phase in the students' lives kept it from threatening a family's good name (Ryan 1953a, 312). He also said that youth in general "speak longingly of romantic marriage" but that in the end they would sacrifice romance for a good arranged marriage that would preserve family bonds (1953b, 151). I have heard that women university students would never admit, even to their closest friends, that a love affair had become sexual. If the relationship ends, the information about a woman's loss of virginity absolutely cannot be known—or it would add up to bad *kaṭakatā* for her future marriage prospects.

While Ryan states that romance was popular among elite university students in the 1950s, my conversations with people of various backgrounds indicated that only recently have people in villages begun to understand *love* and *marriage* as distinct. The Good girls of Shirtex and Serendib seemed to be working at a way to cast their love affairs in terms more or less easily accommodated within traditional notions of the proper relationships between men and women. Thus, even in their constructions of their own love affairs, these women were attempting to do something new. For instance, it may have been the case that although some relationships did involve sex, factory women did not speak to me (nor to their coworkers, from what I could tell) of their relationships as being sexual because they worried about *kaṭakatā*.

Typical in many ways was the love affair of Kanthi, who operated a sewing machine at Shirtex and whose parents I quote in the previous chapter. Kanthi had met her boyfriend Harsha when she and a group of coworkers took a trip on one of their Sundays off from work. When I met Kanthi, she and Harsha had been together for two years, but for the past year Harsha had been in the army. Kanthi carried Harsha's photo and love letters with her all the time and when she spoke of him her eyes glimmered. She referred to Harsha as her husband (*mahattaya*, literally "master"), she performed *bodhipūjas* for his safe return from the army, and in the same way that wives seek their husband's permission for most things they do, she sought Harsha's permission before going on a trip or to a party with coworkers.

My conversations with a number of workers and their parents led me to believe that the parents allowed their daughters to have boyfriends, and that so long as the daughters came home before dark they were considered Good girls and remained above suspicion. Parents told me that their daughters' respectable character was evidenced by the facts that they lived at home, participated in village social and religious life, and generally returned home by dark.[3] In essence, parents consented to the relationships because they believed that as long as their daughter remained a virgin, a more appropriate marriage could be arranged later.

But some may also have permitted these relations in part because they feared that their daughter might commit suicide if the relationship were prevented. This fear was not unfounded: Sri Lanka has one of the highest suicide rates in the world and the ostensible cause for suicide is often problems with love affairs (Marecek 1998). Because Harsha was of a lower caste than Kanthi, her *govigama* parents had not approved. However, they did not prohibit her from continuing the relationship. Kanthi's father told me that a worse problem than his daughter marrying her lower-caste boyfriend Harsha would have been her drinking poison (the preferred method of suicide in Sri Lanka).

Because the factories were still relatively new at the time of my field research, it was not entirely clear to me if parents would easily be able to arrange suitable marriages for their garment worker daughters. While I knew of a number of workers whose marriages were arranged, I was not able to ascertain if those matches were considered good or merely acceptable. But in contrast with the parental wishes for arranged marriages, all the women I knew with boyfriends told me that they would marry their boyfriends. Whether or not that would turn out to be the case remained to be seen as of the completion of my field research. I do know that Kanthi did not marry Harsha, because he died in a battle with the LTTE. I did know of a number of elopements, and it was generally said that parents would refuse to accept such marriages only until the birth of the first grandchild.

These women with boyfriends had different aspirations and values from those of their parents, even as they cast their love affairs in conventional, even ideological, terms. Along with the style and consumption practices of their new social lives, this break with the aspirations of their parents indicates that the daughters were expanding the domain of women's practices and developing a new model of Good-girl conduct. The Shirtex and Serendib women, then, were not Good girls in a straightforward sense of the term. To have a boyfriend and yet be considered a Good girl was to be something new—it was to be one of the Good girls of Sri Lankan modernity.

Virginity at Marriage

Shirtex and Serendib women situated themselves in complicated ways in reference to the ideal of women's virginity at marriage. Two practices that emerged during the colonial era to test a woman's virginity at marriage were still practiced during the time of my field research. They elicited ambivalent responses from my interlocutors.

The first practice is apparent in a Sinhala idiom (which factory women invoked) that if a woman is not a virgin she will faint on the wedding stage (*pōruwa*, the decorated plank on which the bride and groom stand during the wedding ceremony). In the early nineteenth century Dona Grero, a woman poet from the Matara district (in the south), wrote the following poem in Sinhala for unmarried women: "All those who hope to be familied should protect their virginity carefully and not lose it; then what fear is there to stand on the bridal poruwa?" (Ranaweera 1992, 24; cf. Gombrich and Obeyesekere 1988, 262–63).

The second practice is that some mothers-in-law inspect the white sheets of a newly married couple for blood after their wedding night. This practice, which seems to have emerged in modern times (Gombrich and Obeyesekere 1988, 262), is today still practiced by rural and urban families of various social classes. In an article on the shame concept, Eva Ranaweera (1992, 19) writes: "the greatest shame a lajja baya woman faces is the test of virginity on her wedding night. It has social bearing on family and community and exposure is to a wide public." On numerous occasions unmarried factory women told me they were afraid of this test, asked if Americans also did this, and inquired if I thought there could be any reason other than not being a virgin that a woman would fail to bleed.[4]

One such conversation took place in Serendib's finishing section when Chandra and Kamala were packing knit skirts and tank tops for shipment to the United States. Combined with my presence, the unusual style of clothing they produced for foreign women was often a catalyst for discussions with me about different women's behavior and traditions. While folding what they considered rather risqué tops, these two women complained to me about the bedsheet virginity-test tradition. They told me that because sometimes women don't bleed from their first experience of sex, some women have resorted to putting red dye on the sheet to substitute for blood. But they said that was not a good solution since the shade of red is never quite right. Chandra and Kamala both professed to disagree with the tradition but complained that because their parents were of the old (*paranay*) generation they were firm in their ideas. Sharmini Fernando (1997, 22), coordinator of an HIV/AIDS prevention project in Sri Lanka, has written about how women in sexual health workshops "wonder about the requisite bleeding as the only proof" and "jokingly ask me to give workshops to future mothers-in-law." In a different conversation, a small group of Shirtex women told me that it was good that the mother-in-law checked for blood in this way, since, as one woman put it, it is important that women "protect their virtue" before they marry.

Chandra and Kamala also derided the wedding-stage virginity test. But, as with the bedsheet test, they questioned the practicality of the test rather than the virginity ideal itself. Their continued adherence to the ideal was evidenced by their repeated reference to unmarried women who had lost their virginity as *honda nä*—not good. I mark this complex positioning regarding virginity tests as another aspect of their attempt to be a new kind of Good girl, who can enact new social practices while maintaining certain traditions.

Good-Girl Style and Sociability

In the previous chapter, I note that workers, managers, and parents draw stark contrasts between village and city garment workers, and that these contrasts confirm previously held assumptions about the degradation of tradition that occurs in cities. But in practice the contrasts were not so stark. Various people noted ways in which women in Kandepitiya were changing due to their employment in local factories—and some of these changes meant they were becoming more like city people. For some parents in particular, the changes they saw were simply "bad." But for the women engaging in new social practices, these changes were indications of access to a modern world that is exciting, fun, and desired. Clearly these women had ambivalent attitudes toward being garment workers, as with the fast-food workers in Harlem for whom their work was both a blessing and a curse (Newman 1999).

Piyasena, the sixty-five-year-old father of a Serendib finishing-room worker, nicely captured concerns about social change in the area. In an interview he spoke of the changes he observed in terms of a distinction between Kandyan and Low Country people. "Kandyan" (also "Up Country," *uḍa raṭa*) describes the people and area of the precolonial Kandyan kingdom, today roughly delineated by the Central Province where the town of Kandy is the capital. It is usually contrasted to the southwest coastal region that is so dominated by Colombo that when people refer to the Low Country (*pahata raṭa*) they often just mean the capital. After he had determined that my research assistant was Kandyan by asking for her surname, Piyasena immediately complained to us that with factory employment village girls started wearing rings, nail polish on their fingers and toes, and hairstyles (*konḍe mōstara*). He said: "That Kandyan way has changed completely. That is very bad. When going somewhere they redden these [fingernails], redden the lips. You can't say whether it's a Kandyan girl or what kind of girl. Meaning that they have adjusted themselves to that way which was borrowed from these [indicating me] Western [*baṭahira*] people's countries. In that way they became very bad."

Piyasena clarified that what he meant was that now Kandyan girls were behaving like Low Country girls. He said that behaving like Westerners was something city people had been doing for a long time, but now, with factories in villages, villagers were also beginning to act like that. Piyasena added that his daughter remonstrated that if she did not behave in that way, the other factory girls who had "adjusted to city ways" would think she was like unsophisticated, rural people (*goḍēma minissu*), and she would be marginalized (*kōn wenawa*). For Piyasena, the presence of garment factories in villages had sparked concerns about the disintegration of village tradition.

Piyasena saw his daughter performing production and consumption practices considered urban, but he wanted to defend her from charges of immorality associated with village women who work in Colombo. While he viewed his daughter's behavior negatively, he also implied that her motivations were somehow nobler than if she were simply attempting to fulfill new consumer desires. Her motivations were rooted in the desire for social acceptance. But in our numerous conversations, Indrani, his daughter, indirectly contested her father's claim. She was not merely motivated by social acceptance—she wanted to practice new behaviors, and she enjoyed those new behaviors, yet she still wanted to be considered a Good girl.

Indrani and her coworkers did not articulate these changes in the same terms as Piyasena. They saw them as elements of a desired new kind of life. Asoka Bandarage (1988, 68) has written that despite the harshness of their work in FTZs, women employed there were proud of being factory workers because it was their entry to the modern urban sector and the new lifestyle associated with it. Sandya Hewamanne's (2002, 2003) more recent research on FTZ women has demonstrated similar excited engagement with a new kind of world. Various comments from Shirtex and Serendib women show that they, too, thrived on their new social lives—even as they worked hard to balance their new life with traditional expectations for women. As I show below, these women do not consider what they do to be bad because they know that in the end they are still morally upright women, since they adhere to the core feature of traditional women's behavior—sexual chastity.

I examine these various changes in terms of three different categories: changes having to do with a new social life, those that have to do with hygiene, and those that have to do with appearance.

New Social Life

Cultivating a Good-girl identity made a new social life possible for the women at Shirtex and Serendib. Compared with unemployed village women, they behaved in a new manner simply by getting out of their houses more and through interacting with urban, middle-class male managers as well as male and female coworkers from various villages and castes. The social lives of village women of the same age group who did not work in the garment factory were considerably more restricted. The nonfactory women did not have the money or the social networks that formed the basis of this new social life. On their days off, garment workers frequently went to parties (mostly for weddings) and on trips with one another. For parties they sometimes donned nail polish and lipstick, cosmetics that although increasingly popular even among villagers were often associated with "outside" (*bāhira*) and immoral behavior—at the extreme, with prostitution.

If practiced by urban Juki girls, many of these behaviors would have been the focus of intense social criticism. But these women returned to their parents' homes at night and participated in village social and religious life. Even their trips confirmed their traditional nature: they usually went to Buddhist religious sites—which was appropriate in that one of the marks of a Good girl was concern with earning religious merit (*pin*). However, I went on a number of these pilgrimages and noted that they were punctuated by dancing and singing on the bus, flirting with boys in passing vehicles, and buying tourist trinkets at every stop along the way.

Even the trip to Samarakoon Sir's father's funeral was like this. The mood on the four-hour bus ride was festive, although the dancing and singing which normally occurs in a bus on a road trip was reserved for the return trip. There was a considerable amount of jokes, laughter, and gossip on the way to the funeral, but when the staff van passed the buses, the workers would become solemn, as if only mourning and social responsibility were on their minds. In the back seat of one bus, a few machine operators smiled and waved at men in passing vehicles. One motorcycle driver passed his address to them through the bus window, and a candy truck driver gave them lollipops. The women were performing an important social obligation and in so doing demonstrating that they were good. But they were also having a lot of fun—as they said, this funeral trip was both *full jolly* and *dukay* (sorrowful). These women were clearly carving out a way to be Good girls plus something else.

Wedding parties were an important aspect of this new social life. When a woman married, she usually hosted a special party for her coworkers on a Sunday near the day of her wedding (which, being scheduled whenever the astrologer deemed most auspicious, generally would fall on a weekday). One Sunday morning I stood at a bus stop in the center of a small town with the entire Serendib cutting section as we waited for a rented van that would bring us to a coworker's wedding party in a distant village. The women wore gorgeous ornate silk saris and matching blouses, golden sandals, shiny clutch bags, gold bangles, rings, and necklaces. Suddenly a small group huddled in a circle. I joined the circle to discover that they were passing around lipstick! When I expressed surprise, the women quickly told me that they would remove the lipstick before they returned home to their parents, brothers, and husbands who would object. Although they had the freedom to go off for a trip on the one day they could have done housework, they did not want to be perceived as too different from traditional women. They noted that the fact that the wedding was in a distant village clearly helped—nobody at the bride's

JUKI GIRLS, GOOD GIRLS

Figure 5. On one of their rare days off from work, these Serendib button section workers, dressed in their finest gold-threaded Kandyan saris, waited for a bus to take them to a coworker's wedding party. The woman on the right has a perfect "bump" hairstyle. Photo by Caitrin Lynch.

village would know them.[5] Indeed I never saw anybody wear lipstick to a local wedding.

A new style was central to this new life: Even a brief glance at unemployed village women showed that the factory workers had learned to behave, dress, and consume products in a new way. Garment workers participated in new consumption practices made available through economic liberalization and made desirable partly through the advertising, especially on television, that permeated the countryside (cf. Kemper 2001). Many factory women spent significant amounts of their wages on jewelry, clothing, and other personal items, as well as on household luxuries such as cassette players, televisions, and sewing machines.

When walking through a village, one could instantly distinguish garment workers from other village women by a certain style that included fancy sandals or shoes, umbrellas, neat skirts and blouses, and an imitation leather pocketbook with embossed Egyptian designs so common that I heard it referred to as "a garment bag" (*gāment bag ekak*). There was also a certain hairstyle especially popular among garment workers. Referred to as "the bump" (*bump eka*), the hair was pulled into a bump (or puff) at the front, clipped into place with a barrette, and the braid started up high. In itself, this hairstyle mediated a perceived divide between urban and rural Sri Lanka. Urban women were disparaged for wearing their hair cut short, but the factory women also wanted to distinguish themselves from village women who parted their long hair down the middle and braided it from the nape of the neck. Workers would often describe to me as a transformative moment when so-and-so coworker's hair went from a middle part to the bump hairstyle. No doubt because both short hair and bangs were widely said to signify moral looseness, there was only a handful of workers whose hair was either cut short or who had their hair at the front cut into bangs.

With their own cash to spend and new friends to accompany them, factory women frequently took shopping trips to Kandy, often without the supervision of parents or brothers. When I went with them, some would want me to tell the shopkeepers that we worked together at a garment factory, while others instructed me to keep mum in this regard. Sometimes they asked me to speak English to them when walking down the street so people would think they also know English. Similarly, some garment workers explicitly wanted to pass as white-collar workers. In spite of its disrespectable associations, many women desired garment work because it bestowed an aura of generic professionalism: They could wear nice clothes and go to work looking like any other commuter on the bus (cf. Mills 1999, 129). Though some women expressed a desire for the factory to require uniforms so that they would not ruin their own clothes, many said uniforms would make them too easily identified as garment workers.

Some women worked quite hard at passing as white-collar, buying certain kinds of clothing and traveling in less obvious garment factory groups than others. But even those who did not at least took the basic step of brushing off their bodies the telltale signs of factory employment: fabric dust and pieces of thread. A considerable amount of fabric dust floated through the factories, and by the end of the workday the hair of many factory workers would be covered with dust particles. At the end of the day the factory women would grab their bags and stand just outside the canteens, brushing their hair in unison and shaking thread off their clothes. Some women did not do so and rushed out the factory gates as fast as they could—but I sometimes heard critical comments from the others to the effect that such women did not care about their reputations. Nevertheless, as nice as they made themselves look at the end of the workday, the garment workers still were not quite right for society's moral critics. Chinta once told me that people could still smell their sweat in the bus ride on the way home, and it was because of sharing crowded buses with smelly garment workers that others looked down on them.

But even this everyday practice of ridding one's body of fabric dust hints at the workers' ambivalent attitudes toward their public profile. Efforts to pass as white-collar employees notwithstanding, my interlocutors often expressed their pride in being garment workers. As I indicated earlier, some women would invite me to tell other people that we knew each other from the factories. Likewise, many women carried the "garment bag" pocketbook, even though it worked as a visual cue that allowed critical comments to be directed against them in public.

Being Dirty and "Goḍē"

Recall Chandra's comments that when some women first came to work at Serendib they did not wash properly and smelled of sweat. "But then when they get a month's wage or two . . . they come looking beautiful the next month wearing perfume and powder. . . . Then they have fallen into society. Before that they lived with dirt dripping from their clothes. There are a lot of workers in our factory like that who have become stylish. People who came here in a rural [goḍē] manner." Piyasena used the same word when he said his daughter engaged in new social practices because she did not want to be perceived as being like rural people (goḍēma minissu). Derived from the noun goḍa (village), goḍē is an adjective that can mean "rural," with no negative connotation. It was generally used as such by the older generation of villagers. But when goḍē was used by younger villagers (such as the garment workers) and by city people it usually carried with it a very pejorative sense of being unsophisticated and backward. For instance, after waiting three hours in a village for a bus, which finally arrived dilapidated and overflowing with passengers, a factory friend remarked that it was an unacceptably goḍē thing to happen and would never occur in cities. My urban friends used goḍē as an adjective in English conversations to mean tacky, unsophisticated, and lacking style, as in "You can't wear such a goḍē shirt to the rugby match." The noun form (goḍaya), referring to villagers (rustics), was present in a popular expression urbanites used to describe the awe with which villagers met city life: *goḍayaṭa magic* (the city is so strange it is magical for the rustic).

The term *goḍē* is often contrasted to the term *diyunuy* (developed, progressive, modern). Garment workers often told me that they worked or studied in order to *diyunu wenna*, or prosper, improve, develop. There is a long history of an association between being clean and being civilized in Sri Lanka, as evidenced by Dharmapala's efforts to introduce a new sanitized and moral daily behavior among Sinhalas. The anthropologist Susan Reed (2002, 255) has discussed this correlation between cleanliness and modernity in reference to transformations in the status of Kandyan dancers and drummers in the late twentieth century. She writes of how these artists' bodies became respectable through changes in dress, hair, and shoe style, and how "comportment and cleanliness became important in their redefinition as respectable teachers and artists." Reed quotes an informant: "Now the performers are clean, they have changed. That is what is called development" (2002, 255–56).

Chandra's comments about women using perfume and powder once they got their first paycheck and no longer having "dirt dripping from their clothes," along with Chinta's observations about people looking down on garment workers on buses because of body odor, are both meaningful in terms of Sinhala Buddhist nationalist concerns about hygiene, discipline, morality, and modernity. They resonate with Premadasa's promises about the advent of discipline in the countryside through the introduction of factories. Recall this 1992 Sinhala-language newspaper article about the social effects of the 200 GFP factories: "The young men and women in villages will get in the habit of dressing smartly and going to work. . . . Rustic [*goḍē*] village young men, women, and their parents will become disciplined by learning various things about traveling, food, clothing, housing, good habits [*cāritra*], etc." (Hettigoda 1992). Related to this vision was one of the points on Anthony Fernando's list of changes brought on by the establishment of rural factories: "They started taking a closer look at what they were wearing and went in for smarter clothing" (Fernando n.d.).

Chandra spoke here about consumption in relation to hygiene and modernity. Not only was she speaking of a newly hygienic modernity in which women participated, but she was also speaking about how they spent their money. Women spent their factory wages in different ways—supporting their families, saving for a dowry or for building a house, spending on educational ventures, and consuming things that could be considered "luxury" items, such as the latest fashionable skirt, purse, cassette tape, or perfume. Chandra's comment about girls with dirty clothes was about modernity refracted through the lens of hygiene and beauty. Various coworkers spoke of the ways in which they were exposed to "society" (*samāje*) through factory work, and Chandra spoke of modern hygiene indicating entry into society. But for her the entry was almost accidental—they have "fallen" into society.

Chandra was one among many Shirtex and Serendib workers who correlated being stylish with being less rural. Nevertheless, theirs was also a hygienic stylishness that demonstrated that they were disciplined, and therefore Good girls. Although she was speaking of her own cohort, Chandra and the 200 GFP commentators alike made moral claims about the social transformations resulting from garment factory employment. They all spoke from within a social environment in which discipline, morality, and tradition were important ideals. However, whereas the 200 GFP commentators wrote about Premadasa's promise to raise backwards villagers to acceptable standards of hygiene, bodily practice, and so on, Chandra was speaking with obvious pride about how she and her coworkers had incorporated a greater measure of modernity.

Dark Skin and Paddy-Field Work

Shirtex and Serendib women's ambivalence about the new, modern lives that factory work made possible is also seen in their reactions to an anecdote that I discussed with workers and others on many occasions. Through an American friend, I had heard of a woman who chose to work in a garment factory because she did not want to get dark (*kalu*, also the word for "black") working in a paddy field. This anecdote encapsulates notions about race, class, modernity, and gender that I was exploring in my research, and it was a dependable conversation-starter whenever I wished to discuss such issues with my factory friends.

Many women told me that if they did not have their jobs they would likely have stayed home, being "bored" (*kammäli*) and doing household work. They said they would have also done work in paddy fields on an occasional basis. If their family owned land, this would have been unpaid labor. If not, they would have worked in exchange for rice or a small wage. Many rejected the option of working in Colombo out of hand, either out of fear for their safety and reputation, or because their parents or husbands would have ruled it out for the same reasons. If their only choice was between paddy field and garment factory work, they preferred a permanent indoor job at a factory to irregular outdoor daily wage labor (*kulī wäḍe*). Garment factory jobs yielded higher wages, from which they could purchase items for their own use that made them feel, and look to others, like modern people (for instance, cassette players, the latest fashionable pocketbook, or gold jewelry). They also preferred factory work because it gave them the chance to pass as office workers—something not possible for agricultural workers for one significant reason that I describe below.

When I would relate this story of a woman preferring garment factory work over getting dark in a paddy field, my factory friends would pause only briefly before asking, "That means, when you work in a factory you get pretty? Like that?" Often they would immediately debunk this idea by explaining that factory labor made them weaker and worse-looking than they would be otherwise. Some noted that they lost weight because of not eating properly (losing weight was negatively valued: body fat is a marker of wealth and surplus). They also pointed out that they were often ill with stomachaches and headaches. Some noted that their skin had indeed become lighter but that was attributed to the effect of the florescent lights. As Kumari put it, "In one way it's better to stay outside, feeling the wind, better than getting boiled [*tambanawa*] inside because of the lights."

Despite these protests, the women all agreed on what the story meant. Sita explained that working in the sun made your skin get dark and made you look ugly and old. Others would say that boys did not like girls with dark skin. These points were clearly supported by the prevalent ideals of beauty in Sri Lanka, epitomized by the models for Fair and Lovely skin bleaching cream that was for sale in even small village *kadē*s (cf. Fuller 2006). It was fair-skinned girls who were consistently chosen as the princesses (*avurudu kumāri*) at Sinhala New Year's festivals, and indeed fair skin was one of the traditional criteria for their selection. At another 200 GFP factory I asked the only female manager I ever met if the women workers had changed since they began work two years previously. Without a moment of hesitation she responded, "Yes, truthfully, the girls were dark" (*ow, kalu wela hiṭiya, ättaṭama*). She explained that they had been dark from working in the fields outside, but now they never went out in the sun. She added, "They look better now." I later asked some women at this factory why they did not like to do agricultural work and the conversation immediately turned into joking banter about not wanting to be dark.

The valuation of fair skin as an index of beauty is connected to ethnic and class divisions in Sri Lanka. It has implications for the relationship between Sinhalas and Tamils in contemporary Sri Lanka, where the Orientalist construction of Aryans and Dravidians has a strong place in the popular imagination: Sinhalas are considered fair-skinned Aryans, and Tamils are considered dark-skinned Dravidians. The historian R. A. L. H. Gunawardana has explored how the association of Sinhalas with fair skin developed in line with the application of Orientalist linguistic and racial constructions to Tamils and Sinhalas. He has shown that the association between fair skin and beauty is a post-Orientalist development, which today is understood as ancient (Gunawardana 1990; cf. Trautmann 1997). In modern Sri Lanka these notions are so ingrained as to be common sense. One day a factory friend and I encountered a woman we didn't know on a village path. After a casual conversation that included some comments about recent government defeats in the war, my friend asked the woman if she was Tamil and the woman said, "No, I'm just dark because I do farm work."

As a result of the colonial legacy, high-paid, salaried government positions are considered a social ideal, and people with such jobs are generally thought to have lighter skin than others, their offices keeping them from being darkened by the sun. Having a white-collar job also means having money for consuming luxury items. Garment workers were often able to pass as such white-collar workers when they went to town for shopping expeditions. Dark skin thus projected a set of negative connotations: rural origin, backwardness, separation from the modern white-collar world. The overall picture is reminiscent of Orientalist constructions of dark-skinned savages. Thomas Trautmann (1997, 70) describes the short-lived theory on skin pigmentation of the early anthropologist James Cowles Prichard, according to which the process of civilization lightens the skin. The associations among class, tradition, and fair skin in Sri Lanka imply a similar construction, but here it is the modern that enables fair skin.

Workers' ambivalence about associating themselves with Sri Lankan modernity is seen in their dual reactions to the story of the woman who did not want to get darkened by paddy-field work. The workers wanted to be associated with the rural because it was socially and physically safe, but it was also backward and they wanted to be seen as developed/progressive (*diyunu*), not *gode*. Because many young people refuse to work in paddy fields, parents are forced to hire people to work their land. As Susila once put it, factory workers are the people who used to work in fields, "but now they think the factory is better than the fields. . . . I think it's because their nails become black and because they get mud on their nails or because their nails get dirty, and then there's no time to polish them." Likewise, Piyasena also told me that girls who used to work breaking stones in quarries now refuse to do that work. He said that they would rather dress proudly and go for a job. But even Piyasena seemed to have contradictory opinions on what garment work meant for the society. He, as well as other people, said that the positive aspect of these factories was that the factory women had become more "used to society" and less shy than unemployed village women.

As this paddy-field anecdote and Chandra's comment about "dirt dripping from their clothes" indicate, for many Shirtex and Serendib women being stylish was about being less rural. In certain aspects of their appearance and behavior these women distanced themselves from both their rural and class origins. But despite the new styles and behaviors they displayed, whether in choice of clothing or boyfriends, they did not go beyond a certain level of departure from village norms. Like other Sinhala Buddhists, garment workers conceptually linked together villages, paddy-field work, and Sinhala tradition and female morality; and they thus struggled over their distaste for agricultural work, both admitting and denying it in their reactions to my story.

Consumption and Discipline

Shirtex and Serendib women were sometimes criticized by other villagers for aping Western behavior through consumption practices that were said to obscure their village roots, causing them to stand out from other villagers and appear more like city people. Similarly, I heard middle-class urban people express concern that it was difficult to differentiate between garment factory girls and Kandy girls in shopping centers in Kandy. Such censure was an attempt on the part of people from different social positions to maintain a dichotomy between the rural (the traditional, authentic Sinhala) and the urban (the modern, Westernized, corrupt Sinhala). Different interests converged in the same ideology: For villagers, staying on the rural side of this dichotomy carried with it a sense of pride (for being authentic); for city people, staying on the urban side carried with it a sense of power (for being wealthy and forward-looking).

But neither category of people maintained the dichotomies without contradiction. While city people often saw villagers as backward, they simultane-

JUKI GIRLS, GOOD GIRLS

ously valorized their identity as authentically Sri Lankan. And while villagers saw in Colombo social danger, many still desired to be associated with the city, particularly through consumption practices. Since economic liberalization in 1977, global commodities had flooded the Sri Lankan market. These new goods were generally associated with Colombo, perhaps because they first became available in Colombo, and moreover because through the mass media such items had been portrayed as urban—this was especially true of television advertising and teledramas (Kemper 2001).

According to villagers with whom I spoke, in the Udakande area changes in consumption practices became more pronounced after the garment factories opened in 1992. Monthly factory wages put more money into circulation and demand expanded for staple and luxury items alike. Many new *kadēs* opened and old shops expanded. The Provincial Council minister told me that whereas prior to the factory openings villagers had had to go to Kandy to buy items as basic as "a watch, a shirt, or a skirt for a child," now village shops carried those items and more—"things like plates, cups, aluminum houseware, clothes, sewing machines, radios, and clocks."

I frequently heard comments about the spending habits of 200 GFP women from people other than workers—from their parents, local government officials, managers, and factory owners. Whether critical or supportive, the mere fact that this was a topic deserving comment revealed the pervasiveness of nationalist concerns about disciplined female behavior. Such concerns with spending and discipline were part of the 200 GFP program design from the start. Perhaps because these concerns were constitutive of the program, all factory owners and program officials invariably spoke to me about the vast amounts of money released for circulation in the villages—thus drawing together a newly disciplined citizenry with access to consumption practices. The Provincial Council minister told me in an interview in Sinhala that he had once met a garment worker he knew depositing money at the bank. He cited her transformation as indicating development (*diyunuy*): "She was so poor that when she first came to work at the garment factory she didn't even have a pair of sandals. That day she had come to the bank to deposit money. She had 70,000 rupees in her account. The girl who came to the garment factory without even two sandals now has a gold bangle on her hand, a nice gold chain around her neck, and had saved 70,000 rupees. This is development." The amount in her bank account was the equivalent of two years' salary. Being clean, building a proper home, eating well, and saving money: all good things for the nation's development, according to this politician.

I often heard from managers, owners, and officials this heroic discourse about the promise for the nation of the consumer practices of a disciplined (and self-disciplined) citizenry. But there was another somewhat hidden discourse about this relationship between consumption and discipline. I picked up on this undercurrent more often in speaking with parents and managers who were closer to the action, but it was also present in the comments of others. I offer four out of many possible examples.

The Politician

Immediately after his comment about the girl who saved 70,000 rupees, the minister added: "Now a lot of girls think it is a good thing if you have a chain around your neck and gold bangles on your arm, and if you have put on two nice sandals and an outfit. It is a custom of Sri Lankan society that people are judged like this. If a girl wears good shoes and dresses well then people think she is a good person. . . . If these people are taught that a person is not measured by gold then they will save money and invest in economically fruitful ventures."

Managers

Many managers told me that there was a relationship between personal appearance and factory productivity, that neat women were productive workers. They would take this correspondence into account in making hiring decisions and hire a neatly dressed worker over someone with a missing button on her dress. But some managers also complained to me that some workers dressed as if they were going to a party and not coming to work on a factory production line.

A Scholar

In a discussion about Shirtex and Serendib workers, a university lecturer commented to me that "these people" spend money as though they were in a higher social class than the one they really belonged to; their spending habits were not in line with their income. Because of this, she said, once they stopped working they would not have raised themselves to a higher social standing; their incomes were not being used toward future development.

A Father

Kanthi's father complained to me about his daughter's frivolous spending. He had many examples, but the main one that he repeatedly mentioned was that his daughter owned not one but *two* cassette players. When I asked Kanthi about this she told me she had bought the second one because a friend was selling it for a really good price.

These four critical comments about women's spending habits point to a problem of disproportionate spending—disproportionate, that is, from the perspective of others who want to monitor workers' spending habits and who want to see the new access to money open opportunities for them to become a certain kind of citizen, not necessarily something of their own making. In fact, these were critiques of the workers' active construction of a new Goodgirl style. For instance, regarding the way they dressed at the factories, the workers' perspective was simply that they were enjoying the new modern world of style they were constructing while at the same time managing to pass as respectable workers on their commute. But some managers seemed to be concerned about keeping class divisions straight: this was not the correct way for girls like that to dress and spend their money.

These conflicting readings of what women should and should not do with their wages indicate a deficiency in the 200 GFP response to the underwear critique. The notion that garment workers would remain Good girls because villages were natural bastions of tradition could hold true only if local women's ability to respond creatively to the transformation in their social position were not taken into account. The women themselves would have generally agreed that their new consumer practices and behaviors kept them within the realm of nationalist discipline; they were not suddenly acting nontraditional. But they were at the same time becoming associated with new styles and ways of being that marked them with the urban and modern.

In the previous chapter I introduced Gamini Sir, who worked as a manager when Shirtex first opened. I quote extensively an exchange that occurred well into an English-language interview with him. It is provocative for its explication of how factory work affects villagers. I encourage readers to ask: Was Gamini Sir speaking of an emergent mode of being Good girls?

Caitrin: Have the workers changed since they came to the factory?
Gamini Sir: They have got posh. They have got social, right? So that is

very important. They were very timid and all and now they are social in the sense, they can share their views with anybody in the society. They are not afraid to talk. Even their eating habits would have developed. I can remember at the beginning, when they had the canteen, there were girls who used to come and eat and just at the beginning they would make the place untidy. But in time to come, they develop and they learn how to eat properly and where to keep their plates and all. . . . They would have learned to wear clean clothes. Now if they were just at home they would have just lived untidily, and by looking at the other people, nice looking, their nice clothing and all, so they would have definitely learned something in their life.

Caitrin: How do they become more social? Why?

Gamini Sir: More social in the sense they have the opportunity to move with various types of people. Right? Otherwise they were just at home, they were in the villages. You know, they don't, in a funeral or something or a wedding or something like that only [do] they get the opportunity to talk to each other. Otherwise they will just talk to their neighbor and their ideas are same. They don't know new things. But when they get together in the factory . . . one fellow is coming from one area, another is [from] a different area. So they discuss. And they discuss about their school period [when they went to school]. They will ask which school you went [to] and how their school [was]. And it might apply to their family members. I mean they will say, "This school is good, we will put our sister or brother in this school. So-and-so told me this school is better, this teacher is good." Like that, you know, even they will learn something about the area. "That area is better than our area. Our neighbor[hood] is not that good." They will say, "Our neighbors are just, they are good, or they are bad. But so-and-so said their neighbors are [incomplete thought]." They will discuss about various societies you get in these various village places. They have, like, this Lions Club and all, in the villages also you get, organizations. So they will say, "In that village they have better *samitiya* [organizations]. So it is better to start in our village also something," they will say. Like that, there is an improvement, an unseen improvement.

Caitrin: Do some people think that is bad, that women are becoming less traditional?

Gamini Sir: But still they haven't gone out from their culture. Right? They are still in their villages. Still they are with their parents. While they are learning something they are still with the culture, no? They are not corrupted. That is very important. That is very important for any society, as long as they protect their culture and they are well behaved, that is very useful. Whether they earn millions and millions, if their culture is not changed, if their behavior pattern is not changed that is . . . most important. Behavior pattern, as long as it develops in a good way. Because they are always bound to somebody. Villagers. Even when we were in the village, we . . . used to listen to our parents always. What they used to guide us. But when you are living alone, we have our own ideas, right?

Gamini Sir's responses were given in terms by now familiar to readers: that workers have learned how to eat and dress better (paragraph one), that they have learned things about society (paragraph two), and that because they stay in villages they are well-behaved and traditional Good girls (paragraph three). Gamini Sir did not offer any of the critical comments about the behavior of factory workers that I heard from many other people—for example, comments about how they dressed and what they spent their money on, or their "love affairs." Like Gamini Sir, reporters and other 200 GFP supporters who wrote in 1992 when the program started also provided this sort of uncritical and fulsome assessment of the new factories' effect on villages and village women. Officials and factory owners also spoke like this, rarely including critical comments.

Throughout the interview whenever I asked Gamini Sir questions about factory policies on productivity, discipline, leave, and the like he repeated that because he had only been at Shirtex for the first year he could not be too sure what things were like now. But he did not seem to have the same caveat in regard to comments on social change. His comments did not really take into account what was happening on the ground. So while the women would have agreed that they were learning new ways of being from their factory experiences (paragraphs one and two), his comments on whether or not culture is changing (paragraph three) may not have been quite on target; they did not take into account how women were actually constructing a Good-girl identity out of their new factory lives.

The Attraction and Repulsion of the Urban

In the face of the changes in wealth distribution and the access to new consumption practices introduced among rural Sri Lankans as a result of the 200

GFP, how has a new division between rural and urban been produced in everyday discourse and practice? Jonathan Spencer (1992, 385) has argued that various words (in Sinhala and English) for *urban* and *rural* carry with them implications of differential access to wealth, power and knowledge. Of the village in which he did research, he writes that urban (*tavumbaḍa* [*town-baḍa*]) and rural (*gambaḍa* or *piṭisara*) "are key diacriticals in the language of local class relations" (1990a, 127). Spencer also says that rural people use the terms in a straightforward manner, to refer to rich people (urban) and poor (rural). He then explains that although for urban and rural people the terms are used easily, and with seeming clarity, "the simple dichotomy of town and country may serve to obfuscate and conceal other powerful divisions—between rich and poor, powerful and powerless, knowers and known-about" (1992, 385).

While this can certainly be said to represent the case in the community I studied, there are yet other divisions that this simple urban and rural dichotomy obscures: divisions between the poor and the rich *within* urban and rural Sri Lanka and divisions along the lines of gender between the experiences of poor men and poor women generally in both urban and rural Sri Lanka. A young village woman imagines at least two Colombos, and imagines them with ambivalence. There is Colombo as the elite power center—the Colombo of Royal College, Majestic City shopping mall, Mercedes-Benz cars, and Parliament. But there is also Colombo as the magnet for the landless rural poor—the Colombo of the shantytown dwellers by the Kelaniya River and low-paid workers in the Katunayake FTZ. Both these Colombos symbolize the polluting or corrupting power of wealth. Urban elites are maligned for economic, political, and cultural corruption; and the urban poor are maligned for succumbing to such evil influences. But both Colombos also hold some appeal for some villagers: the former for the world of money, fashion, and modernity; the latter for a chance at accessing this world.

Compared to village women, village men seemed more able to meet success and tap into the wealth of Colombo, since they were less socially vulnerable to a spoiled reputation. In fact, social and biological reproduction are conjoined here: as I was often told, since men were not in danger of coming back to their villages with their bodies marked by transgression—that is, being pregnant—they were more mobile and could live the urban life with a higher degree of social ease, more easily accessing its opportunities. The urban therefore meant something different for rural men and women. Women think of it as a place where poor village women are forced into prostitution. Their desire is to participate in a modern, urban life that is nevertheless safe, both physically and socially. They want to inhabit an imagined urban social space somewhere between that of the corrupt elite and the downtrodden poor.

Why is the urban at all attractive for rural women in spite of its obvious negative features? For the rural poor, and particularly for women who feel constrained by their families, the urban offers a chance at social status, wealth, power, and generally the possibility of more control over their lives. It also offers a chance at an escape from the stigma of being rural. But because there are risks in attempting to inhabit such an urban space, new production and consumption practices in villages brought along with the 200 GFP social transformations have offered women a chance at the advantages of urbanity in the comfort of their own villages. The Good girls at Shirtex and Serendib saw themselves as, and took pride in being, modern working women and not simply *goḍē* villagers. Yet their behavior still needed to be respectable, falling on the "good" side of a good/bad moral dichotomy pervasive in Sinhala life. They were at pains to give the impression that they adhered to what are considered traditional Sinhala Buddhist values, especially the cardinal one of sexual morality. Given the association between village locatedness and moral purity, staying at home enabled these women to construct a new mode of being Good girls. Finally, there was even a certain moral protection offered by being known as Good girls from Shirtex and Serendib.

GΣΣTA

Untitled

Free Trade Zones in Sri Lanka are important for industrial development and as a means of job growth.

When you analyze the garment factory concept in Sri Lanka, you could see the weaknesses of the concept and the system.

The weaknesses of the system could be summarized as follows.

The garment industry mostly uses women's labor. As a developing nation, Sri Lanka has a surplus of labor supply. It is easy to exploit the economically unstable women to obtain cheap labor for industry. Although the freedom of women is a widely discussed subject nowadays, it is obvious that the women employed in the garment industry have become slaves.

The normal work shift begins usually at seven o'clock in the morning and ends at four o'clock in the evening. This is a health hazard. Women employed in this industry have being diagnosed with illnesses such as blindness, headache, heart problems, and so on. They may be subjected to reduced life expectancy. We cannot be satisfied about the pay we get after working hard for eight hours.

In addition, the freedom of speech, the freedom of expressing ideas has been suppressed. Freely expressing ideas will most certainly lead to dismissal. Working at night is a great threat to the continuity of lives. Marriage breakups could happen. Lifestyle and routines may worsen. Night work also causes transportation problems for many women. That had led to instances of some women becoming prostitutes. Though it is possible for workers to continue their education while employed, night work has become an obstacle to such activities as well as a hindrance to their kids' educational activities. People are turned into machines. There are many instances where the parents' night work has forced kids to become distanced from their parents.

A division of labor results in women not learning the whole trade, and they are stressed as they engage in monotonous work throughout the day.

They should have the privilege of obtaining leave whenever it is necessary.

It is a hindrance to the social respectability of the women. The decline of cultural values is a common occurrence. Even though the women get economic freedom, they are forced to neglect part of their duties to kids and family.

If you conduct research on women working in the garment industry, it is easy to realize that unjustifiable and unreasonable treatment of women is a widespread problem. Often these women are subjected to abuse and insult.

6. PATERNALISM AND FACTORY CONFLICTS

Investors and managers understood their own efforts to bring industry to villages within Sri Lankan conceptions of the rural and the urban, tradition and modernity, masculinity and femininity. When factory representatives implemented policies that were attuned to these challenges, they created a manager-worker dynamic that was structured by paternalism and face-to-face relations. In this chapter I examine the administration of these policies through the frame of "welfare capitalism," a widespread managerial doctrine that mandates employers to monitor workers' lives inside and outside factories, on the assumption that high worker morale leads to increased factory efficiency and productivity. I analyze manager-worker relationships under such a system from the perspectives of both the management and the workers. The second half of the chapter turns to an examination of conflicts within and around the factories in the context of paternalistic and face-to-face managerial practices as well as that of the Juki stigma.

An analysis of several examples of conflicts that cropped up at the factories can shed light on how Sri Lankans involved in the garment industry were wrestling to make sense of and live comfortably in a social world that had changed considerably since the country's 1977 economic reforms. Through discussion of three ethnographic vignettes—a walkout, a skit about "love sickness," and a Western dance contest—I demonstrate that conflicts inside and outside the factories were occasions on which village women struggled to forge positive identities in the face of conflicting messages they received about the value of their labor and their new lives as female factory workers.

President Premadasa hoped to attract business owners to invest in the 200 Garment Factories Program out of "social conscience." Over and above the economic incentives, Premadasa offered less tangible benefits: the investors could understand their profits in terms of "traditional" values. In the 200 GFP inaugural speech, Premadasa forecast that the rural workers will "respect and honour the people who invest, realising that it is because of them that they are earning a livelihood" (Special Correspondent 1992a). In various speeches, he described uplifting the poor and reviving the dormant but innate value of discipline as program goals. He quoted one investor who addressed the simultaneous economic and social incentives for investing: "A certain investor participating in the two hundred garment factories program said at the opening of his factory recently that the capitalists in the country were today becoming philanthropists because of the economic policy of the government. That investor by that statement aptly and succinctly summed up the economic vision of our government" (Fernando and Fernandopulle 1992, n.p.). Premadasa was quite careful to describe the attendant values as native to Sri Lanka. By invoking notions such as the "open economy with a human face" and "capitalists-as-philanthropists" he worked to make economic liberalization and capitalist development consistent with Sinhala Buddhist values.

Investors were told that they were performing a public service by providing greatly needed jobs to poor villagers. Investors were also strongly encouraged to treat their workers charitably in order "to bring about a meaningful relationship between the rich and the poor for their mutual benefit" (Fernando 1992d, 15). Reporters described the "social conscience" required for investors to participate:

> The President said the rich, the haves—would not think that the wealth they had acquired or inherited was their own for their own enjoyment—for them to do anything with.
>
> "On the contrary, they should think their wealth is something they had in trust, for the benefit of the entire society. This type of social conscience is a must for any success of any system of government," he pointed out.
>
> Even in the society in the time of our ancient kings, economic activ-

ity was guided by social conscience and collective effort. (Fernando 1992e, 17)

All the Sri Lankan investors whom I interviewed cited economic incentives to invest; most also said they were motivated in large part by the ability to provide a social service to the rural poor. Some of these investors interviewed had also been quoted to this effect in the newspapers when the 200 GFP began. For instance, one article quoted the chairman of the Sri Lanka Apparel Exporters' Association at the time, a prominent industrialist whom other investors looked to for leadership. The chairman invoked the notion that participating in this program is a social service, and he also implied that investors were true patriots. He said: "Our entrepreneurs should have a worthy intention and aim. What is that? It is the desire to build up our motherland. There is no use for entrepreneurs who have no feeling for the country. Only those who really feel for the country should join this garment industry program. The most important thing that they should realize is that the development that is gained through this program cannot be achieved even in a hundred years without such a program" (Amararatne 1992a, n.p.). Another article noted that a managing director "said that his company decided to participate in the garment factories program as they wished to contribute towards the efforts to provide employment to rural youth and upgrade the quality of living of the country's peasantry" (Fernando 1992f, n.p.).

Welfare Capitalism at Shirtex and Serendib

For many 200 GFP investors, it was a logical step from establishing factories out of social conscience to implementing paternalistic factory policies. Factory paternalism has a long history, but it has been especially associated with the American industrialist Henry Ford. Ford famously adopted a "welfare capitalist" system where the employer focused on worker morale to increase efficiency and productivity (Meyer 1981). With productivity and workplace loyalty as his ultimate goals, he instituted various methods to ensure that his autoworkers were healthy, satisfied with their jobs, but also internally competitive and divided. Bonuses became linked to production rates, and his "Sociological Department" monitored outside-of-work behavior (clothes styles, household cleanliness, spending habits) to ensure that the employer had total control over the workers. As other American corporations adopted the Fordist model in subsequent decades, the period from the 1920s to the 1960s witnessed the height of welfare capitalism and its built-in paternalism: "Companies built cafeterias and health clinics, sponsored baseball and bowling leagues, and granted days off for the opening of deer season" (Gross 2004, n.p.).

The paternalistic monitoring of workers' lives was key to the Fordist model and has been adopted in other places in the world in industrial as well as nonindustrial work settings. In her study of early to mid-twentieth-century Colombian industrialization, the historian Ann Farnsworth-Alvear (2000, 17) describes the adoption of a model of welfare capitalism. Although much in the Colombian methods was similar to the Fordist model, Farnsworth-Alvear uses the term "welfare capitalism" in a more general sense "to describe employers' interest in combining an older paternalistic tradition with the progressive adoption of imported technology, as well as their self-positioning as social engineers."

Research about women workers in factories and on plantations elsewhere has demonstrated that often company self-interest is disguised as benevolent paternalism (D. Wolf 1992, 124). Managers deploy local social hierarchies (including gender norms) to create a disciplined workforce (Farnsworth-Alvear 2000, 115). Paternalistic practices have included management calling female workers "our girls" and using familial pronouns, keeping track of women's after-work behavior, or offering classes in nutrition, mothering, and domestic education. The company philosophy at one electronics factory in Malaysia is posted throughout the building: "to create one big family, to train workers, to increase loyalty to company, country and fellow workers" (Ong 1987, 170). At the same factory, parents are given tours to reassure them that their daughters work in a protected environment.[1]

Shirtex's Asanka Sir and Serendib's Tissa Sir, the managing directors and primary investors, were strong advocates of the social service orientation of the 200 GFP. In newspaper articles as well as in discussions with me, they both said that they invested in the program at least in part because it allowed them to help poor villagers. They endeavored to create a work environment that was intensely personal, paternalistic, community-related, and localized. They frequently discussed with their managers the importance of personal connections to workers and the area villages; and they implemented various policies that encouraged personal connections between the factory representatives and the workforce, their families, and other villagers.

JUKI GIRLS, GOOD GIRLS

Factory production and discipline revolved around face-to-face, personal relationships. A dominant theme I heard from managers was the sense of their duty to help workers lead proper lives. When I discussed manager-worker relations with workers, the themes that most often arose were their personal connections to managers, their respect for managers, and the complicated effects of status hierarchies within the factories. I turn now to examine managerial perspectives on paternalism, and then workers' perspectives on personal connections and status.

Managerial Perspectives on Paternalism

Factory representatives considered their interest in workers' personal lives to be a natural part of their job duties. On a case-by-case basis, managers frequently contributed to workers' family funeral costs, awarded time off for exams or classes, hired workers' relatives, and advised women workers on proper relationships with men. One of the main forces behind these informal arrangements at Serendib was Ralph Sir, the production manager, who hailed from an English-speaking Colombo family. Ralph Sir took his job seriously and was intensely concerned with factory productivity, which he considered to be related to workers' lives outside of work. In our frequent conversations about the factories, he continually came back to women workers' personal lives. Ralph Sir's sisters and fiancée were roughly the same age as the Serendib workers. He often compared his strategies for looking after Serendib women's welfare to how he would watch out for his sister and fiancée.

One afternoon, as we stood at the head of the production lines having a conversation in English about the usual topics of production, discipline, Good girls, and so forth, Ralph Sir told me the following story. That morning a machine operator had shown up for work after a two-week unexcused absence. Ralph Sir was very angry with her, and he called her into his office for an explanation. He said he spoke to her very "lovingly" and asked her why she was absent. She immediately began to cry and so he sent her back to her machine. Her line supervisor then came and told him that the truant worker had been raped. Ralph Sir called the woman back to his office and told her that she could not have her job back unless she married the man who had raped her and returned to show him the marriage certificate. He told me he did this because Sri Lankan women cannot be unwed mothers—she would be kicked out of her house and become a beggar in the street. I assume here that the implication was that this woman had been raped some time ago but had missed work after finding out she was pregnant. Ralph Sir argued that the only solution for this woman's future would be for her to marry the rapist.

I remember being shocked that not only was Ralph Sir policing this woman's personal life, but also that he would require her to marry a man who raped her. He considered it his role to teach women and to protect them. Women in various parts of the world have been expected to marry their rapist to recoup the woman's honor.[2] Although it is not a widespread and legally sanctioned practice in Sri Lanka, it certainly is conceivable that some Sri Lankan parents might force their daughter to marry a man who raped her.[3] The assumption here would be that if a woman loses her virginity before marriage and does not marry the man to whom she lost it, she will either become a prostitute or will at least be considered one. Better than the stigma of unwed motherhood is marriage to a man with poor character.

So, why would Ralph Sir require her to marry her rapist? Perhaps he had a complicated interpretation of what the woman meant by "rape." Although this may have been a case of what we would call "stranger rape" or "date rape," Ralph Sir may have assumed that the man who raped this woman was her boyfriend, and that what the woman was calling *rape* was consensual sex. Ultimately, I do not know whether the woman was raped or engaged in consensual sex, nor do I know whether or not the woman would have wanted to marry the man. I regret that the woman's perspective on this story is absent from my analysis, since Ralph Sir, appropriately, never told me who she was. It would be extremely unlikely for an unmarried woman to admit to having gotten pregnant after engaging in consensual sex. To protect her honor, it would be more respectable for a woman to say she was raped—though in both cases her reputation would be negatively affected since she had lost her virginity. Since morally it is simply unacceptable for a woman to have premarital sex, and since the woman will not be accepted by society afterward, her reputation and morality can be recovered only through marrying the boyfriend. In this conception, then, Ralph Sir may have been trying to help the woman by telling her to marry her boyfriend—and as her manager, he felt he could essentially hold her job hostage until she complied. Even if Ralph Sir thought the woman was raped, either by her boyfriend or by someone else, he might have been ultimately concerned to make sure she was not an unwed mother.

Regardless of what Ralph Sir thought the woman meant when she said she had been raped, he may have been motivated both by concerns about the woman's future and concerns about factory productivity: Why lose a good worker to the strictures of moral purity and reputation? Moreover, if there had been an unwed mother working at Serendib, that would have affected the image of the factory as a whole, as well as the reputations of the other women who worked there and other prospective employees. His strict action of requiring her to marry her rapist or leave the factory may have reflected his concern about keeping and attracting a productive workforce in the future.

Ralph Sir habitually brought women's moral behavior into our discussions about factory productivity. Many workers spoke of the relationship between themselves and the managers in terms of a student-teacher model; and Ralph Sir took the model to heart, adopting the role of the teacher who imparts moral instruction in addition to instructions on operating a sewing machine. On another occasion, Ralph Sir told me that he once saw a worker's boyfriend waiting for her eagerly outside the factory on payday. Workers were paid in cash, which meant the boyfriend would have gotten instant gratification by dipping into his girlfriend's wage. The next day Ralph Sir called the worker in and talked to her about "protecting her wage for herself."

He and his colleagues generally considered the workers at the two factories Good girls. However, when factory productivity was at stake, accusations of being bad girls surfaced, and female sexual morality was central to this anxiety. Typical of his consistent concern with policing women's morality, Ralph Sir told me that he once fired three bad girls who had worked in FTZ factories before Serendib was built near their villages. These girls, he explained in English, had become "corrupted" in the FTZ, and after returning home to work at Serendib they tried to teach "stunts" to the other workers. He recalled how these women would lie to their parents about their hours of employment. They had become accustomed to having boyfriends in the FTZ, so they misreported the factory work schedule in order to have time for illicit liaisons in the village. They would leave work at 5:30, meet their boyfriends for an hour, and go home at seven, telling their parents that they had worked until 6:30. The three also pulled other stunts. They did not report for work on days required for overtime, and they took unexcused absences on normal workdays. Ralph Sir eventually fired them by referring to violations of factory rules.

Although some of these "stunts" would not directly affect productivity, by eroding parents' trust in management's ability to control and protect their daughters such behavior could lead to parents prohibiting their daughters from working at the factory, thus diminishing the available workforce. Often parents allowed their daughters to work because they trusted the management to act in loco parentis. Ralph Sir was exemplary—but not alone—in his concern with women's morality and factory productivity. Similarly, Serendib's Chanaka Sir, an assistant production manager, told me in an interview in English that he had once "chased off" a worker named Champi after he found out she was "going here and there" with a boy. He told her supervisor to tell her not to work for a day because of this behavior. Instead Champi came to him and apologized, which Chanaka Sir took to mean she would change her ways. He let her resume work. He told me he did this "to guide her properly, in life." He said that by doing this he tells girls, "Don't do this kind of thing, you will get lost and you will lose your family life, everything."

Ralph Sir told me many times in English that he preferred to hire women straight out of school who had not yet become "spoiled." He especially did not like to hire women who had previously worked in the FTZs, although he sometimes did so because of labor shortages or for other reasons. He and other managers frequently used the term *Good girl* in conversations with me and among themselves about specific workers and factory production. Decisions about discipline in certain instances were influenced by whether or not the managers considered the worker a Good girl. For instance, almost every day after lunch one Good girl named Mallika returned to the Shirtex production floor late but was never punished, whereas a worker who was not considered a Good girl would be reprimanded for returning late just once. Productivity was key: Mallika could come late because she always worked at or above the target rate. Likewise, managers did not stop me if I sat down to chat with a Good girl at her machine. But Yohan Sir, the Shirtex production manager, often called me away from speaking with (and hence distracting) certain workers who he would then tell me were sewing under target or producing damaged garments. For managers, productivity was the main determinant of whether or not a woman was a Good girl—but that did not prevent managers from concerning themselves with women's moral behavior outside the factories.

Workers' Perspectives: Personal Connections and Status

Workers' responses to managerial discipline, particularly to the scolding of workers, were quite varied. These distinct responses illustrate the breadth of the issues involved as the women worked to make sense of the inequalities of economic liberalization that were so pronounced inside the factories.

JUKI GIRLS, GOOD GIRLS

Workers considered their relationships to supervisors, managers, and investors in personal terms, and frequently expressed their thankfulness for their jobs in conversations with me. As if to demonstrate their personal connections with the owners, workers often recounted to me personal conversations they had with the two factory investors. They referred to these men as Asanka Sir and Tissa Sir; the use of their first names (rather than last names) with "Sir" indicates relative familiarity. They would often tell me that the owners really cared about the workers, and they would cite the following as a demonstration of their care: whenever they visited the factories (about once a month) these men walked through the production area and stopped to talk to workers. Workers told me in many ways that they felt that they owed the owners their loyalty because they provided them with jobs.

Workers frequently offered the investors, managers, and supervisors gestures of thanks and respect appropriate in circumstances outside the factory setting. For instance, around the time of the Sinhala and Tamil New Year's holiday in April, individuals brought managers the sweets that are typically exchanged to celebrate the new year, like *kavun* (a deep-fried oil cake, made with rice flour and treacle) and *kokis* (a crisp sweet made of rice flour and coconut milk). When Yohan Sir got married, Shirtex workers pooled their money and presented him with wedding gifts. When Samarakoon Sir's father died, more than half the Shirtex workforce visited the funeral home and presented him with an envelope full of money for funeral expenses. When a Serendib manager broke his leg in a motorcycle accident, workers in his section visited his home, where they gave him sweets and he offered them tea with sugar (sugar in tea being a relative luxury). Workers also tried to leverage these personal connections for specific advantages. One woman wrote Asanka Sir a letter asking him to hire her sister. Another wrote to Tissa Sir asking for money for a sick child's medical treatment. On one of my first days at Shirtex, I was talking to Asanka Sir just outside the factory entryway when a woman entered the grounds, dropped to her knees and prostrated before him (a traditional gesture of respect), and asked him for a job. Her husband had been killed by the JVP, and a local Buddhist monk who knew Asanka Sir had sent her to the factory to seek employment.

Serendib's Chanaka Sir once organized a day trip with workers from his production lines to Nuwara Eliya, a popular hill resort. Although this happened before my field research period, I often heard about this trip when workers told me about how much their managers cared about them. Some workers told me that they normally were not allowed to go on trips but their parents allowed them to go on this one since a manager was leading it. One worker described the outing as follows, "The trip really removes the workers as much as possible from their lives that are full of difficulty. The garment factory is a bit tiring for the body, and when you have to work in the night as well it's uncomfortable. So at a time like that, we went on a trip to Nuwara Eliya, and from going on a trip like that Chanaka Sir showed us that life in the garment factory is very important." That is, by taking them on an outing like this, Chanaka Sir showed them that what they did in the factory was very important and that they should be rewarded for working so hard.

The same worker said that through this effort Chanaka Sir had gained a lot of respect from the workers. In fact, workers constantly spoke about Chanaka Sir and other managers in terms of their respect (*gauravaya*) and love (*ādaraya*) for these managers. One worker who had been quite ill for months, and eventually had to stop working, told me how Chanaka Sir had made specialist doctors' appointments for her and driven her home when she was too ill to work. Others—including pleased parents—told me that he would sometimes drive them home when they had to work after dark.

A worker named Kamala spoke eloquently about the relationships between workers and managers. She explained that when Samarakoon Sir's father died, all the workers wanted to show a unified face and go to the funeral.

> Because a lot of workers love Samarakoon Sir, they went to share Samarakoon Sir's sadness among the workers. And, Yohan Sir gave us cake for his marriage ceremony. So, because he didn't forget us, we can't forget him either. We got together and said that we must also give him a present that will make him remember us. . . . Even on his birthday, Yohan Sir gives us each a piece of cake on his birthday. . . . All of us thought about it, about the fact that he doesn't forget us, and we thought we mustn't forget him either, and we fulfilled our duty. Sir's duty gets fulfilled by Sir.

Kamala was one of many workers who invoked the concepts of duty (*yutukam*) and respect (*gauravaya*) in reference to how they treat managers ("we fulfilled our duty") and how managers treat workers (Sir fulfills his duties). By raising these principles, which structure many Sinhala Buddhist social relationships, she showed the terms in which she and her coworkers tried to accommodate the inequalities that were so apparent in the manager-worker relationship.

In addition to participating in their managers' funerals and weddings, workers also offered help at times of illness. The first day I was at Serendib, I went to a *bodhipūja* with hundreds of workers to benefit the factory manager's ill daughter. Teja later told me in an interview that during that period, she and her coworkers all prayed frequently to the gods and the Buddha to heal the daughter. Teja was also among the group that went to the manager's house when he broke his leg. When she told me about this, I asked her what now, on reflection, seems a decidedly leading question (I found this sometimes to be a useful fieldwork tactic). Her lengthy reply is a wonderful articulation of the reasoning by which workers made sense of the social inequality that was so apparent in the factories.

Caitrin: Isn't there a danger that when workers do that kind of thing they will think they're good friends with the manager once they get back to the factory?
Teja: No, no. We're not so foolish to think that. . . . The workers are not so dumb as to think, "I helped him like that, I am connected to him like that." There is respect when they go to see him, and after they return to the factory there is also the same kind of respect. The way I see it, there is a great respect between manager and employee. . . . There is a saying that if there is a high-low status difference, it should be kept at that level. If the status is leveled, the work won't be accomplished. There must be a certain gap between the employee and the manager. . . . If they try to work as friends, then there would be a lot of sacrifices that would take place. If the workers weren't producing at a sufficient level, the managers wouldn't be able to scold [if they had close bonds with the workers]. When they scold, that means we develop. Both groups develop. If Sir thinks the way we work is good, if Sir doesn't say anything, thinking, "These workers are good, they helped me in a time of trouble," and he doesn't do anything about low production, then he'd have to accept our production level even if we only gave him ten items. That's really the death of the factory. They can't do that. We're not angry. They determine the target amount required for that order. There's nothing to get angry for if they tell us that target amount. . . . There must be inequality. It won't be right if there is equality. If both parties come to the same level, if the state arises where I don't listen to what Sir says, there is no development there. . . . I'll be compelled to work the way I want to. Though we do our work by using our brains, Sirs do their work by using their

business intelligence. We must respect that and we must get used to their business method. It's then that the business will prosper.

Workers often told me that they wanted the factories to prosper so that they will continue to be employed. They were keenly aware of competition from other countries and other firms within Sri Lanka and they did not want their factory to shut down in the face of competition.

Although Teja referred to the importance of managers scolding workers, and Kamala stated that workers loved Samarakoon Sir, there was also a prominent sense at both factories that, in scolding, managers sometimes overstepped the line of what was appropriate. Workers often said that rather than reforming, they simply got angry when they were harshly scolded. Sita, who was a mother of small children, said the following, pointing out an inherent problem with the use of the term *lamay* (children) to refer to workers. "When shouted at, the workers are even more disobedient. They won't do any work at all. They get angry. Though they are workers/children [*lamay*] they are not simply children [*lamay*]. Though we are workers/children, we are mothers, too. There are times when after being scolded we don't feel like doing what we are told to do." Another worker said that after they were scolded sometimes they ended up damaging the garments because they were upset. Many workers said that after scolding, managers would often approach them later and speak nicely, not actually apologizing but, as one woman said, "setting things right by being kind."

Many workers said that the managers showed compassion and love toward the workers and that they only scolded when it was absolutely necessary. They argued that the managers were only doing their jobs, and that the managers themselves risked being scolded by their own bosses. Some echoed Teja in arguing that scolding helped the workers to improve, and one said that it was being scolded that had allowed them to develop into such good workers over the past three years (since the factory first opened). Susila explained that in the same way that parents must act lovingly to their kids, "if managers act lovingly toward the workers, the girls will feel like working." However, she conceded that "a certain amount of shouting is needed by the managers, or the girls will try to climb onto their shoulders." But another woman explained that the managers should scold "with control," rather than speaking to the workers as if they were slaves.

I saw many cases of harsh scolding but also many where managers spoke about problems to workers gently, quietly, and, it seemed, kindly. Workers frequently explained to me that the latter approach was much more effective than the former. One said, "If they speak nicely and ask for the target amount, then the worker, feeling good about it, will somehow try to give her amount. If they speak in an unpleasant manner, frequently the target lessens even more." One worker explained that because there is a close relationship between the mind and body, when a worker's "feelings are pounded" it becomes difficult to work. From being insulted the worker becomes physically uncomfortable, ailments increase, and she becomes less productive. "But if the sirs and supervisors speak well and lovingly, no matter how difficult it is to work, it is not a big deal. We can do the job happily."

Factory Conflicts

These were new factories where managers and workers alike negotiated the workplace division of labor in relation to hierarchical models familiar from outside the factories. There were many instances in which the correct relationship between managers and workers was debated and discussed. Disagreements over suitable modes of behavior often were expressed in conflicts, many of which came down to the question of the displacement of expected social hierarchies.

When new cultural practices emerge, conflicts are arenas in which people test shared assumptions and in which values are negotiated and made explicit. Here I am following Pierre Bourdieu (1977, 168–69), whose work is used so aptly by Jane Collier in her analysis of disagreements among Spanish villagers. Collier (1997, 12) writes that "it is through constant and recurring arguments that a people establish and perpetuate the shared, usually implicit assumptions that constitute their tradition and that make it possible for them to understand how they disagree with one other." Explicitly raising concerns helps people identify their desires and realize where they are similar despite disparities of experience or expectation.

Disagreements, grievances, and conflicts at these factories arose among women workers, between workers and supervisors or managers, and among managers and supervisors. Some conflicts were directly related to work, like those about unjust managerial preference or promotions, cruel treatment by managers, unfair wage calculations, the quality of the factory's medical facilities, inability to get required leave, or poor work habits. Other conflicts referred to issues outside of work, like family or village enmities, caste divisions, electoral politics, or love affairs. Even what looked like internal factory conflicts cannot be understood out of the wider social context: people were making sense of the world around them, and much of what happened within the factories was interpreted in the context of the larger social discourses about economic liberalization and social change. Many conflicts invoked gendered concerns about Good girls, Juki girls, and appropriate femininity.

I offer one small example of how nonfactory issues were brought to bear on factory productivity. A small group at Shirtex once complained to me about a worker named Shirani who was allegedly having a sexual relationship with a married male coworker. Arguing that Shirani was a bad girl and that she was giving the rest of them a bad name, they requested that I report Shirani's behavior to Yohan Sir to get her fired. I was thrust into an uncomfortable situation. These women were calling attention to my position of relative power, which they were trying to use for their own ends. But I could not comply. I still do not really know what had been going on, but clearly the women assumed that management would want to eliminate such a bad element from the otherwise productive workforce. If indeed Shirani had been having an illicit affair, since they obtained social and work advantages from being considered as Good girls by management and the wider society, her coworkers may have been fearful of being tainted by her bad behavior. Note that the cheating husband did not concern the women—they did not try to get him fired. This was one of many cases in which it became evident that women were defining themselves in reference to other women more than in reference to men (Farnsworth-Alvear 2000, 27).

At least two types of conflict arose among workers because the complicated question of how to be a Good girl and a factory worker at the same time was of great significance to them and because there were different ways of negotiating this new subject position. Both could be said to have aided management. First, there were conflicts among workers within a factory. Second, there was competition between workers at the two factories, which was often articulated in terms of differences between the factories at the level of tradition and modernity. Differences in the layout and atmosphere of Shirtex and Serendib were frequently read alongside supposed differences between the women of the two factories. Noting these differences and conflicts between the factories helps bring into focus the contradictions, complexity, and strain that characterized the cultural work of learning to be Good girls.

Workers, managers, and the two owners alike often asked me to compare the factories. I cannot count the number of times workers at each place asked me questions such as "What is Serendib like? Our sirs are good, aren't they?" or "Do you think we are different from the workers at Shirtex?" Serendib managers would often ask me if I thought they were better managers than those at Shirtex; at least, were they kinder? Shirtex workers and managers often cast Shirtex workers as unequivocal traditional Good girls, and therefore better workers; whereas Serendib managers and workers made comments that conveyed a pride in Serendib's women being more modern than the workers across the wall, but still insisting they were Good girls and good workers.

Shirtex managers who professed to know the production figures (which I did not corroborate) said that compared to Serendib their factory was much more efficient, produced higher-quality garments, and had a lower employee turnover rate. Several Shirtex managers and their predecessors told me that when the original 200 GFP hiring was conducted in 1992, Serendib managers selected women based on appearance—they only wanted pretty girls. But at Shirtex they chose workers strictly on the basis of poverty, that is, on whether or not they were Janasaviya recipients. These Shirtex managers contended that because they did not hire on personal caprice, Shirtex was a more productive factory. By highlighting Janasaviya status when speaking of why Shirtex was more productive, Shirtex managers and also workers correlated poverty with cultural authenticity: It was not just that "Good girls make good workers," but that "poor girls make Good girls make good workers."

Serendib Janasaviya workers also correlated poverty with authenticity, but at the expense of coworkers who had come from the previous non–200 GFP Serendib factory. I sometimes heard intrafactory criticisms from the two different batches of women within Serendib that paralleled the interfactory comments I heard from Shirtex and Serendib workers about the other factory's workers as a body. These comments paralleled the ambivalence I describe in the previous chapter as the simultaneous attraction and repulsion of the urban and modern. The non-Janasaviya women took pride in being positioned as (and positioning themselves as) more modern, but they no doubt worried about the Juki reputation; the Janasaviya women took pride in being positioned as (and positioning themselves as) more traditional, but they surely enjoyed the new style and social life I describe in the previous chapter.

How do these points of criticism, comparison, and competitiveness affect the "Good girls make good workers" formulation? Together, they indicate that although all the 200 GFP dramatis personae were working with the same cultural models about Good-girl conduct in the context of the shared construct of the rural-urban divide, there was no easy solution for any of the parties concerned to the question of whether a garment worker could be a Good girl. The women in the two factories were working with the same sets of experiences and desires to carve out new subjectivities—but it was only through highlighting what they saw from afar as contrasts that they were able to articulate their own desires. The refashioning of subjectivity is a difficult project; there was no simple, functional solution to the contradictions the women encountered and the conflicting messages they received about how to be from the different people in their lives—their brothers, parents, boyfriends, managers, and coworkers.

The Shirtex Walkout

Paternalism and the focus on face-to-face relationships meant that workers did not have a comfortable forum for lodging their many grievances. The vast majority of workers at both factories were afraid to complain about anything. I heard a variety of reasons for this fear. Some were afraid that managers might take complaints as a personal affront. As Farnsworth-Alvear (2000, 124) corroborates in another context, "in workplaces marked by face-to-face relationships of power, joining a strike involved a personal kind of insubordination." Some cited the fear of losing their jobs. Women would frequently state that there would always be ten or more people waiting outside the factory gates for their jobs. (Though the specter of an infinite labor pool haunted these women, managers often expressed concern to me about the dearth of people applying for jobs.) Another problem was that they were afraid to speak up: they have been raised as *läjja-baya* women to not speak with persons of authority unless spoken to, and they were also generally afraid of speaking with managers. These women also did not want themselves and the village to get a bad name. They said they were *läjjay* to raise issues when their relatives would hear about them. Finally, they did not want the factories to close down. I often heard this last point from workers and other villagers: many were concerned that people not protest working conditions simply because they wanted to keep the factories in Udakande, but they mused that there had to be some effective way to get problems addressed without scaring off investors. These last two points raise the important complication posed by the factories' location in a village. While some people said that the surveillance of the factories by villagers prevented abuse from occurring at the factories, others said that the kinds of deep connections forged with managers also meant that there was no arena for lodging legitimate protest.

The workers had no formal mechanism for lodging complaints that avoided face-to-face confrontation. There was no trade union at either factory. Managers believed there would be few complaints, and they often told me that workers should simply come to them with any concerns. They also sometimes told me that the company's Workers' Committees could deal with problems, but during my field research, there was no formal committee at either factory. Workers' Committees (often called Workers' Councils) are a common alternative to unions in many Sri Lankan factories. According to Premadasa's 200 GFP rules, there was supposed to be a Workers' Committee at each factory. Serendib held a committee election by secret ballot near the end of my field research, but the results had still not been announced two months later—a delay that many workers attributed to vote rigging by management. In lieu of a committee, about once a month a dozen or so Shirtex workers selected by Yohan Sir would meet with senior Colombo-based administrators to discuss concerns. Obviously this was a fraught procedure, and I often heard complaints that Yohan Sir only selected women who would never speak against him or were too shy to speak at all. At times, anonymous letters of complaint were sent to the owners of both factories, but anonymity often prevented the factory owners from taking the concerns seriously. Furthermore, some people were so afraid of losing their jobs that they would not write letters because they feared that their identity could be found out through their handwriting. Filing official complaints with the Ministry of Labour was a complicated process that workers told me was confusing and intimidating and offered no hope of easy resolution of grievances.

It was in this context that anonymous posters critical of Yohan Sir appeared at Shirtex. Before dawn on a Tuesday morning in February 1996, white posters with red painted lettering were pasted on the walls, buildings, and pavement along the roads within a one-mile radius of the factories.[4] The largest occupied a wall near the turnoff to the factory: four feet long by one foot high, its huge letters proclaimed in Sinhala "Chase Out Yohan Sir." All the posters expressed similar sentiments, and all were directed against Yohan Sir, Shirtex's production manager. The posters, most signed "from the workers," variously proclaimed Yohan Sir a demon, arrogant, and inhuman. Others read as follows: "At the factory they get work not from workers but from slaves"; "Protect the factory from Yohan Sir who is arrogant"; "We don't want Yohan

Sir, fire him"; "We're not slaves"; "Yohan Sir demands labor that is too much for the workers' bodies" (this is a Sinhala expression for exploitative labor conditions); "Factory directors, why aren't you taking steps to fire Yohan Sir?"

Workers and staff members from both factories encountered these posters as they arrived at work that morning. Yohan Sir did not come to work that day, nor the next two, for he had gone to Colombo the previous afternoon for his wedding. He was from Colombo but lived during the week in a rented house down the lane from the factories. I also was in Colombo that day, conducting research at some urban factories. When I walked to the factories from the clock-tower junction two days later, I immediately wondered what I had missed. I found scraps of posters littering the roads and some large, legible poster remnants still in place—despite villagers' efforts to remove them, some were still hanging because of the powerful adhesive.

On that Tuesday morning, after they entered Shirtex, a number of workers, led by three women who usually acted as leaders, announced that they disagreed with the sentiments of the posters. They then refused to work until they could leave the factory to hang posters of their own and march in support of Yohan Sir. Shirtex's owner, Asanka Sir, was immediately contacted by telephone at the home office in Colombo. Kumari, the same woman who organized the trip to Samarakoon Sir's funeral the previous year, spoke with Asanka Sir. She apparently expressed the workers' shame (*läjja*) about the incident, and asked for permission to counterdemonstrate.[5] Permission was granted for Kumari and five others to leave the factory. But about one hundred women rushed out before the guards managed to close the gates and prevent others from leaving. Evidently most of the total of 350 workers had been ready to depart, but there was a small number (I heard estimates of around 30) still inside the factory, for various reasons unwilling to leave. Not aware that Yohan Sir was in Colombo, the workers marched around the village and then down a lane to Yohan Sir's house. Assuming he was at home and afraid to come to work, they hoped they could change his mind. Numerous villagers came out of their houses to watch the procession. It was only after the police arrived and forced the workers back into the factory that production began. By then it was noon.

This was thus an unusual walkout: the workers refused to work to support management, not to oppose it.[6] Violet, one of the walkout leaders, later told me that if they had been silent the villagers would have assumed they had hung the posters. She said that to prove that Yohan Sir was innocent of these charges and that they supported him, they wanted to march through the vil-

.   JUKI GIRLS, GOOD GIRLS

lage and post new signs proclaiming the truth. This second batch of posters was made that morning in the factory's cutting room with the markers and paper normally used for patternmaking. Two succinct posters were generated at this time: one said "Sir for us and us for Sir" and the other said "We want Sir." During the procession, workers also used the factory markers to alter some of the original posters. For instance on a poster that had originally declared in red paint "Yohan Sir, are you a demon?" there was writing added in blue marker that read "No, who says?"

In addition to these rather straightforward rebuttals written on the original posters, there was also written on some posters another rejoinder of which I heard two versions. (These posters were removed before I saw them.) They said either "The bed is ready, come at night" or "The bed is ready, bathe and come." The numerous people with whom I discussed these retorts were uniform in their interpretations: they were a clear sexual invitation that challenged the authors of the original posters to prove the integrity of their accusations against Yohan Sir by demonstrating their sexual prowess. There was a correlation drawn here between honesty and masculine sexual power. These sexual retorts—and not the accusations against Yohan Sir—became the major focus of village discussion about the day's events. The villagers thought the women must have written the sexual phrases, which was not appropriate feminine behavior. By the end of the same day, the workers who marched in the procession were being accused of sexual impropriety. With the focus switched to the sexuality of the women workers, the critiques of management that had been raised in the posters were instantly forgotten.

Starting on my very first day at Shirtex, I often heard and saw Yohan Sir shouting at workers. As some workers noted to me, even his normal tone of voice and facial expressions were harsh and seemed to express disgust, so when he raised his voice people cowered. He would sometimes call workers idiots and fools. Workers complained to me about these epithets. They noted that he would call them "cattle" and would sometimes address them with the degrading and disrespectful Sinhala pronoun *tamuse*.[7] I knew of a number of women who quit their jobs because of his harsh treatment, one explained to me that she left because "there is no need to be insulted for 2,000 rupees." There was no formal mechanism for registering concerns about this ill treatment. It was in this context that the posters appeared.

The posters were signed "the workers," but no workers took responsibility for the action once they arrived at work that day. Perhaps the anonymity of the original posters was related to the various concerns women had about agitating for change in their paternalistic and face-to-face work environment. The grievances in the posters were largely about Yohan Sir's treatment of workers. They focused on emotional and interpersonal relationships, not on objective criteria such as wages, health care, or target rates. This focus is consistent with the approach taken in factories elsewhere where management policies are structured by paternalism and face-to-face power dynamics. Farnsworth-Alvear (2000, 141) notes that disputes in Colombian factories centered on the interpersonal world, and were "about workers' control over the tone of workplace interactions involving specific persons." Regardless of who really penned the posters, their approach is significant. When they wrote that Yohan Sir was "arrogant" they seemed to be flagging his violation of accepted rules of hierarchy and subordination, and they may have expected that agitating about that claim would have been effective in a factory where interpersonal relations were so important to everyday factory productivity and discipline.

In the days following the walkout there was intense speculation by workers, managers, and villagers as to who might have hung the original posters and why. I spent considerable time discussing what had occurred with all these people, who were themselves busy with their own speculations, queries, and analyses. I certainly never uncovered any one story about the incident that I could call "the truth." In fact, I was not seeking out "the truth," because I knew full well that individuals remember and experience an event according to their own subjective biases and perspectives. I sought instead to learn what people were saying about this incident, how they were making sense of it, what their discussions told me about how they made sense of the wider social world. Even if it could be discovered, I would not be particularly interested in "what really happened." Instead, my analysis focuses on how people remembered and made sense of this event (cf. Israeli 2002, 1; Roy 1994).

My inquiries yielded a number of explanations about who hung the original posters and why—that is, the agents and their motivations. Agents included the following, all placed in very different stories: the brothers, husbands, or boyfriends of workers; the women workers themselves, led by a sewing-machine operator named Sunila, who joined Kumari in the efforts to counterdemonstrate; disgruntled area van drivers; and a prominent local Buddhist monk. Motivations focused on three main areas: actual managerial abuse, national party politics, and competition between managerial factions.

A few explanations focused on Yohan Sir's managerial techniques—the posters, I was told, were put up by the boyfriends, husbands, or brothers of women who had quit their jobs because they believed Yohan Sir had been too harsh. According to this story, because women would not have been able to go out in the night or early morning to hang posters (Good girls must stay inside when it's dark), their male associates would have hung the posters. Explanations focusing on managerial abuse, however, were in some sense the least prevalent. It was as if most people seemed to be looking for another, more "real" motivation.

Many of the explanations stated or implied that the posted comments on Yohan Sir's managerial style were not necessarily true; they were just intended to get him fired. For instance, a significant portion of rumors focused on party politics, particularly the opposition between supporters of the opposition UNP and the PA. There were rumors that Yohan Sir was a supporter of the UNP and that workers loyal to the ruling PA had hung the posters to have him fired and replaced by a PA production manager. In one version of this story, a prominent PA monk from Udakande provided the paper and paint to workers or their male relatives. Given how party politics in Sri Lanka has been another means of discussing tradition and modernity, these arguments could be interpreted as referring to an effort by PA workers to make the factory more traditional (the PA/SLFP is considered Kandyan and, hence, close to tradition) and not run by crass materialists (the UNP, Low Country–associated party).

Others said the posters were hung by van owners and drivers who were angry that Yohan Sir did not employ them to drive workers home at night after overtime shifts. Another explanation focused on internal managerial disputes, arguing that lower-level supervisors and managers who opposed Yohan Sir hung the posters. Others said Yohan Sir himself orchestrated both the poster campaign and the walkout to take place on a day he would be away— his absence had thus not been coincidence—in order to show his superiors that the workers supported him over the rival managers. Even these explanations referring to management rivalries were cast as a Kandyan-Low Country (traditional/modern—local/foreign) dispute, with the Kandyan managers trying to oust the outsider whom, some said, they opposed precisely because he was an outsider.

A number of people said that those who wrote the posters also participated in the walkout. While there were several people involved, the leaders in both activities were said to be Kumari and Sunila. According to this story, Kumari and Sunila orchestrated the posters and the walkout to elicit support for Yohan Sir, whose position was being threatened by rival managers and by a few disgruntled former workers. Some said they were asked to do this by

Yohan Sir; others said they did this on their own. In any event, according to this story, Kumari and Sunila (with the help of others) hung the posters, then led the walkout to show that the workers supported Yohan Sir.

Many people told me that Sunila had penned the sexual rebuttals. Kumari, Sunila, and their coworkers denied it and said that the authors were the local unemployed young men who loitered on the village streets and on the cricket pitch located immediately outside the factory. But not only the young men but also other villagers and the Shirtex workers who did not go on the procession told me that the culprits had been the factory women with Sunila in the lead. Serendib workers, who only saw the procession through their factory windows as they continued to work, also generally told me that the sexual rebuttals were Sunila's doing.

It was easy for everyone to imagine that Sunila would have led the workers in the original poster campaign and in writing these sexual rebuttals. Sunila was a twenty-seven-year-old married mother of two young daughters who lived with her widowed mother. Her husband worked in a textile factory in Colombo and returned home for two days each month. Along with Kumari, Sunila was an unofficial factory leader who played a large role in organizing trips, parties, and other social events. Sunila also was a vocal UNP supporter. In this case rather than her leadership qualities, her sexuality was at issue. I was told that with no man to watch over her, Sunila could have easily made and hung posters *in the dark*, despite being a woman—the assumption here was that no respectable woman would be out in the dark.

Some observers seem to have considered Sunila a woman who was *läjja-baya näti* (without shame and fear). In this formulation, Sunila talked too loudly, was too forward with the managers, and carried her body in an anything but demure fashion. There was no man around to control her behavior. One other woman whom I heard described in similar ways was a young widowed childless woman whom workers characterized as *social*, the same word that Teja used to describe her mother in chapter 4. Several workers told me that this woman's outgoing and unsubmissive behavior was characteristic of a woman who is not proper and complete because she has not endured the pain of childbirth. In his study of violence as an object of anthropological study in Sri Lanka, the anthropologist Pradeep Jeganathan (1997) describes a woman who inhabits the cusp between being *läjja näti* (without shame) and *baya näti* (without fear). He argues that the identification of a woman as being without *läjja* produces a social space for her to be sexualized. Similarly, her lack of *baya* produces a space for violence. Sunila seems to be situated in a similar manner.

Though I heard all the above interpretations of the posters and walkout from workers and villagers in Udakande and the surrounding villages more generally, key members of the Shirtex management conveyed a different, unified interpretation of the event to me and to the workers. They all refused to use the word *strike* to describe the events and would reprimand anyone—including me—who used the word in English or Sinhala. Unequivocally attributing the sexual phrases to the boys on the street and explaining the poster content as a means of ousting Yohan Sir for other reasons, these managers interpreted the walkout as a sign of the strength of the factory. Yohan Sir told me he was proud that the "girls" supported him. I also heard him tell the women this directly when he called a factory meeting on his first day back and thanked the workers for their support. He was staunchly confident in his comments to me that the posters had not come from the workers, and he argued that it reflected well on the girls that they had demonstrated to show the villagers what they thought of him.

Asanka Sir told me he had given permission for the small group to leave the factory premises in order to "let off steam." When I reminded him that more workers than he had intended departed and that the entire morning's production had been lost as a result, he said, "That doesn't matter. There must have been some frustration to get so worked up. It's good for people to shout like this." A month later, in the conversation in which he argued that their attendance at his father's funeral demonstrated how good the village girls were, Samarakoon Sir added the following point: "If those posters had been put up in Colombo, the workers would have said nothing about it." Samarakoon Sir saw the walkout as a way to protect Shirtex and Yohan Sir. Many workers (as seen in Violet's comments about wanting to make sure villagers did not think they hung the posters) spoke of it this way, too. They were also concerned to protect their own reputations. The Shirtex Sirs were able to sidestep the sexuality questions to use the walkout as an affirmation of their workers' status as good, respectable girls—an affirmation in which parents and the workers themselves would have taken comfort.

In comments to me, Serendib managers used the walkout and the sexual aspersions as clear evidence of the superiority of their factory and its workers to Shirtex's. They would have wanted to distance themselves from the event in order for their factory and its workers to avoid getting a bad reputation. This would have been especially important for Serendib's management because it was already their company, and not Shirtex, that worried some locals for perhaps being exploitative. Serendib workers consistently worked overtime, which was paid, and technically optional, but in practice was extremely difficult to refuse to do. They often were informed of required overtime moments before the end-of-day bell rang, and they had no way to inform their families that they would be home late. Serendib workers often did not even get a holiday on Poya days, the monthly national full moon holidays (holy in the Sinhala Buddhist calendar). Workers in the embroidery room sometimes worked overnight.

Serendib workers joined in this comparison between the factories: I heard from many that the Shirtex workers were simply "naughty" (in English) or *honda nä*. Some said that if there were actually problems as stated with Yohan Sir, the workers should have just "kept their mouths shut." Others conceded that something would have had to be done, but in a unified fashion—with some workers refusing to walk out, it made all the workers look ridiculous.

Villagers whom I surveyed about the day's events (including parents of workers at both factories, the boys who loitered at the cricket field, and nearby shop owners and neighbors) immediately dismissed the possibility of true worker grievances and focused instead on the bad character of the women— epitomized by Sunila—who presumably wrote the sexual phrases. Jayasuriya Sir, Shirtex's personnel manager, told me that on the afternoon of the walkout a group of fifteen villagers (members of the village "civic order committee") came to the factory to speak with him. With the sexually suggestive altered posters in hand, they complained that the language was inappropriate for women and that it gave the village a bad name. They did not discuss the posted accusations of exploitation, inhumanity, slavery, and so on. The mother of a worker at Shirtex whom I asked about the entire day's events (and not just about the altered posters) responded instantly with the run-together words "*Ci, käte wäda, sauttuy*"—"Yuck, filthy, rotten." She then explained that Good girls shouldn't do such things: they should neither complain about their work conditions nor write bad words on posters. Others used the same phrases, mostly the words *naughty girls* (in English), *ci*, and *sauttuy*.

With the focus directed toward Sunila, the significance of the event was minimized—an explanation could be found in the idiosyncrasies of one actor. Likewise, the political arguments and the complex stories about management rivalries eclipsed the arguments about true worker grievances. The accusations about Yohan Sir's managerial techniques were being read as *about* something else. The sense seemed to have quickly emerged that the posters could not really point to labor issues. The sexual retorts turned the conversation into a means of talking about something other than the dynamics of capital and labor.

What mattered was that women were acting up, not being proper and traditional, displaying bad character, and giving themselves and the village a bad name. This worker protest, and especially the walkout, were unworthy of good, traditional, village girls. Because the poster hanging and the walkout raised the possibility that the women workers were not ideal factory workers—not a compliant labor force, that is—it was as if villagers had then begun to wonder, "Well, if they are not good workers, can we still assume they are Good girls?" There seemed to be speculation that despite their village locale perhaps the modern garment factories *could* corrupt village women. Moral panic about urban factory workers, which had itself contributed to the gendered transformation of the 200 GFP, suddenly was brought to Udakande. When sexuality was broached, it created an easy scapegoat. In the end, the women who had marched around the village in a walkout became the objects of public scorn. Posting critiques of management was rendered a profoundly ineffective form of protest.

Factory New Year's Festivals

The only occasion when the Shirtex and Serendib workers officially interacted was the annual New Year's festival, hosted jointly by both factories in April.[8] Children of workers were also invited to these festivals, which were held on a Sunday before New Year's from ten to three. I attended in 1995 and 1996. Workers from both factories competed in games involving skills such as cracking a clay pot while blindfolded (a game for both sexes), thatching a palm frond and scraping coconuts (for women), and climbing a greased pole (for men). There were other games and contests, including the New Year's Princess competition, a mainstay at New Year's festivals throughout the country, and a costume competition. There were prizes (cash or saris) for all these contests, and workers took them all quite seriously.

These factory festivals were events at which management hoped to help construct a community of Good girls aligned with the factory. Managers hoped that because they sponsored traditional activities such as the festival, villagers would see the factory as a place where traditional values were maintained and not a corrupt locale where parents would be wary of sending their daughters. Moreover, since workers would be happier in the morally safe environs, it was also a way to create a cohesive and content and disciplined workforce. An overproduced clothing sale at the 1996 festival could be interpreted in this vein since it was a boon to workers who might not otherwise have been able to participate fully in the New Year's tradition of presenting gifts of clothing or fabric. Because of Serendib's sale they could give these gifts to their families without spending too much of their wages.

Workers experienced and made sense of these festivals in their own ways. Incidents at the 1995 and 1996 festivals show that workers considered the festivals as arenas to have fun, reframe their experiences, and make statements about who they were (cf. Farnsworth-Alvear 2000, 184–85). Each year there was a laughing contest in which management judged the funniest and most authentic-sounding laugh. At the 1995 festival, the contest included a performance by a worker who prefaced it with this introduction: "Pardon me, I have come here to laugh. They do not allow me to laugh during work, so now I have come here to laugh in front of everybody. Just yesterday they scolded me for laughing." This open commentary on factory discipline was playfully transgressive because it was a critique of management in front of management, and because it was done at the New Year's festival, an event designed to help construct a community of Good girls aligned with the factory. The same year, in the fancy dress contest a woman dressed as a beggar threw bits of crumbled bread (leftovers from the bun-eating contest) at the audience members and especially at her manager, who said loud enough for many people to hear, "I know she doesn't like me, but she doesn't have to throw things at me." Another woman dressed as an officer from the Special Task Force (STF, the police's elite commandos) lay down on the ground with a toy gun and fired directly at her production manager.

The women here—the laughing worker, the bun-throwing beggar, the STF officer—were performing critiques about factory production by highlighting divisions between workers and management. At the festival the following year, held less than two months after the Shirtex walkout, I saw no such explicitly production-oriented critiques. The divisions that I noticed that year were among workers themselves. There were two events that took on lives of their own afterwards for the questions they raised about women's moral behavior. In fact, in the period following the walkout I began to notice, overhear, and be drawn into many more conversations than previously about sexuality, moral behavior, and Good girls.

Figure 6. At the annual factory New Year's festival in April 1995, this Serendib worker dressed as a male officer from the Sri Lankan police's elite commandos, lay down on the ground with a toy gun and fired directly at her production manager. Photo by Caitrin Lynch.

Love Sickness Skit

At the 1996 festival, a Shirtex group performed a skit that centered on "love sickness" (*love māndama*). The skit itself as well as its reception demonstrates that the question of how to be a Good girl was at the crux of an ongoing process of identity formation and was subject to negotiation, contestation, and disagreement. The skit was performed in front of workers, supervisors, and managers, as well as the two factory owners. It was a comedy written by Manel, a Shirtex cutting-room helper known for her writing talent. Manel was often recruited to help write love letters for friends. In the midst of working she also wrote hilarious poems about the factory, featuring alliteration and puns, that were surreptitiously passed around the cutting room. The performers included Manel and Kumari and three other workers named Pushpa, Nandani, and Padma.

A girl meets a boy on the bus on her way to "tuition" (a private tutoring class) and catches "love sickness" (*love māndama*). The girl is dressed in *salwar kameez*, the "boy" (all parts were played by women) in jeans, striped shirt, and a baseball cap. The man's and the woman's outfits indicate a certain kind of modern fashion. While the man's clearly refers to a Western modernity, the woman's is more complicated. The *salwar kameez* is an outfit consisting of a long shirt worn over loose-fitting pants. Worn by North Indian women in particular, it became the accepted outfit for unmarried Muslim girls and women in Sri Lanka in the 1990s. By the mid-1990s it was becoming a fashionable outfit for Sinhalas and Tamils as well, especially in Colombo. Yasmin Tambiah (2005, 257) describes the *salwar kameez* as "a marker of a contemporary, mostly urban, supranational hybridity." I rarely saw non-Muslim garment workers in *salwar kameez*, except for the occasional outfit worn instead of a sari or fancy shirt-and-blouse kit to a wedding party.

After several flirtatious encounters on the bus and at the bus stop, the lovesick girl stops eating and complains to her parents of numerous aches and pains. Her concerned parents take her to an Ayurvedic doctor, a practitioner of indigenous medicine, who diagnoses her with *love māndama*, but only after a humorous series of questions about her symptoms. By now the audience was in hysterics, including Tissa Sir, Serendib's owner, who was sitting tightly surrounded by a laughing group of workers' children. To describe the girl's ailment, the doctor uses the English word "love" together with *māndama*, a Sinhala word for infectious disease. But the girl's parents mishear the word *love* as "*ilawwa*," a term for funeral. This is a subtle and insightful commentary by Manel, who is known for her clever use of puns. Sinhala-speakers tend to adopt English words into Sinhala, and they utter an *i* sound in front of some foreign words that start with consonants. (For instance, the Sinhala word for school is *iskōlaya*.) Similarly, the English phonemes *v* and *w* overlap in Sinhala, and many native speakers do not hear or produce a distinction between them. Thus, some people pronounce *love* as "*ilove*" and sometimes the *v* sound comes out like a *w-* or even a *b-* sound in English. By showing that the parents cannot identify the word as *love*, Manel alerts the audience that the parents are steeped in tradition. They are immersed in village society where funerals are a frequent (and important) social topic; they are not accustomed to recognizing the foreign concept or word *love*. The following exchange occurs between the parents and the doctor:

Doctor: It is *love māndama* [love sickness].
Father: What sickness? *ilawwa māndama* [funeral sickness]? From going to funerals?

Doctor: No, no, love sickness, love sickness.

Mother: Our daughter didn't go to any funerals recently. So how did she get this sickness?

Doctor: No, no. You don't have to go to funerals to get it. You must stand at a bus stop and go to classes.

Father: She went for classes on three days.

Mother: She went this morning also. So that must be it.

Doctor: She must have gotten it [collided with it] when going by bus.

Mother: What does that mean, doctor? That she got it while going on the bus? We haven't been on the bus [so we don't know what happened on it].

Doctor: Oh, well then ask your daughter. Ask your daughter about love sickness.

The doctor says there is only one medicine to cure it, but curiously he doesn't say what that medicine is. The family leaves, the parents even more mystified than when they arrived. Later the girl meets the boy again on the bus, and they decide that they must tell the girl's parents about their love. At the same moment that they arrive home to inform her parents, the Ayurvedic doctor also shows up and exclaims, "Ah, I see the medicine has arrived!" The parents quickly understand and, after a few shocked comments about their daughter getting involved in such things while acting sweet "like a kitten," they concede that they will let the affair continue.

The skit over, the performers then sang the following song (also written by Manel). "Perera Sir" refers to the owner of Shirtex, whom they referred to here by last name:

Hey ho! In Perera Sir's garment factory
Boys and girls get together and sew mischievously
Manel, Nandani, Padma, Kumari, and Pushpa and another load of girls
This is Shirtex where cutting and sewing are done
This is the Reuters office
La la
Spending time jolly and fighting
Everyday we come to Shirtex
In the middle of thousands of problems we spend our time being jolly.

The song and skit were met with laughter and applause. When I later asked Kumari the meaning of the "Reuters office" line, she said it was about spreading gossip (*opadupa*) and that "anything that happens anywhere is valuable information for us." The factory was thus like the Reuters news agency—receiving and transmitting all sorts of information as news. Rather than being spoken of as another difficult thing in the workers' problem-filled lives, factory work was characterized as an escape from problems. A research assistant who translated the song for me interpreted the comment about boys and girls getting together and sewing mischievously as referring to relationships between boys and girls that parents wouldn't approve of. In song, Shirtex was characterized by gossip, love affairs, and fun—not the expected descriptive phrases about a factory. The song and the skit both emphasized the importance of love and humor in these women's lives.

But that did not amuse all the audience members. Though the song and skit seemed well received at the time (as indicated by the laughter and applause), I heard numerous critical comments about the skit in the next hours and over the next few days, from both Shirtex and Serendib workers. One Shirtex woman told me that this was Kumari's idea of a good skit, but that really it just showed that Kumari was naughty and not a Good girl. As they stood at a table checking for damaged garments, a group of Serendib women told me with considerable concern and animation that the performers were naughty and that they themselves easily could have written a better skit in just an hour. One of these women said that it seemed as though the Shirtex performers had been making fun of women, and she stated that the skit was humiliating (*nōṇḍi*) for the workers. She seemed to be saying that by making fun of women for having nothing on their minds but boys, the performers reinforced men's ideas about women's priorities, confirmed the moral panic about Juki girls, and made all the women look like bad girls. In this same vein, one could focus on the writer's choice of public transportation as the site of the boy and girl's meeting—this could be said to reinforce the moral panic about Juki girls that focuses in part on their public mobility, since it facilitates inappropriate contact between men and women.

Manel showed her skill in using a single skit to raise numerous issues at the heart of her coworkers' struggles to be considered Good girls—issues ultimately at the heart of Sri Lankan struggles over modernity. Further analysis could probe into the following questions: Why did the parents go to an Ayurvedic doctor and not a Western doctor? Why did the writer use the English concept of *love* rather than a concept with an older Sanskrit or Pali-based history such as *ādareya* or *prema*? Why was the girl on her way to tuition class? Why the modern clothes? Why the Reuters office and not a Rupavahini office (the Sri Lankan government-controlled news bureau), or even a village *kadē*?

While creating a content and disciplined workforce at the New Year's festival may have been one reason management hosted this festival, such responses to the skit suggested competition and conflict between workers. It elicited moral criticism between workers within Shirtex and across the two factories, criticisms framed as a matter of good versus bad girls. There were complicated negotiations taking place here about how to be a good woman in light of the new roles made available to women in the liberalized economy. Conflicts within the factories were arenas in which values were being negotiated, assumptions were being aired, and meaning was being made.

Western Dance Contest

As if that was not enough, a second event at that 1996 New Year's festival also elicited moral criticism among workers. At the end of the day, after the New Year's Princess competition, the coconut scraping, the crying contest, the skits, and the awards for the best workers at each factory, when some people had already begun to depart, a "Western dance contest" was held in the Serendib canteen. A hired disc jockey had set up his stereo system. More than one hundred workers and all the Serendib managers crammed into a small section of the canteen for this contest, the first of its kind at these factory festivals (1996 marked the fourth festival since the factories opened in 1992). The rules were announced, and to the disappointment of a number of male workers it was designated for women only. The dancing was to be Western, though the music was a combination of Sinhala "debate baila" music and music from the West, such as the kind heard on the Colombo-based radio station YES-FM (in 1996, artists such as Celine Dion, Oasis, and Madonna, to name a few).[9] The judges were the Serendib managers: Standing behind the DJ table, some with their fashionable wives or girlfriends by their sides, they looked like a group of big, stylish men proudly surveying their possessions.

The music started, and about thirty women began to dance, with a crowd of one hundred or more male and female workers—and some of their children—jammed in, watching the spectacle. There was a gradual selection out, first to ten workers, then five, and then the final three. The finalists were ranked and awarded cash prizes that corresponded to the amounts for the New Year's Princess competition, the competition with the largest kitty—

1,000 rupees for first prize, 500 for second, and 250 for third. (The base salary for all 200 GFP workers was 2,000 rupees/month.) All three winners were from Serendib (although there were Shirtex workers in the top ten), and all were women I had seen but never met. The first-prize winner was wearing a tight-fitting black dress and her long hair was let down. I can only describe her dancing as extremely provocative and sexy.

The music resumed after the contest ended and many people entered the makeshift dance floor to strut their stuff—male and female workers, at least five of the Serendib sirs, and me. I was dancing next to Kumari when the dancing finally ended, so she and I left together. On our way out of the gates we encountered Ravi Sir, a Shirtex manager who was also leaving. Few Shirtex workers and not even one Shirtex manager had been at the contest. Kumari good-naturedly scolded Ravi Sir for not being there and complained that no Shirtex managers attended. Later, in Kandy, I ran into Chinta and her coworker Podi Kamala from Serendib. When I told them what they had missed they exclaimed that they would have loved to be there, but they had left the festival early so Podi Kamala could pick up a new gold bracelet she had ordered (for 3,000 rupees, she told me as she proudly showed me the bracelet).

In the next weeks a number of Shirtex workers mentioned the Western dance contest to me in us-versus-them terms. Although there were Shirtex women (not only Kumari) at the contest, most who mentioned it to me seemed to regard the contest as an example of the kind of questionable thing that happened at Serendib and not at Shirtex. When I was visiting a Shirtex worker's home, her father mentioned it to me in the midst of talking about something else. He suddenly dropped it into our conversation, asking if I thought it was a good thing? Clearly there was some concern about it as perhaps not the right kind of event to be happening at the factory. The contest must have transmitted highly conflicting messages to the women at both factories. A big financial reward—half of one month's base wage—was given for sexy Western dancing, dancing that was definitely something neither the women generally nor the managers seemed to consider Good-girl behavior suitable for the factory's productivity and reputation. None of the three winners were women I knew of as good workers from my extensive conversations with Serendib managers. Moreover, because there is a history of a Sinhala nationalist association between dancing and Westernization but also social mobility, and because popular music has been deemed shaming and un-Aryan by Sinhala nationalist revivalists, this dance contest would have brought on feel-

JUKI GIRLS, GOOD GIRLS

ings of conflict for the women who knew they were supposed to be bearers of tradition (de Alwis 1998, 112; Kemper 2001, chap. 3; Sheeran 1997, 211, 234–35).

While creating a content and disciplined workforce at the New Year's festival may have been the aim of management, responses to these two events at the 1996 festival suggested competition and conflict among workers. The love sickness skit elicited moral criticism among workers within Shirtex and across the two factories, criticisms framed as a matter of good versus naughty girls. The Western dance contest elicited moral criticism that mapped onto an underlying dichotomy of traditional Shirtex and too-modern Serendib. These criticisms arose in the post-walkout period when the question of what it meant to be a Good girl and good worker had become prominent. In addition to criticizing urban Juki girls, the Shirtex and Serendib women were also now criticizing each other.

CONCLUSION

The Sri Lankan economy was liberalized in 1977. By 1979, the Juki-girl stigma had emerged. As I complete this book in 2006, this stigma still stands as a powerful critique leveled at the hundreds of thousands of women employed in the garment industry. The moment in Sri Lankan history examined here can provide critical insights into global processes that obtain in many postcolonial nations today. By studying the ways in which gender became a key element of Sri Lankan responses to globalization, we can begin to understand the centrality of cultural norms and expectations concerning gender to economic processes around the world.

People in nations that experienced colonization often fear that globalization, in practice, means neocolonialism. Of course, there are numerous indicators in the United States that Americans fear globalization, too. Witness the intense contemporary concerns about outsourced white-collar labor, the flooding of the apparel trade by imports from China, or the dearth of engineering students in the United States as compared with India and China, to name a few examples (Friedman 2005a and 2005b). But, postcolonial concerns about globalization are markedly different from those concerns in the United States. Among Sri Lankans, from politicians and business leaders to factory laborers and the parents of small children, these fears are manifest in a daily struggle: How to access the material benefits of globalization without sacrificing their cultural identity in a world perceived as increasingly homogeneous?

This book appears when a shift in global trade regulations portends socio-economic changes in Sri Lanka. On 1 January 2005 the worldwide Multifibre Arrangement (MFA) for trade was discontinued, concluding a phaseout that was begun in 1994. The MFA was inaugurated in 1974 to regulate global trade balances, placing trade restrictions and allotments on exporting countries. Small countries such as Sri Lanka benefited greatly from this "quota system." It will take time to assess the effects of this shift, but it is likely that many Sri Lankans will lose their jobs because garment production is expected to move to larger countries such as China. Prior to the MFA's end, some analysts had predicted that 60 percent of the Sri Lankan garment industry could be in danger of failing.[1] Layoffs on this scale could affect many of the people I have introduced in this book. Some who could lose their jobs include those who currently eke by on their factory wages—people like Kumari, the factory leader; Manel, the scribe; and Geeta, the sociologist. But an industry collapse would also threaten those who enjoy middle-class or elite standards of living, such as Serendib's Ralph Sir as well as Asanka Sir and Tissa Sir, the managing directors and primary investors at Shirtex and Serendib.

The global dimensions of the work at Shirtex and Serendib became apparent in myriad ways during my field research but were made especially clear to me and to the workers at the Serendib shipping dock one day. In the process of loading boxes onto the container, one man found a small strip of white, flexible plastic wedged in the container door. Once he tugged the item out, he found it to be a packet that was torn on one end; a dried red substance lined the torn opening. Unable to make out what the artifact was, he sent a message through the factory for me to come to the loading dock. He had found a used packet of McDonald's ketchup labeled for consumption in the United States. The small group of workers who had gathered around me eagerly awaited my explanation. They knew what ketchup and French fries were (colonialism left behind certain culinary delights), but they did not know about single-serving ketchup packets or McDonald's (the first of these restaurants would arrive in Sri Lanka a few years later, in 1998). After I explained, we all laughed together and talked about American dock laborers eating French fries dipped in ketchup. When some of the group exclaimed in Sinhala, ṣōk! (Wow!), I truly do think that we shared a sense of amazement about the connections between laborers that the packet symbolized—about the idea of someone on the importing end of the commodity chain, perhaps in Baltimore, New York, or Los Angeles, taking a well-needed break from unloading the very boxes that the Sri Lankan workers load in.

Contemporary globalization is not always characterized by sameness and connections, and even in this story of the ketchup we can see differences of power and access in the global economy. Arjun Appadurai (2000, 6) describes globalization as "a world of disjunctive flows." There are far-ranging disjunctures in how people, things, images, and ideas flow through the world during this current era of globalization. When we account for differences in speed, access, and directionality, we can begin to see the distinctive ways people, even those in the same society, engage with and are acted on by globalization. Emphasis on such disjunctures enables us to pay careful attention to the simultaneous pleasures and pains of people who stand at the forefront of these flows, people such as Manel, whose song captured the ambivalent nature of garment workers' encounters with globalization:

Spending time jolly and fighting
Everyday we come to Shirtex
In the middle of thousands of problems we spend our time being jolly.

In this book I have examined these disjunctures on many levels. Diversely situated Sri Lankans morally disciplined the female workforce in 200 GFP factories, and those workers themselves responded to new forms of discipline. Discourses about culture, authenticity, and morality came to be central to the political configuration of the 200 Garment Factories Program as well as to workers' and managers' everyday experiences of the program. Questions of culture, gender, labor, and globalization—as argued out locally in terms of underwear, Good girls, Juki girls, shame, and control, to name a few tropes—pointed to complicated attempts at addressing and resolving anxieties about globalization and modernity.

Appadurai (2000, 6) argues that globalization "produces problems that manifest themselves in intensely local forms but have contexts that are anything but local." A number of studies of different times and places (for instance, nineteenth-century Massachusetts and Paris and late twentieth-century Malaysia and Mexico) have examined associations made between women's factory work and immoral sexual behavior. While one may be tempted to see in this conjuncture a tendency for capitalism to cause universal effects, ethnography reveals the locally mediated effects of capitalism on the lives of women workers. The Sri Lankan articulation of female purity and morality has taken on a particular spin under capitalist production. I hope to have described not only what that spin is, but also what its implications are on the ground for managers and workers alike as they work in factories that are simultaneously sites of hypermodernity, in terms of production, and hyper-conservativism, in terms of culture, authenticity, and morality. The points of criticism and competition between the factories presented in the previous chapter indicate some of the difficulty involved in bringing together these different value systems, despite the widespread assumptions and claims that an easy reconciliation would be found in the figure of the Good girl.

Although this book is replete with conversations, quotations, and narratives by and about individual Sri Lankans, it is not a book about those individuals per se. I tacked between political discourses and workers' hopes, managerial strategies and parental concerns, and factory policies and nationalist visions to demonstrate the complex contexts that affected individual choices and the meaning that people gave to those choices. Women like Mala, who ambivalently accepted a position as a garment worker after she could not find a better job, crafted something of their own out of those contexts. Leading lives that were admittedly filled with suffering, Shirtex and Serendib women did not overtly contest forms of domination and oppression that they daily encountered inside and outside the factories. Their efforts were focused elsewhere, and careful analysis allows us to look beyond victimization to see agency in their lives. They creatively fashioned a place where they could be Good girls who were also garment workers. This was not a simple project. Never questioning their deep commitments to their nation, they nevertheless endeavored to make sense of their own ambivalent feelings about their work and to reconcile their pride in the work they did with the stigma attached to it.

I was once in a factory in Colombo at the end of the workday when I noticed that the workers were brushing cotton dust from their hair before they left the factory grounds. Arjuna Sir, the manager who was escorting me through the factory, turned to me and said in English, "Look at them combing their hair. All they are interested in is not looking like they work at a garment factory. In Kandy they just shake the dust off and go." When I told Arjuna Sir that the Shirtex and Serendib workers also brushed their hair before they left he said, with obvious disappointment, "Well, then Kandy girls must be changing." He then predicted that the "Kandy girls" would soon start to copy the "Colombo girls" who were accustomed to spend 900 rupees of their 2000-rupee monthly wages on clothes.

These comments were made at the end of a long factory tour and interview with Arjuna Sir, who had worked at Serendib when it first opened in Kandy. Throughout the day, he had made a number of comments about the differences between Kandy and Colombo that undergirded a complicated and at times contradictory understanding of gender, national identity, culture, and globalization. I quoted him earlier saying "Kandy girls are easy to handle. It's in the village, no?" This statement attributed an inevitable, inherent controllability to the village woman. His comments about hair brushing implied that Kandy women were superior to Colombo women for not being overly concerned with appearance. But with his disappointed reply to my comments about Kandy women combing their hair he seemed ready to concede that the village might not be the impervious moral sanctuary he had assumed. Arjuna Sir joined others in Sri Lanka who endeavored to understand the social transformations brought on by economic liberalization in terms of dichotomies between *rural* and *urban*, *good* and *bad*, *Sri Lankan* and *foreign*, *tradition* and *modernity*, *East* and *West*, and *us* and *them*. When faced with the evidence of the new kind of Good-girl identity under construction by Kandy women, evidence that revealed the historical contingency of these apparent dichotomies, Arjuna Sir and others seemed to concede defeat.

Near the end of my field research, Shirtex and Serendib workers, their families, and other villagers from the area seemed to be slowly coming to the realization that their communities were not impervious to change. The evidence pervaded their villages, chipping away at the dichotomous understandings that permeated Sri Lankan society and complicating President Premadasa's promises about the factories. For instance, we saw that observers understood the Shirtex walkout, the love sickness skit, and the Western-style dance contest in terms of appropriate norms of femininity. We can see in their discussions of these events certain anxieties about social change and about women workers' creative solutions to the question of how to be both Good girls and good workers.

I have noted throughout this book the urgent attention Sri Lankans pay to factory women's morality in economically liberalized Sri Lanka. We can understand the Juki-girl stigma only by examining its deep and cross-cutting social, cultural, economic, and political contexts. Of these contexts, key elements are Sri Lankan notions of female respectability and social hierarchy; cultural and material responses to globalization, youth rebellion and labor migration; and state economic policies and everyday practices of capitalist production. The 200 Garment Factories Program was designed and understood to address

specifically Sri Lankan postcolonial debates about whether or not globalization caused cultural homogenization. In the ensuing history we can see how
such variously situated participants in the 200 GFP as politicians, factory
managers, and garment workers worked to make economic globalization consistent with Sri Lankan cultural practices and meaningful in terms of Sri
Lankan social life.

I end this book by returning to the image of women brushing cotton dust
out of their hair before exiting the factory grounds. One must understand
much about the Sri Lankan context to make sense of this action of brushing
hair—an act that could appear to be almost mechanical, or a strictly aesthetic
issue. Anthropological analysis allows one to move from a minute, everyday
action, like brushing hair, to the wider political, economic, and social context.
Similarly, when I first read Mala's survey comment about her reluctance to
work at Shirtex because of the widespread insults leveled at garment workers,
I did not understand much of what she meant. This book is the result of ab-
stracting out from her statement to its wider context in an effort to understand its premises.

In various places in his published diary, the twentieth-century American
writer H. L. Mencken (1991) wrote about "lintheads," that is, the poor white
southern textile workers who had moved to his native Baltimore during
World War II.[2] Mencken was unequivocally critical of lintheads, as the following entry from 11 May 1945 evinces:

> Miss Peach says that linthead girls of twelve or thereabout come into the
> square at night to pick up men and boys. If this is true I have not noticed
> it. . . . As for the damage to their virtue, it is purely imaginary, for only
> a rare linthead girl remains a virgin after the age of twelve. Her deflow-
> ering, in fact, is usually performed by her brothers, and if not by her
> brothers, then by her father. Incest is almost as common as fornication
> among these vermin, and no doubt it is largely responsible for their
> physical and mental deterioration. Everyone who knows the Southern
> poor whites knows this, but it is not mentioned in official reports.
>
> The other day, walking down Baltimore Street, I happened to fall in
> behind two linthead girls further along in years—perhaps sixteen or sev-
> enteen. They were talking loudly and I could not help overhearing.
> Their gabble was almost incredibly obscene—an endless stream of dirty
> words, repeated over and over again. They must have heard me walking
> behind them, but they showed no sign of it. Save from an occasional

JUKI GIRLS, GOOD GIRLS

drunken soldier, I have never had the honor of hearing so gorgeous a display of indecency. (Mencken 1991, 365)

We can almost feel Mencken's disgust with lintheads in this passage, and it comes through in other diary entries as well, in references to the sexual immorality, slovenliness, and wretchedness of lintheads and an equation of them with animals in their "habits and ideas" (1991, 325–26; cf. 396–97). There is a striking similarity in Mencken's response to lintheads and the types of critical comments many Sri Lankans make of Juki girls. However, just as Mencken's characterization of linthead women gives us no sense of those women's own perspectives, ideas, and experiences, the criticisms that are leveled against Juki girls in Sri Lanka beg for the perspectives of the women themselves.

Whenever I have taken up the cases of garment workers in this book, I have focused on the ways in which they made sense of their collective identity, as defined by a stigmatized profession. I have tried to show why it might be that someone like Mala would come to see great value to their labor and their skills even though "that cannot be seen by the outside world since it is enclosed within the four walls." As I have done for women often stigmatized as Juki girls, authors have tried to write against the negative portrayal of lintheads. The historian, teacher, and storyteller Shannon Brooks (1999) has done that with her introspective discussion of models of Appalachian womanhood and women writers, especially in her work on the fictional writings of the nineteenth-century Appalachian feminist Emma Bell Miles. Brooks is herself from a family of lintheads, and she explains that when she grew up in the 1980s, her mother exhorted her daughter to not "act like a linthead," an accusation that would be leveled if, for instance, one wasn't well traveled and gawked at planes at the airport (157–58). Brooks discusses a 1909 short story by Miles entitled "The Dulcimore." The main character, Selina, tries to convince her daughter not to marry a "mountain man." Brooks writes:

Like Selina, though, many mountain women have dreamed of a different future for their daughters. Some have helped bring it about through speeches and marches. Like Miles, some have written articles and stories. But most have simply worked on, silently and steadily, saying, if anything at all, "Here is the substance of my life. Take from it what lesson you will." The lesson I have taken is that there is no life free of struggle, nor does any life lack value. The trick is being able to see and appreciate the fullness of all lives, of lintheads and professors and writers and mothers. (Brooks 1999, 170)

In this book, I have tried to provide a glimpse of the fullness of the lives of women like Kumari, Geeta, Mala, and Teja, allowing them to speak of their personal aspirations, their hopes for their daughters, what they love and merely endure at these factories, and how they make sense of their worlds. In both speech and action these women capture the complexities of working under a stigma when what they wanted was to be considered Good girls for themselves, their factory, their village, and their nation.

GLOSSARY AND ABBREVIATIONS

Frequently used acronyms

200 GFP	200 Garment Factories Program
FTZ	Free Trade Zone
JVP	Janatha Vimukthi Peramuna (People's Liberation Front)
LTTE	Liberation Tigers of Tamil Eelam
PA	People's Alliance
SLFP	Sri Lanka Freedom Party
UNP	United National Party

Frequently used Sinhala words

AHIṆSAKA: innocent, harmless; connotes simplicity, purity, and naïveté

BODHIPŪJA: a form of ritual that one offers at a *bodhi* tree

CARITAYA: moral character

DHAMMADĪPA: literally, the island of the *dhamma* (the Buddha's teachings); many Sinhala Buddhists believe that the Buddha designated Sri Lanka as the island that would exemplify and preserve the Buddha's teachings.

GAURAVAYA: respect

GOḌĒ: rural; connotes rural naïveté (like the English term *country bumpkins*)

HONDA NĂ: not good

KADĒ: a small shop

KAṬAKATĀ: orally transmitted information about people, bizarre conduct, or events; gossip

LĀJJA-BAYA: respectability; literally, "shame-fear"

SAṆWARA: discipline, decency; connotes not acting up or not being flashy, showy, or demonstrative; having self-control

NOTES

Introduction

1. Whether they were speaking Sinhala, English, or Tamil, Shirtex and Serendib workers addressed and referred to managers, who were all male, by their first names followed by the English title "Sir." They referred to male supervisors in the same way and to female supervisors with their first names followed by "Miss," if unmarried, and "Madam," if married. It is common in hierarchical situations in Sri Lanka to use Sir, Miss, and Madam in this way, either with the addressee's first or last name. Using the first name indicates more familiarity. Schoolchildren refer to their teachers with their first name plus Miss or Sir.

2. The factory names in this book are pseudonyms, as are the names of villages (such as Udakande) and people other than national political figures. I have done this to protect the privacy of the individuals about whom I am writing, including the industrialists who allowed me into their factories. To protect the privacy of workers, I have taken further precautions in certain sensitive situations, for example, those concerning family relations and labor relations. In some cases I have conflated the stories of two or more workers or changed certain cosmetic details of their stories.

3. In this book I have used established conventions for transliterating Sinhala words, and in particular I have followed the system employed by the anthropologist David Scott (1994, xiii), who writes: "The vowels *a, ā, ä, a, ä, e, ē, i, ī*, are pronounced like the first vowels in *sun, salt, may, bad, end, made, in*, and *feel*, respectively. Among the consonants, *c* is pronounced *ch*; the *s* gives a *sh* sound; *ṭ* and *ḍ* are palatals pronounced with the tongue far back; and *g* is always hard." The letter *ṇ* produces a nasal sound. For ease of reading, I often pluralize Sinhala words with the English letter *s*.

4. The two main ethnic groups in Sri Lanka are Tamils and Sinhalas (also known as "Sinhalese"). Seventy-four percent of Sri Lankans are Sinhala, most of whom are Buddhist (a small minority are Christians). The minority ethnic groups in Sri Lanka include Tamils (18 percent—mostly Hindu, some Christian), Muslims (7 percent), and small populations of other groups. (The U.S. Library of Congress cites these 1981 census figures at countrystudies.us/sri-lanka/38.htm. There was no census in 1991. For results of the incomplete 2001 census see www.statistics.gov.lk/census2001/index.html.) The terms *Sinhala* and *Tamil* also refer to the languages spoken by Sinhala and Tamil people; the first language of Muslims is generally Tamil. The shorthand *Sinhala Buddhist* is now a common designation for the majority population.

5. I place "tradition" in quotation marks to indicate that beliefs and practices that are

constructed as "traditional" today (and, earlier, for instance in anticolonial movements) are often quite new and may have been newly created or adopted from elsewhere. The term is deployed throughout the book with the caveat that we must always historicize and contextualize the term.

6. I use the term *subjects* rather than a more common term like *people* to invoke the modern philosophical figuration of individuals as thinking agents and not simply victims of the world around them. The intended connotation is the grammatical subject of a sentence, the active party, rather than a political subject ruled by someone else. This use of the term *subject* is consistent with my discussion of *agency* in the pages that follow, in which I argue for the importance of seeing how individuals act on the world around them but within certain structural constraints.

7. Mala is the author of one of three essays written by a garment worker at Shirtex or Serendib that appear in this book. These three women—Geeta, Mala, and Rohini—each wrote essays for me during my field research. They separately told me that they wanted to help me with my research by recording their formal thoughts about the situation of women garment workers in Sri Lanka. I regret that I cannot acknowledge the authors of these eloquent essays by their real names due to privacy concerns.

8. In using the term *discourse* I am invoking more than the concept of speech. I am referring to the concept used by social theorists (particularly Michel Foucault) in which the way people talk about the world reflects invisible ways of thinking and seeing that are connected with structures of power. Thus, when one analyzes discourse, one examines the underlying assumptions and relations of power embedded in forms of speech.

9. The Juki Corporation, a Japanese company, is the world's largest manufacturer of industrial sewing machines, and it has been selling sewing machines in Sri Lanka since 1976 (Perera 1998). The "Juki girl" nickname emerged by 1979, the year after the nation's first free trade zone for export-oriented manufacturing opened.

10. Using *lamay* in this way is common in other situations in Sri Lanka among peers and by bosses or teachers in structured hierarchical situations.

11. *Bodhipūja* is a form of ritual that one offers at a *bodhi* tree (*ficus religiosa*), the species of tree under which the Buddha achieved awakening (Gombrich and Obeyesekere 1988, chap. 11; Seneviratne and Wickremaratne 1980).

Chapter 1. Globalization, Gender, and Labor

1. The phrase "global feminization of labor" is common in studies of globalization and labor. It refers to the processes, since the 1970s, in which there has been an increase in women's participation in labor markets while at the same time newly created employment falls within the category of "women's work." See Standing 1999.

2. The term "scientific management" (also called Taylorism) refers to Frederick W. Taylor's 1911 treatise *The Principles of Scientific Management*, which was a prescriptive account of modern management principles. He offered a "scientific" method for dealing with management problems based on his systematic study of work behavior. Time and motion studies emerged from his principles, as did forms of work regulation such as piecework,

incentives, and bonuses. Taylorism was most popular in industrial production in the early twentieth century, but its principles remain important in industrial and other forms of management today.

3. In contrast to an assembly line, this system is more of a branching "assembly tree." Serendib was organized as an assembly line, Shirtex as an assembly tree. At Shirtex, numbered garment components moved through the factory in bundles and different components were stitched together in different places until they all converged in the spot where the final garment came together. The factory consisted of sections of workers who performed distinct operations such as sewing shoulders, collars, cuffs, or side seams. At any one time two distant workers could be working on the same garment—one attaching cuff to sleeve and the other sewing together shoulder seams. The pieces only met up later in the process.

4. As other scholars have amply demonstrated, this simultaneous valuation of the traditional and the modern is an attribute of modern societies; indeed, the very concept of *tradition* only emerged in modernity. The anthropologist Jean Jackson (1995, 18) describes how people turn to "tradition" in their struggles to make sense of social change and to preserve "self-respect, autonomy, and a life with meaning." Jane Collier (1997, 217) describes the same phenomenon of the "invention" of tradition as a way in which "modern people experience ethnicity as a tool for resisting modern forms of rationalized power."

5. This expression could also be translated as "shocked," or "taken aback," but "spooked" evokes the supernatural aspect of the phrase and seems apropos when combined with Kumari's invocation of "heaven."

6. Beyond a narrow understanding of factory discipline, all these modes of learning could also be understood in terms of a wider concept of "discipline," as discussed by Michel Foucault, whose thesis in *Discipline and Punish* (1977) is that in modern societies individuals internalize structures of power and discipline themselves by enacting particular modes of behavior and belief.

Chapter 2. Localizing Production

1. From the fifth century B.C.E. to the twelfth century C.E., this city in the dry zone of Sri Lanka was the capital of a vibrant kingdom. Today it is an important pilgrimage site for Sinhala Buddhists.

2. The Sri Lankan government allocated quotas to garment manufacturers in line with the Multifibre Arrangement (MFA), a system that regulated global trade balances by placing trade restrictions and allotments on exporting countries between 1974 and 2005.

3. In April 1996, when I was completing my field research, 161 were in operation, 5 were under construction, and 12 had been closed. These figures were compiled for me in April 1996 at the Board of Investment (BOI), the government office that administers the program.

4. Sindhis and Gujaratis are ethnic groups from India and Pakistan. Some members of these groups emigrated to Sri Lanka after the 1947 partition of India into India and Pakistan, and today they make up an important segment of the Colombo business class.

5. UNICEF figures on literacy available at www.unicef.org/infobycountry/sri_lanka_sri_lanka_statistics.html.

6. The recommendations on industrializing rural areas, making English accessible, and giving incentives to return to agriculture appear in the commission's report (*Sessional Paper I* 1990) on pages 61, 64, and 79, respectively.

7. The term *dhammadīpa* is frequently used by Sinhala Buddhist nationalists today to describe Sri Lanka as the "island of the *dhamma*," *dhamma* here referring to the Buddha's teachings. Although many nationalists would argue that this epithet has ancient origins, as Steven Collins notes (1998, 598–99 n. 17), the term appears only once in the *Mahāvamsa* (the sixth-century chronicle of Sinhala presence on the island). It refers to the "light of the *dhamma*," playing off the idea of "light of the world" (*lōkadīpa*). The term was first used to mean "island of the *dhamma*," Collins writes, "in 1942, in an article written in English by a western monk, who seems to be attributing it to a speech by Lord Passfield made in the House of Lords: a fine colonial irony." See also Seneviratne 1999, 194 n. 11.

8. For studies of Sri Lankan FTZ workers see Fine 1995; Gunatilaka 2001; Hettiarachchy 1991; Hewamanne 2002 and 2003; Joint Association of Workers Councils of Free Trade Zones 2001; Labor Video Project 1993; Rosa 1991; Tennekoon 2000; Voice of Women 1983; Weerasinghe 1989; Weerasuriya 2000. See Heward 1997 on the 200 GFP and Ryan and Fernando 1951 on Colombo factories in the 1940s.

9. According to the Sri Lanka Export Development Board (a state body), in 2001 the industry employed 338,000 workers and was the country's largest source of foreign exchange (above tea and remittances from housemaids in the Middle East): www.srilankabusiness.com/trade_info/srilankaproduct/apparel.htm.

10. Richardson (2004, 48) refers to the UNP as promoting "capitalism with a Buddhist face." Goonewardena (1996) refers to a PA motto of "capitalism with a human face."

11. I use the term *nationalist imagination* following Benedict Anderson's (1991, 5–7) discussion of nations as "imagined communities": although a nation's inhabitants will never know most of their fellow inhabitants, they imagine deep connections to one another. The "nationalist imagination" refers to the ways in which members of a nation imagine these connections and the stories a nation tells itself about its origins, values, and beliefs.

12. Alles 1990; Amnesty International 1990; Chandraprema 1991; de Silva 1998; Gunaratna 1990; Moore 1993.

13. By contrast, the 1971 JVP revolt, which predated economic liberalization, was more anticapitalist than antiforeign. Scholars debate the question of the later JVP's agenda; for instance, Moore (1993: 629–39) and Uyangoda (1992) argue emphatically that it was antiforeign but not anticapitalist, whereas de Silva (1998) says it was both.

14. Moore (1993, 627) is emphatic that the 1980s JVP revolt cannot be mapped onto rural-urban problems, and that the 1980s JVP enjoyed a much larger urban base than the 1971 JVP.

15. When factory labor first emerged in England, peasants had to be made into workers. The requisite transformations were accomplished through the use of discipline systems that rewarded and penalized workers. Karl Marx and Michel Foucault, in addition to labor historians such as E. P. Thompson, discuss the role of discipline in the Industrial Revolution.

16. I was unable to find a definitive explanation for Premadasa's intentions behind the construction of clock towers. In stark contrast to other aspects of the program that were repeatedly covered in the media and in government-issued pamphlets, there appears to be nothing written about this requirement.

17. E. P. Thompson (1967, 69–70) describes similar use of watches in newly industrialized England.

18. Susil Sirivardana, interview, 31 March 1996.

19. Stupas are dome-shaped monumental structures that contain relics of the Buddha or of prominent Buddhist figures.

20. Interview, 14 March 1996. A number of his English-language newspaper articles from that era were quoted in this chapter, under the byline of A. S. Fernando or sometimes with no byline at all.

Chapter 3. The Politics of White Women's Underwear

1. I have found no firm figures on the composition of the JVP by gender, though it is commonly noted that it was mostly male. See de Mel 1998, 2001; Gunaratna 1990. Hettige (1992, 65) writes, "Only a small minority of female youth have taken part in militant youth politics."

2. The concept of *ahiṃsaka* has been critiqued by the Sri Lankan feminist journal *Options*. In early 2001, *Options* commented on Ahinsa, a new insurance policy for women, noting that the insurance policy played on expectations for women to be innocent and harmless such that it could be positioned "for those who possess the essentially female qualities of innocence, harmlessness and 'weepiness'" (*Options* 2001).

3. Sandya Hewamanne (2002, 1, 367–78) corroborates the negative connotations of underwear in her fascinating discussion of FTZ women's transgressive acts involving the display of underwear on publicly visible clotheslines.

4. The term *suddi* could refer to "foreign women," although it usually refers to white women. In this case the sexual connotations of the critique clearly recommend its translation as "white."

5. See, e.g., Dalzell 1993; Dublin 1979; Farnsworth-Alvear 2000; French and James 1997; Lee 1998; Mills 1999; Ong 1987; Peiss 1983; Prieto 1997; Salzinger 2003; Sandel 1996; Scott 1999.

6. This is particularly true for studies of South Asia. Cf. Chatterjee 1989; Das 1996, 2000; de Alwis 1997, 1998; Jayawardena 1986, 1992; Jayawardena and de Alwis 1996; and Mani 1989, 1998.

7. It is beyond the scope of this project to investigate a third historically significant period: the period between independence in 1948 and economic liberalization in 1977. Such an analysis would be fruitful in elucidating the work put in by contemporary subjects to create a distinctively postcolonial way of being Sri Lankan.

8. See also Gombrich and Obeyesekere 1988, 256, 262–63; Grossholtz 1984, 125; Knox 1981 [1681], 133; Obeyesekere 1984, 449; Perera 1987, 3–5; Ranaweera 1992; Weerasinghe 1989.

9. Although emigration for employment overseas was not a direct feature of liberalization policies, there are two ways in which liberalization was linked to foreign migration. First, changes in emigration laws were implemented around the same time as the economy was liberalized. This meant that demand for foreign employment for working-class Sri Lankans arose at the same time as demand for laborers in the export industrial sector increased. Second, with liberalization, there was a lack of state investment in the agricultural sector, and so not only was there an increased demand for workers in the Middle East, but there was also a labor force eager to go (since there were few jobs in Sri Lanka).

10. See de Alwis 1998; de Mel 1998; Jayawardena 1992; Perera 1996; Tennekoon 1986.

11. Reuters SLNet newsgroup posting, 12 August 1997.

12. Xinhua SLNet newsgroup posting, 12 August 1997.

13. See Trautmann 1997 for a discussion of skin color and the Aryan construction, and for a history of the Aryan and Dravidian linguistic and racial categories in general. Briefly, although the terms *Aryan* and *Dravidian* were originally Orientalist linguistic and racial constructions, they have a strong place in the popular imagination in Sri Lanka. The term Aryan was developed to refer to people and languages spanning from North India to Europe, while Dravidian referred to South Indian languages and people. In Sri Lanka currently, Sinhalas are considered Aryan (and fair-skinned, after their European Aryan relatives) and Tamils are considered dark-skinned Dravidians (Gunawardana 1990).

14. The quote about *istiripura* is from Voice of Women 1983, 69. The usage of the term *vēsakalāpaya* is noted in Weerasinghe 1989, 319; and *premakalāpaya* is a term I frequently heard.

15. Ajit Serasundara, personal communication (18 October 2001).

16. I have yet to come across usages of the term that do not have these negative connotations, although one might imagine that garment workers who are referred to as Juki girls might make their own sense of it. The factory women I know used it negatively to describe other workers. Hewamanne (2003) argues that some urban garment workers who would be labeled as Juki girls actually celebrate the Juki identity.

17. Ajit Serasundara, personal communication (18 October 2001).

18. This brothel incident, and the complex relationships between army men and garment women, was later depicted in Vithanage's 2003 film *Ira Madiyama* (August Sun).

Chapter 4. Juki Girls, Good Girls, and the Village Context

1. *Locatedness* is a term used frequently in academic parlance to refer to how people make sense of the places they inhabit and construct meaningful connections to the immediate world around them. As residents of places, we all engage in important work to make those places meaningful localities—we construct histories of these places and tell stories about them, and we feel certain emotions toward them like deep attachment and affiliation.

2. A pseudonym.

3. At the time, this hiatus added up to a period of several years because of a backlog of students caused by university closings during the second JVP revolt.

4. On caste and national politics, see Jiggens 1979. For a classic sociological study of changes in caste in general, see Ryan 1953a; more contemporary accounts are Gunasinghe 1990 and Roberts 1997. For the role of caste concerns in the JVP and LTTE, see *Sessional Paper I* 1990, 84–85.

5. In 1996, the existence of camps was still circulating at the level of rumor. But human rights groups had by then documented the presence of "rehabilitation camps" where thousands of youth were detained and some eventually released. There remained rumors about secret camps, and it has been documented that suspected JVPers were kept in various official and unofficial locations, many of them never to appear again. See Keenan 2005 and *Sessional Paper V* 1997.

6. Chandra used the English word "upset" to mean "problem."

7. Unlike in the United States, in Sri Lanka body fat is desired because it indicates that one has sufficient financial resources that one does not need to do physical labor. This norm seems to be changing, though, with the influence of Western images of thin women as attractive.

8. This is a rehabilitation center for treating soldiers with physical injuries and those experiencing psychological trauma.

9. In 2003, an association of garment factory industrialists sponsored a pop music CD about garment workers, which was intended to help raise their status. At the time of its release, an English-language newspaper article described one song, a rosy, hopeful feminist vision, as follows (Uvais 2003, n.p.):

> The theme of "bread winner" was the foundation of this piece of music elaborating on the many reasons, all noble, that result in a woman becoming a garment industry employee. Whether it is to help her family, maintain the home and to keep her family fed or even, for some, to save money so that their children have access to greater academic or career opportunities than she had, the role of a garment factory employee as the bread winner of the family has led to a new position of respect in the family. Patriarchies have now turned to matriarchies with women now being the highest earner and being seen as the rescuer of the family, finally getting a strong and clear voice in this male world.

Chapter 5. The Good Girls of Sri Lankan Modernity

1. Workers accrue state-mandated financial benefits of two types, both calculated from the worker's wage rate. EPF stands for Employees Provident Fund, a fund consisting of 8 percent of the wage contributed by the worker plus 12 percent of the wage contributed by the employer. The money is made available for women after age fifty or immediately if they stop work to marry, and for men after age fifty-five. ETF stands for Employees Trust Fund, a fund consisting of 3 percent of the worker's wage, contributed entirely by the employer. It is available to workers after the current job ends (either through resignation or termination).

2. Although women often said they would like to be paid more, they also acknowl-

edged that garment work paid more than other jobs available to women. At the time of this field research in 1995 and 1996, when one U.S. dollar equaled approximately 55 Sri Lankan rupees, every worker in the 200 GFP earned a state-mandated minimum of 2,000 rupees (approximately $37) per month. Machine operators who worked overtime, met production targets, and had perfect attendance could take home more than 5,000 rupees ($90) per month in wages and bonuses. This take-home wage was better than that of a starting police officer or a bank employee, and it was far better than a teacher's. Although the dollar figure may suggest otherwise, 5,000 rupees provided basic subsistence for an individual (but *not* for a family, for whom the workers were often providing). In 1996 a loaf of bread cost 7 rupees; a kilo of lower-quality rice, 15 rupees; two aspirin tablets, 1 rupee; a two-mile bus fare, 2 rupees; and rubber sandals, 175 rupees.

3. Sometimes workers at Shirtex and Serendib worked overtime into the night, and occasionally overnight. When they needed to travel after dark, vans hired by the factories would bring them home.

4. This fear contradicts the claim by Gombrich and Obeyesekere in 1988 (262–63) that the bedsheet virginity test was practiced by Low Country Sinhalas, but not by Kandyans.

5. The same point would come up in reference to caste, too: if the wedding was for a low-caste coworker, high-caste women could attend more easily if it were in a distant village.

Chapter 6. Paternalism and Factory Conflicts

1. Cf. Cairoli 1998, 1999; Fernández-Kelly 1983; Fuentes and Ehrenreich 1983; Hall 1992; Kondo 1990; Nash and Fernández-Kelly 1983; Prieto 1997 [1985]; Siddiqi 1996.

2. For instance, according to Italian law from the 1930s to 1996, criminal charges would be dropped against a rapist if he agreed to marry the woman he raped—all for the sake of the woman's future (Stanley 1999, A6).

3. I thank Michele Gamburd for her thoughts on this situation with Ralph Sir, which have helped me immensely with my analysis. Gamburd noted that she has heard rumor and innuendo that suggest that it is possible that some Sri Lankan parents might force their daughter to marry her rapist (Personal communication, August 2005).

4. Posters are a popular medium of mass communication in Sri Lanka. They are used particularly in politics, covering walls throughout Kandy and Colombo and even appearing in smaller towns and villages during elections and strikes. See Moore 1993, 627 n. 92; Ratnapala 1991, 179.

5. I learned this in an interview with Asanka Sir after the incident. He spoke in English, but said he was reporting what the workers had said in Sinhala: "*apiṭa läjjay*"—we're ashamed.

6. The only other work stoppage that I know of at either factory also was in support of Yohan Sir. This happened in late 1999, when workers refused to work because they had learned that Yohan Sir was leaving the factory under what were rumored to be less-than-favorable conditions. The workers who wrote to me about this later incident said that the

workers wanted to express their support for Yohan Sir if he was in fact being fired. Indeed, Yohan Sir did then leave Shirtex.

7. *Tamuse* is one of several forms of the pronoun *you* in Sinhala. Colonial-era Sinhala-English dictionaries indicate that it is polite and civil, like *thou*. However, the contemporary valence is the diametrical opposite of polite and civil, unless it is used in an affectionate and joking manner with close friends or relatives.

8. Sinhala and Tamil New Years are celebrated on April 13 or 14 each year, with the precise time determined by astrologers. The New Year festival marks the annual harvest and is one of the most exciting festivals for Sri Lankans. People prepare sweets weeks in advance and purchase clothes as gifts for relatives. Shirtex and Serendib workers get a one-week paid holiday at this time and receive a New Year's bonus.

9. "Debate baila" is a form of Sinhala pop music, a hybrid Sri Lankan musical form that incorporates elements of Portuguese and indigenous music. See Kemper 2001, chap. 3; Sheeran 1997, 2002.

Conclusion

1. United Nations Industrial Development Organization, "Trade Capacity Building: Case Studies: Sri Lanka," www.unido.org/doc/27889. Other analysts have said that Sri Lanka will fare well because it produces quality garments that are in demand and cannot be produced just anywhere. See, for instance, Karp 1999. See also Kelegama 2005.

2. The presence of cotton dust led to the branding of Southern U.S. male and female cotton-mill workers in the early twentieth century as "lintheads" (Brattain 2001; Brooks 1999; Hall et al. 2000). According to Jane Collins, the lint implied a certain sense of being "fresh off the farm," uncultured, and "perhaps having the poor morals that accompanied a hand-to-mouth existence." (Personal communication, 26 June 2002.)

REFERENCES

Abeysekara, Ananda. 2002. *Colors of the Robe: Religion, Identity, and Difference*. Columbia: University of South Carolina Press.

Abeysekera, Sunila. 1989. "Women in Sri Lankan Cinema." *Framework* 37: 49–58.

——. 1997. "Penalising Women's Sexual Autonomy: A Look at Contemporary Sinhala Cinema." *Options* 9: 3–7.

——. 2005. "Garment Girls and Army Boys: Foretelling the Future." *Cinesith* 4: 23–29.

Adam, Barbara. 1990. *Time in Social Theory*. Philadelphia: Temple University Press.

Afterimage. 1997. *From The Background to the Foreground: The Photo Backdrop and Cultural Expression*. 24, 5.

Alles, A. C. 1990. *The JVP: 1969–89*. Colombo: Lake House Investments.

Amararatne, R. M. R. 1992a. "The Garment Factory at Patha Dumbara That Brightens Dumbara." *Dinamina* (Colombo), 18 September, n.p. (in Sinhala, trans. Nandana Galpaya).

——. 1992b. "Kaluwaragaswewa Garment Factory Built in Memory of Mother." *Dinamina* (Colombo), 12 October, n.p. (in Sinhala, trans. Nandana Galpaya).

Amnesty International. 1990. *Sri Lanka: Extrajudicial Executions, "Disappearances," and Torture, 1987 to 1990* (ASA 37/21/90). London: Amnesty International.

Anderson, Benedict. 1991. *Imagined Communities*. Rev. ed. New York: Verso.

Appadurai, Arjun. 1996. *Modernity at Large: Cultural Dimensions of Globalization*. Minneapolis: University of Minnesota Press.

——. 1997. "The Colonial Backdrop." *Afterimage* 24, 5: 4–7.

——. 1998. "Dead Certainty: Ethnic Violence in the Era of Globalization." *Public Culture* 10, 2: 225–47.

——. 2000. "Grassroots Globalization and the Research Imagination." *Public Culture* 12: 1–19.

Asad, Talal. 1993. *Genealogies of Religion: Discipline and Reasons of Power in Christianity and Islam*. Baltimore: Johns Hopkins University Press.

Bandarage, Asoka. 1988. "Women and Capitalist Development in Sri Lanka, 1977–87." *Bulletin of Concerned Asian Scholars* 20, 2: 57–81.

Behar, Ruth. 2003. *Translated Woman*. 2d ed. Boston: Beacon Press.

Beynon, John, and David Dunkerley. 2000. "General Introduction." In *Globalization: The Reader*, edited by J. Beynon and D. Dunkerley. London: Routledge.

Biyanwala, Janaka. 1997. "A Letter to Susanthika." *Options* 10: 25, 27.

BOI. 1993. "Free Trade Zone" pamphlet. Section on "Garment Factories, From Village to Village," June (in Sinhala, trans. Rosemary Chunchie).

——. n.d. "200 Garments Industries in 200 Pradesheeya Areas: A Brief Step by Step Guide on How to Implement Your Project" (pamphlet).

Bond, George. 1988. *The Buddhist Revival in Sri Lanka: Religious Tradition, Reinterpretation and Response*. Columbia: University of South Carolina Press.

Bourdieu, Pierre. 1977. *Outline of a Theory of Practice*. Cambridge: Cambridge University Press.

Bowen, John. 1992. "Centralizing Agricultural Time: A Case from South Sulawesi." In *The Politics of Time*, edited by Henry J. Rutz. Washington, D.C.: American Anthropological Association.

Brattain, Michelle. 2001. *The Politics of Whiteness: Race, Workers, and Culture in the Modern South*. Princeton, N.J.: Princeton University Press.

Brooks, Shannon. 1999. "Coming Home: Finding My Appalachian Mothers through Emma Bell Miles." *NWSA Journal* 11, 3: 157–71.

Brow, James. 1990. "The Incorporation of a Marginal Community within the Sinhalese Nation." *Anthropological Quarterly* 63, 1: 7–17.

——. 1996. *Demons and Development: The Struggle for Community in a Sri Lankan Village*. Tucson: University of Arizona Press.

Burke, Timothy. 1996. *Lifebuoy Men, Lux Women: Commodification, Consumption, and Cleanliness in Modern Zimbabwe*. Durham, N.C.: Duke University Press.

Cairoli, M. Laetitia. 1998. "Factory as Home and Family: Female Workers in the Moroccan Garment Industry." *Human Organization* 57, 2: 181–89.

——. 1999. "Garment Workers in the City of Fez." *Middle East Journal* 53, 1: 28–43.

Caprio, Temby. 1997. " 'Our Anoja': Questions for a National Cinema." *Options* 10: 5–11.

Carby, Hazel. 1997. "Policing the Black Woman's Body in an Urban Context." In *Women Transforming Politics: An Alternative Reader*, edited by Cathy J. Cohen, Kathleen B. Jones, and Joan C. Tronto. New York: New York University Press.

Cat's Eye. 1997. "Susanthika: Sexism, Racism, and the Body Politic." *Island* (Colombo), 26 November: n.p.

Chandraprema, C. A. 1991. *Sri Lanka: The Years of Terror. The JVP Insurrection 1987–89*. Colombo: Lake House Investments.

Chatterjee, Partha. 1986. *Nationalist Thought and the Colonial World: A Derivative Discourse?* London: Zed.

——. 1989. "The Nationalist Resolution of the Women's Question." In *Recasting Women: Essays in Indian Colonial History*, edited by Kumkum Sangari and Sudesh Vaid. New Brunswick, N.J.: Rutgers University Press.

——. 1993. *The Nation and Its Fragments: Colonial and Postcolonial Histories*. Princeton, N.J.: Princeton University Press.

Clifford, James, and George Marcus, eds. 1986. *Writing Culture: The Poetics and Politics of Ethnography*. Berkeley: University of California Press.

Cohen, Stanley. 1972. *Folk Devils and Moral Panics: The Creation of the Mods and Rockers*. London: MacGibbon and Kee.

Collier, Jane Fishburne. 1997. *From Duty to Desire: Remaking Families in a Spanish Village*. Princeton, N.J.: Princeton University Press.

BIBLIOGRAPHY

Collins, Jane. 2003. *Threads: Gender, Labor, and Power in the Global Apparel Industry*. Chicago: University of Chicago Press.

Collins, Steven. 1998. *Nirvana and Other Buddhist Felicities*. Cambridge: Cambridge University Press.

Colombo Calling (Internet magazine). 1997. 14 July (*sic*, August) (received on SLNet news mailing list).

Constable, Nicole. 1997. *Maid to Order in Hong Kong: An Ethnography of Filipina Workers*. Ithaca, N.Y.: Cornell University Press.

——. 2003. *Romance on a Global Stage*. Berkeley: University of California Press.

Daily Mirror (Colombo). 2005. "Women Victims Need More Help." Editorial, 27 May: n.p.

Daily News (Colombo). 1992a. "Export-Oriented Garment Industry Must Meet Economic Aspirations of People—President." 19 February: 15.

——. 1992b. "A Daunting Challenge." Editorial, 20 February: 6.

Dalzell, Robert F., Jr. 1993. *Enterprising Elite: The Boston Associates and the World They Made*. New York: W. W. Norton.

Das, Veena. 1996. *Critical Events: An Anthropological Perspective on Contemporary India*. Delhi: Oxford University Press.

——. 2000. "The Making of Modernity: Gender and Time in Indian Cinema." In *Questions of Modernity*, edited by Timothy Mitchell. Minneapolis: University of Minnesota Press.

de Alwis, Malathi. 1994. "The Articulation of Gender in Cinematic Address: Sinhala Cinema in 1992." In *Images*, edited by Selvy Thiruchandran. Colombo: Women's Education and Research Centre.

——. 1995. "Gender, Politics, and the 'Respectable Lady.'" In *Unmaking the Nation*, edited by Pradeep Jeganathan and Qadri Ismail. Colombo: Social Scientists' Association.

——. 1996. "Sexuality in the Field of Vision: The Discursive Clothing of the Sigiriya Frescoes." In *Embodied Violence: Communalising Women's Sexuality in South Asia*, edited by Kumari Jayawardena and Malathi de Alwis. London: Zed.

——. 1997. "The Production and Embodiment of Respectability: Gendered Demeanours in Colonial Ceylon." In *Sri Lanka: Collective Identities Revisited*, vol. 2, edited by Michael Roberts. Colombo: Marga Institute.

——. 1998. "Maternalist Politics in Sri Lanka: A Historical Anthropology of Its Conditions of Possibility." Ph.D. diss., University of Chicago.

de Certeau, Michel. 1984. *The Practice of Everyday Life*. Berkeley: University of California Press.

de Mel, Neloufer. 1998. "Agent or Victim? The Sri Lankan Woman Militant in the Interregnum." In *Sri Lanka: Collective Identities Revisited*, vol. 2, edited by Michael Roberts. Colombo: Marga Institute.

——. 2001. *Women and the Nation's Narrative: Gender and Nationalism in Twentieth Century Sri Lanka*. Lanham, Md.: Rowman and Littlefield.

de Munck, Victor. 1998. "Lust, Love, and Arranged Marriages in Sri Lanka." In *Romantic Love and Sexual Behavior: Perspectives from the Social Sciences*, edited by V. de Munck. Westport, Conn.: Praeger.

de Silva, Jani. 1998. "Praxis, Language, and Silences: The July 1987 Uprising of the JVP in Sri Lanka." In *Sri Lanka: Collective Identities Revisited*, vol. 2, edited by Michael Roberts. Colombo: Marga Institute.

de Silva, Pramod. 1992a. "Fearing a Threat to Their Supremacy . . . Some Aristocrats Out to Destroy Govt Programs—President." *Daily News* (Colombo), 20 October: n.p.

——. 1992b. "Remarkable Economic Growth Despite On-Going War, Says President." *Daily News* (Colombo), 3 November: n.p.

——. 1993. "We Seek Support on the Strength of Our Record—President." *Daily News* (Colombo), 16 March: n.p.

Department of Government Printing. 1988. *"For Mother Lanka: A New Vision, A New Deal." The United National Party's Manifesto of Action for Investing in People*. Colombo: Department of Government Printing.

——. 1989. *Address to Parliament by the President on 9th March, 1989*. Colombo: Department of Government Printing.

——. 1990a. *Address to Parliament by the President on 4th April, 1990*. Colombo: Department of Government Printing.

——. 1990b. *Progress of the People: Implementation of the UNP Manifesto, February 1989–October 1990*. Colombo: Department of Government Printing.

——. 1992. *Progress of the People: Implementation of the UNP Manifesto, February 1989–October 1992*. Colombo: Department of Government Printing.

Dickey, Sara. 2003. Discussant comments at panel on "Women and Everyday Conflicts in Sri Lanka." American Anthropological Association annual meetings, 19 November. Chicago.

Dublin, Thomas. 1979. *Women at Work: The Transformation of Work and Community in Lowell, Massachusetts, 1826–1860*. New York: Columbia University Press.

Elson, Diane, and Ruth Pearson. 1981. "Nimble Fingers Make Cheap Workers: An Analysis of Women's Employment in Third World Export Manufacturing." *Feminist Review* 7: 87–107.

Enloe, Cynthia. 1989. *Bananas, Beaches, and Bases: Making Feminist Sense of International Politics*. Berkeley: University of California Press.

Evans-Pritchard, E. E. 1940. *The Nuer: A Description of the Modes of Livelihood and Political Institutions of a Nilotic People*. Oxford: Oxford University Press.

Farnsworth-Alvear, Ann. 2000. *Dulcinea in the Factory: Myths, Morals, Men, and Women in Colombia's Industrial Experiment, 1905–1960*. Durham, N.C.: Duke University Press.

Fernández-Kelly, Maria Patricia. 1983. *For We Are Sold, I and My People*. Albany: State University of New York Press.

Fernández-Kelly, Patricia, and Diane Wolf. 2001. "A Dialogue on Globalization." *Signs* 26, 4: 1243–49.

Fernando, A. S. 1992a. "Two-Hundred Garment Factories, 100,000 Jobs." *Daily News* (Colombo), 19 February: 14.

——. 1992b. "President Warns of Vicious Campaign to Vilify Government." *Daily News* (Colombo), 27 May: 1, 15.

——. 1992c. "President Promises People 'A Better Living Standard' by Next General Elections." *Daily News* (Colombo), 8 August: n.p.

——. 1992d. "President Charts Path from . . . Rule of Law to Rule of Love." *Daily News* (Colombo), 28 October: 15.

——. 1992e. "New Value to People's Latent Skills and Creative Talents." *Daily News* (Colombo), 31 October: 17.

——. 1992f. "President on Ideas of Some Entrepreneurs: 'Poor Pay Minimum Benefits to Employees Will Result in Bigger Profits—A Myth'." *Daily News* (Colombo), 21 November: n.p.

——. 1992g. "Socio-Economic Revolution in Villages through Garment Factories." *Daily News* (Colombo), 25 November: n.p.

——. 1993. "Garment Factories Only the Beginning of Industrial Revolution in Rural Sector—President." *Daily News* (Colombo), 4 February: n.p.

Fernando, A. S., and P. Dissanayake. 1992. "President Vows to Usher in New Order Bound by 'Spirit of Caring and Sharing'." *Daily News* (Colombo), 29 October: n.p.

Fernando, A. S., and A. C. Fernandopulle. 1992. "Let the 'Haves' Invest to Help the 'Have-Nots.' " *Daily News* (Colombo), 24 November: n.p.

Fernando, Anthony. 1993. "The 200 Garment Factory Programme: A Stitch in Time to the Rural Social Fabric." *Daily News* (Colombo), 24 April: n.p.

——. n.d. "The Concept of Poverty Alleviation through the 200 Garment Factories Project." Unpublished typewritten pamphlet.

Fernando, Sharmini. 1997. "The Women's Sexual Health Project." *Options* 9: 21–23.

Fine, Janice, with Matthew Howard. 1995. "Women in the Free Trade Zones of Sri Lanka." *Dollars and Sense*, November/December: 26–27, 39–40.

Foucault, Michel. 1977. *Discipline and Punish: The Birth of the Prison*. Translated by Alan Sheridan. New York: Vintage.

Freeman, Carla. 2000. *High Tech and High Heels in the Global Economy: Women, Work, and Pink-Collar Identities in the Caribbean*. Durham, N.C.: Duke University Press.

——. 2001. "Is Local : Global as Feminine : Masculine? Rethinking the Gender of Globalization." *Signs* 26, 4: 1007–32.

French, John D., and Daniel James, eds. 1997. *The Gendered Worlds of Latin American Women Workers*. Durham, N.C.: Duke University Press.

Friedman, Thomas. 2005a. *The World Is Flat: A Brief History of the Twenty-First Century*. New York: Farrar, Straus, and Giroux.

——. 2005b. "It's a Flat World, After All." *The New York Times Magazine*, 3 April: 33.

Fuentes, Annette, and Barbara Ehrenreich. 1983. *Women in the Global Factory*. Boston: South End Press.

Fuller, Thomas. 2006. "A Vision of Pale Beauty Carries Risks for Asia's Women." *New York Times*, 14 May: 3.

Gamburd, Michele Ruth. 1995. "Sri Lanka's 'Army of Housemaids': Control of Remittances and Gender Transformations." *Anthropologica* 37: 49–88.

——. 2000. *The Kitchen Spoon's Handle: Transnationalism and Sri Lanka's Migrant Housemaids*. Ithaca, N.Y.: Cornell University Press.

——. 2004. "The Economics of Enlisting: A Village View of Armed Service." In *Economy and Ethnic Conflict in Sri Lanka*, edited by Deborah Winslow and Michael Woost. Bloomington: Indiana University Press.

Goffman, Erving. 1963. *Stigma: Notes on the Management of Spoiled Identity*. Englewood Cliffs, N.J.: Prentice-Hall.

Gombrich, Richard, and Gananth Obeyesekere. 1988. *Buddhism Transformed*. Princeton, N.J.: Princeton University Press.

Goode, Erich, and Nachman Ben-Yehuda. 1994. *Moral Panics: The Social Construction of Deviance*. Oxford: Blackwell Publishers.

Goody, Jack. 1991 [1968]. "Time: Social Organization." *International Encyclopedia of Social Sciences* 16, 30–42.

Goonesekere, Savitri. 1989. "Legislative Support for Improving the Economic Conditions of Sri Lankan Women: The Experience of the Last Decade." In *Women in Development in South Asia*, edited by V. Kanesalingam. New Delhi: Macmillan India.

———. 1996. "Gender Relations in the Family: Law and Public Policy in Post-Colonial Sri Lanka." In *Shifting Circles of Support: Contextualising Gender and Kinship in South Asia and Sub-Saharan Africa*, edited by Rajni Palriwala and Carla Risseeuw. Walnut Creek, Calif.: Alta Mira Press.

Goonewardena, Kanishka. 1996. "Cultural Politics of Global Capital: National Socialism in Sri Lanka." Paper presented at the 25th Annual Conference on South Asia, Madison, Wisconsin, 17–20 October.

Government Printing Department. 1992. "The Free Trade Zone Goes to the Village" (in Sinhala, trans. Rosemary Chunchie).

Gross, Daniel. 2004. "Goodbye, Pension. Goodbye, Health Insurance. Goodbye, Vacations: Welfare Capitalism Is Dying. We're Going to Miss It." *Slate*, 23 September: n.p. Available at www.slate.com/id/2107108/.

Grossholtz, Jean. 1984. *Forging Capitalist Patriarchy: The Economic and Social Transformation of Feudal Sri Lanka and Its Impact on Women*. Durham, N.C.: Duke University Press.

Gunaratna, Rohan. 1990. *Sri Lanka: A Lost Revolution? The Inside Story of the JVP*. Kandy, Sri Lanka: Institute of Fundamental Studies.

Gunasekera, Manisha. 1996. "Jatika Chintanaya and Identity Crisis: A Feminist Reappraisal." Paper presented at the National Convention on Women's Studies, March (Centre for Women's Research [CENWOR], Colombo, Sri Lanka).

Gunasinghe, Newton. 1984. "Open Economy and Its Impact on Ethnic Relations in Sri Lanka." In *Sri Lanka, The Ethnic Conflict: Myths, Realities and Perspectives*, edited by Committee for Rational Development. New Delhi: Navrang.

———. 1990. *Changing Socio-Economic Relations in the Kandyan Countryside*. Colombo: Social Scientists' Association.

Gunatilaka, Ramani. 2001. "Freedom of Association and Collective Bargaining in Sri Lanka: Progress and Prospects." Colombo: International Labor Office.

Gunawardana, R. A. L. H. 1990. "The People of the Lion: The Sinhala Identity and Ideology in History and Historiography." In *Sri Lanka: History and the Roots of Conflict*, edited by Jonathan Spencer. London: Routledge.

Guruge, Ananda, ed. 1965. *Return to Righteousness: A Collection of Speeches, Essays, and Letters of the Anagarika Dharmapala*. Colombo: Government Press.

Hall, Catherine. 1992. *White, Male, and Middle-Class: Explorations in Feminism and History*. Cambridge: Polity Press.

Hall, Jacquelyn Dowd, James Leloudis, Robert Korstad, Mary Murphy, Lu Ann Jones, and Christopher B. Daly. 2000. *Like a Family: The Making of a Southern Cotton Mill World*. Greensboro: University of North Carolina Press.

Hannerz, Ulf. 1992. *Cultural Complexity: Studies in the Social Organization of Meaning*. New York: Columbia University Press.

Hettiarachchy, T. 1991. "A Report on the Socio-Economic Problems of the Workforce at Katunayake Export Processing Zone." *Island* (Colombo), 29 December: n.p.

Hettige, S. T. 2000. "Globalisation and Local Culture: The Case of Sri Lanka." In *Sri Lanka at Crossroads: Dilemmas and Prospects after 50 Years of Independence*, edited by S. T. Hettige and Markus Mayer. Delhi: Macmillan India.

——. 2004. "Economic Policy, Changing Opportunities for Youth, and the Ethnic Conflict in Sri Lanka." In *Economy and Ethnic Conflict in Sri Lanka*, edited by Deborah Winslow and Michael Woost. Bloomington: Indiana University Press.

Hettige, S. T., ed. 1992. *Unrest or Revolt: Some Aspects of Youth Unrest in Sri Lanka*. Colombo: Goethe-Institut, German Cultural Institute, and American Studies Association (Sri Lanka).

Hettigoda, Deshabandu Dr. Victor. 1992. "Garment Factory Program Is a Giant Leap in Development." *Dinamina* (Colombo), 19 December: n.p. (in Sinhala, trans. Nandana Galpaya).

Hewamanne, Sandya. 2002. "Stitching Identities: Work, Play, and Politics among Sri Lanka's Free Trade Zone Garment Factory Workers." Ph.D. diss., University of Texas at Austin.

——. 2003. "Performing 'Dis-respectability': New Tastes, Cultural Practices, and Identity Performances by Sri Lanka's Free Trade Zone Garment-Factory Workers." *Cultural Dynamics* 15: 71–101.

Heward, Susan. 1997. *Garment Workers and the 200 Garment Factory Program*. Colombo: Centre for the Welfare of Garment Workers.

Hughes, Diane O., and Thomas R. Trautmann, eds. 1995. *Time: Histories and Ethnologies*. Ann Arbor: University of Michigan Press.

Ismail, Qadri. 1991. "Boys Will Be Boys: Gender and National Agency in Frantz Fanon and the Liberation Tigers." *South Asia Bulletin* 11: 79–83.

Israeli, Raphael. 2002. *Poison: Modern Manifestations of a Blood Libel*. Lanham, Md.: Lexington Books.

Ivan, Victor. 1989. *Sri Lanka in Crisis: Road to Conflict*. Ratmalana, Sri Lanka: Sarvodaya Book Publishing Services.

Jackson, Jean. 1995. "Culture, Genuine and Spurious: The Politics of Indianness in the Vaupés, Colombia." *American Ethnologist* 22, 1: 3–27.

Jayamanne, Laleen. 1992. "Hunger for Images, Myths of Femininity in Sri Lankan Cinema 1947–1989." *South Asia Bulletin* 12, 1: 57–75.

Jayatilleka, Dayan, and Tisaranee Gunasekara. 1994. *The Premadasa Philosophy: Selected Thoughts of Ranasinghe Premadasa*. Colombo: Premadasa Center.

Jayawardena, Kumari. 1985. *Ethnic and Class Conflicts in Sri Lanka: Some Aspects of Sinhala Buddhist Consciousness over the Past 100 Years*. Dehiwala: Centre for Social Analysis.

——. 1986. *Feminism and Nationalism in the Third World*. London: Zed.

———. 1992. "Some Aspects of Religious and Cultural Identity and the Construction of Sinhala Buddhist Womanhood." In *Religion and Political Conflict in South Asia: India, Pakistan, and Sri Lanka,* edited by Douglas Allen. Westport, Conn.: Greenwood Press.

Jayawardena, Kumari, and Malathi de Alwis. 1996. "Introduction." In *Embodied Violence: Communalising Women's Sexuality in South Asia,* edited by Kumari Jayawardena and Malathi de Alwis. London: Zed.

Jayawardena, Kumari, and Swarna Jayaweera. 1986. *A Profile on Sri Lanka: The Integration of Women in Development Planning.* Colombo: Women's Education Centre.

Jayaweera, Swarna. 1989. "Women and Education." In *The UN Decade for Women: Progress and Achievements of Women in Sri Lanka,* edited by Swarna Jayaweera. Colombo: Centre for Women's Research (CENWOR).

Jeganathan, Pradeep. 1997. "After a Riot: Anthropological Locations of Violence in an Urban Sri Lankan Community." Ph.D. diss., University of Chicago.

Jiggens, Janice. 1979. *Caste and Family in the Politics of the Sinhalese, 1947–1976.* Cambridge: Cambridge University Press.

Joint Association of Workers Councils of Free Trade Zones. 2001. *Slaves of "Free" Trade: Camp Sri Lanka.* Videocassette. Seeduwa, Sri Lanka, Joint Association of Workers Councils of Free Trade Zones.

Kabeer, Naila. 2000. *The Powers to Choose: Bangladeshi Women and Labour Market Decisions in London and Dhaka.* London: Verso.

Kandiyoti, Deniz. 1991. "Identity and Its Discontents: Women and the Nation." *Millennium: Journal of International Studies* 20, 3: 429–43.

Karp, Jonathan. 1999. "Sri Lanka Keeps Victoria's Secret: Island Workers Produce Panties in Cool Comfort." *Wall Street Journal,* 13 July: B1, B4.

Keenan, Alan. 2005. "Making Sense of Bindunuwewa: From Massacre to Acquittals," *Law and Society Trust Review* 15, 212 (June) (available online at http://humanrightsand peace.blogspot.com/2006/03/bindunuwewa-massacre-justice-undone.html).

Kelegama, Saman. 2005. "Ready-Made Garment Industry in Sri Lanka: Preparing to Face the Global Challenges." *Asia-Pacific Trade and Investment Review* 1, 1 (April): 51–67 (available online at www.unescap.org/tid/publication/aptir2362_research3.pdf).

Kemper, Steven. 1991. *The Presence of the Past.* Ithaca, N.Y.: Cornell University Press.

———. 1993. "The Nation Consumed: Buying and Believing in Sri Lanka." *Public Culture* 5: 377–93.

———. 2001. *Buying and Believing: Sri Lankan Advertising and Consumers in a Transnational World.* Chicago: University of Chicago Press.

Knox, Robert. 1981 [1681]. *An Historical Relation of Ceylon.* London: Chiswell.

Kondo, Dorinne K. 1990. *Crafting Selves: Power, Gender, and Discourses of Identity in a Japanese Workplace.* Chicago: University of Chicago Press.

Labor Video Project. 1993. *Women of the Zone: Garment Workers of Sri Lanka.* (Videocassette, 30 minutes). San Francisco, Labor Video Project.

Landes, David S. 1983. *Revolution in Time.* Cambridge, Mass.: Harvard University Press.

Lave, Jean. 1988. *Cognition and Practice.* Cambridge: Cambridge University Press.

———. 1993. "The Practice of Learning." In *Understanding Practice: Perspectives on Activity and Context*, edited by Seth Chaiklin and Jean Lave. Cambridge: Cambridge University Press.

——. 1996. "Teaching, as Learning, in Practice." *Mind, Culture, and Activity* 3, 3: 149–64.

Lave, Jean, and Etienne Wenger. 1991. *Situated Learning: Legitimate Peripheral Participation*. Cambridge: Cambridge University Press.

Lebovics, Herman. 1992. *True France: The Wars over Cultural Identity, 1900–1945*. Ithaca, N.Y.: Cornell University Press.

Lee, Ching Kwan. 1998. *Gender and the South China Miracle: Two Worlds of Factory Women*. Berkeley: University of California Press.

Lloyd, Marion. 1998. "Ban on English-Language Teaching Haunts College Students in Sri Lanka." *Chronicle of Higher Education*, 2 October: A49, A50.

Lukose, Ritty. 2001. "Learning Modernity: Youth Culture in Kerala, South India." Ph.D. diss., University of Chicago.

Maddox, Richard. 1993. *El Castillo: The Politics of Tradition in an Andalusian Town*. Urbana: University of Illinois Press.

Mahmood, Saba. 2001. "Feminist Theory, Embodiment, and the Docile Agent: Some Reflections on the Egyptian Islamic Revival." *Cultural Anthropology* 16, 2: 202–36.

——. 2005. *Politics of Piety: The Islamic Revival and the Feminist Subject*. Princeton, N.J.: Princeton University Press.

Mani, Lata. 1989. "Contentious Traditions: The Debate on Sati in Colonial India." In *Recasting Women: Essays in Indian Colonial History*, edited by Kumkum Sangari and Sudesh Vaid. New Brunswick, N.J.: Rutgers University Press.

——. 1998. *Contentious Traditions: The Debate on Sati in Colonial India*. Berkeley: University of California Press.

Marecek, Jeanne. 1998. "Culture, Gender, and Suicidal Behavior in Sri Lanka." *Suicide and Life-Threatening Behavior* 28: 69–81.

McClintock, Anne. 1995. *Imperial Leather: Race, Gender, and Sexuality in the Colonial Contest*. New York: Routledge.

Mencken, H. L. 1991. *The Diary of H. L. Mencken*. New York: Vintage.

Meyer, Stephen. 1981. *The Five Dollar Day: Labor Management and Social Control in the Ford Motor Company, 1908–1921*. Albany: State University of New York Press.

Mills, Mary Beth. 1999. *Thai Women in the Global Labor Force: Consuming Desires, Contested Selves*. New Brunswick, N.J.: Rutgers University Press.

——. 2003. "Gender and Inequality in the Global Labor Force." *Annual Review of Anthropology* 32: 41–62.

Mohamed, Suresh. 1992a. "Mrs. B's Regime of Shortages and Queues: Govt. Will Never Take People Back to That 'Miserable Era'—President." *Island* (Colombo), 3 June: 3.

——. 1992b. "President Explains Rationale for Garment Factories on Estate." *Island* (Colombo), 24 October: n.p.

Mohanty, Chandra Talpade. 1991a. "Cartographies of Struggle: Third World Women and the Politics of Feminism." In *Third World Women and the Politics of Feminism*, edited by Chandra Talpade Mohanty, Ann Russo, and Lourdes Torres. Bloomington: Indiana University Press.

———. 1991b. "Under Western Eyes: Feminist Scholarship and Colonial Discourses." In *Third World Women and the Politics of Feminism*.

Moore, Mick. 1985. *The State and Peasant Politics in Sri Lanka*. Cambridge: Cambridge University Press.

———. 1989. "The Ideological History of the Sri Lankan 'Peasantry.'" *Modern Asian Studies* 23: 179–207.

———. 1993. "Thoroughly Modern Revolutionaries: The JVP in Sri Lanka." *Modern Asian Studies* 27: 593–642.

Mosse, George. 1985. *Nationalism and Sexuality: Middle-Class Morality and Sexual Norms in Modern Europe*. Madison: University of Wisconsin Press.

Munn, Nancy D. 1992. "The Cultural Anthropology of Time: A Critical Essay." *Annual Review of Anthropology* 21: 931–23.

Nash, June, and Maria Patricia Fernández-Kelly, eds. 1983. *Women, Men, and the International Division of Labor*. Albany: State University of New York Press.

Newman, Katherine. 1999. *No Shame in My Game: The Working Poor in the Inner City*. New York: Knopf and the Russell Sage Foundation.

Obeyesekere, Gananath. 1970. "Religious Symbolism and Political Change in Ceylon." *Modern Ceylon Studies* 1: 43–63.

———. 1984. *The Cult of the Goddess Pattini*. Chicago: University of Chicago Press.

Observer (Colombo). 1993. "Over 50,000 Present at Opening of Two Garment Factories in East." 28 February: n.p.

Onderdenwijngaard, Therese. 1995. "Hema's Story: A Narrative without Plot?" *Pravada* 3, 11: 17–26.

Ong, Aihwa. 1987. *Spirits of Resistance and Capitalist Discipline: Factory Women in Malaysia*. Albany: State University of New York Press.

———. 1991. "The Gender and Labor Politics of Postmodernity." *Annual Review of Anthropology* 20: 279–309.

Options. 2001. "Ahinsa." *Options* 25: 11.

Ortner, Sherry. 1996. *Making Gender: The Politics and Erotics of Culture*. Boston: Beacon Press.

Parker, Andrew, Mary Russo, Doris Sommer, and Patricia Yaeger, eds. 1992. *Nationalisms and Sexualities*. New York: Routledge.

Peiss, Kathy. 1983. "'Charity Girls' and City Pleasures: Historical Notes on Working-Class Sexuality, 1880–1920." In *Powers of Desire: The Politics of Sexuality*, edited by Ann Snitow, Christine Stansell, and Sharon Thompson. New York: Monthly Review Press.

Perera, H. E. Myrtle. 1987. "The Changing Status of Women in Sri Lanka." *International Journal of Sociology of the Family* 17: 1–23.

Perera, Sasanka. 1995. *Living with Torturers*. Colombo: ICES.

———. 1996. "The Social and Cultural Construction of Female Sexuality and Gender Roles in Sinhala Society." Paper presented at the National Convention on Women's Studies, March (Centre for Women's Research [CENWOR], Colombo, Sri Lanka).

Perera, Vernon. 1998. "Juki President Impressed by Local Workforce." *Sunday Observer* (Colombo), 11 October, Business: n.p.

Phillips, Richard. 2000. "The Struggle of the Common Man for Self-Dignity is Very Profound." Interview of Prasanna Vithanage, March 1. Last accessed 1 June 2006 on the World Socialist Web site www.wsws.org/articles/2000/mar2000/pras-m01.shtml.

Pinney, Christopher. 1998. *Camera Indica: The Social Life of Indian Photographs*. Chicago: University of Chicago Press.

Presidential Secretariat, The. n.d. [1991?]. "A Charter for Democracy in Sri Lanka." Colombo: The Presidential Secretariat.

Prieto, Norma Iglesias. 1997 [1985]. *Beautiful Flowers of the Maquiladora: Life Histories of Women Workers in Tijuana*. Austin: University of Texas Press.

Radway, Janice. 1986. "Identifying Ideological Seams: Mass Culture, Analytical Method, and Political Practice." *Communication* 9: 93–123.

Rajasingham-Senanayake, Darini. 1997. "The Sinhala *Kaduwa*: Language as a Double Edged Sword and Ethnic Conflict." *Pravada* 5, 2: 15–19.

Ranaweera, Eva. 1992. "Shame, Woman, Gajaman Nona." *Voice of Women* 3, 3: 18–27.

Ratnapala, Nandasena. 1991. *Folklore of Sri Lanka*. Colombo: State Printing Corporation.

Reed, Susan A. 2002. "Performing Respectability: The Berava, Middle-Class Nationalism, and the Classicization of Kandyan Dance in Sri Lanka." *Cultural Anthropology* 17: 246–77.

Richardson, John M., Jr. 2004. "Violent Conflict and the First Half Decade of Open Economy Policies in Sri Lanka: A Revisionist View." In *Economy and Ethnic Conflict in Sri Lanka*, edited by Deborah Winslow and Michael Woost. Bloomington: Indiana University Press.

Risseeuw, Carla. 1991. "Bourdieu, Power, and Resistance: Gender Transformation in Sri Lanka." In *The Gender of Power*, edited by Kathy Davis, Monique Leijenaar, and Jantine Oldersma. London: Sage.

——. 1996. "State Formation and Transformation in Gender Relations and Kinship in Colonial Sri Lanka." In *Shifting Circles of Support: Contextualising Gender and Kinship in South Asia and Sub-Saharan Africa*, edited by Rajni Palriwala and Carla Risseeuw. Walnut Creek, Calif.: Alta Mira Press.

Rivoli, Pietra. 2005. *The Travels of a T-shirt in the Global Economy: An Economist Examines the Markets, Power, and Politics of World Trade*. Hoboken, N.J.: John Wiley and Sons.

Roberts, Michael, ed. 1997. *Sri Lanka: Collective Identities Revisited*, vol. 1. Colombo: Marga Institute.

——. 1998. *Sri Lanka: Collective Identities Revisited*, vol. 2. Colombo: Marga Institute.

Rofel, Lisa. 1989. "Hegemony and Productivity: Workers in Post-Mao China." In *Marxism and the Chinese Experience*, edited by Arif Dirlik and Maurice Meisner. Armonk, N.Y.: M. E. Sharpe.

——. 1999. *Other Modernities: Gendered Yearnings in China after Socialism*. Berkeley: University of California Press.

Rogers, John D., Jonathan Spencer, and Jayadeva Uyangoda. 1998. "Sri Lanka: Political Violence and Ethnic Conflict." *American Psychologist* (July): 771–77.

Rosa, Kumudhini. 1991. "Strategies of Organisation and Resistance: Women Workers in Sri Lankan Free Trade Zones." *Capital and Class* 45: 27–34.

Rosaldo, Renato. 1989. *Culture and Truth: The Remaking of Social Analysis*. Boston: Beacon Press.

Ross, Ellen, and Rayna Rapp. 1997 [1981]. "Sex and Society: A Research Note from Social History and Anthropology." In *The Gender/Sexuality Reader: Culture, History, Political Economy*, edited by Roger N. Lancaster and Micaela di Leonardo. New York: Routledge.

Roy, Beth. 1994. *Some Trouble with Cows: Making Sense of Social Conflict*. Berkeley: University of California Press.

Rutz, Henry J. 1992. "Introduction: The Idea of a Politics of Time." In *The Politics of Time*,
edited by H. Rutz. Washington, D.C.: American Anthropological Association.

Ryan, Bryce. 1953a. *Caste in Modern Ceylon: The Sinhalese System in Transition*. New
Brunswick, N.J.: Rutgers University Press.

———. 1953b. "The Sinhalese Family System." *Eastern Anthropologist* 6, 3–4: 143–63.

Ryan, Bryce, and Sylvia Fernando. 1951. "The Female Factory Worker in Colombo." *International Labour Review* 64: 438–61.

Salzinger, Leslie. 2003. *Genders in Production: Making Workers in Mexico's Global Factories*.
Berkeley: University of California Press.

Sandel, Michael J. 1996. *Democracy's Discontent: America in Search of a Public Philosophy*.
Cambridge, Mass.: Belknap Press.

Sarkar, N. K., and S. J. Tambiah. 1957. *The Disintegrating Village*. Colombo: Ceylon University Press.

Sassen, Saskia. 1998. *Globalization and Its Discontents: Essays on the New Mobility of People
and Money*. New York: Free Press.

Scott, David. 1994. *Formations of Ritual: Colonial and Anthropological Discourses on the Sinhala Yaktovil*. Minneapolis: University of Minnesota Press.

Scott, James. 1985. *Weapons of the Weak: Everyday Forms of Peasant Resistance*. New
Haven, Conn.: Yale University Press.

Scott, Joan. 1999. *Gender and the Politics of History*. Rev. ed. New York: Columbia University Press.

Seizer, Susan. 2000. "Roadwork: Offstage with Special Drama Actresses in South India."
Cultural Anthropology 15, 2: 217–59.

———. 2005. *Stigmas of the Tamil Stage: An Ethnography of Special Drama Artists in South
India*. Durham, N.C.: Duke University Press.

Seneviratne, H. L. 1999. *The Work of Kings: The New Buddhism in Sri Lanka*. Chicago:
University of Chicago Press.

Seneviratne, H. L., and S. Wickremeratne. 1980. "Bodhipuja, Collective Representations
of Sri Lankan Youth." *American Ethnologist* 4: 734–43.

Senge, Peter. 1990. *The Fifth Discipline: The Art and Practice of the Learning Organization*.
New York: Doubleday.

Serasundara, Ajith [Ajit Serasundera]. 1998. "Youth Politics, Nationalism, and Cultural
Fundamentalism." In *Globalization, Social Change, and Youth*, edited by S. T. Hettige.
Colombo: German Cultural Institute and the Centre for Anthropological and Socio-
logical Studies.

Sessional Paper I. 1990. *Report of the Presidential Commission on Youth*. Colombo: Department of Government Printing.

Sessional Paper V. 1997. *Final Report of the Commission of Inquiry into Involuntary Removal* or *Disappearance of Persons in the Western, Southern, and Sabaragamuwa Provinces*. Colombo: Department of Government Printing. Available online at www.disappear ances.org/mainfile.php/frep_sl_western/.

Shastri, Amita. 1997. "Transitions to a Free Market: Economic Liberalization in Sri Lanka." *The Round Table* 344: 485–511.

Sheeran, Anne. 1997. "White Noise: European Modernity, Sinhala Musical Nationalism, and the Practice of a Creole Popular Music in Modern Sri Lanka." Ph.D. diss., University of Washington.

——. 2002. "Is It 'Normal'? Baila Music, Hybridity, and the Sinhala Nationalist Project." In *The Hybrid Island: Culture Crossings and the Invention of Identity in Sri Lanka*, edited by Neluka Silva. London: Zed.

Siddiqi, Dina. 1996. "Women in Question: Gender and Labor in Bangladeshi Factories." Ph.D. diss., University of Michigan.

Silva, K. Tudor, and Merrill Eisenberg. 1996. "Attitude Towards Pre-Marital Sex in a Sample of Sri Lankan Youth." Paper presented at the National Convention on Women's Studies, March (Centre for Women's Research [CENWOR], Colombo, Sri Lanka).

Smith, Donald E. 1979. "Religion, Politics, and the Myth of Reconquest." In *Modern Sri Lanka: A Society in Transition*, edited by Tissa Fernando and Robert N. Kearney. Syracuse: Syracuse University Press.

Special Correspondent [Our]. 1992a. "Investing in the People—A Durable Security against Violence." *Observer* (Colombo), 23 February: 4.

Special Correspondent [A]. 1992b. "200 Garment Factory Program—A Bold Bid to End Rural Poverty." *Daily News* (Colombo), 30 September: n.p.

Spencer, Jonathan. 1990a. *A Sinhala Village in a Time of Trouble*. Delhi: Oxford University Press.

——. 1990b. "Writing Within: Anthropology, Nationalism, and Culture in Sri Lanka." *Current Anthropology* 31, 3: 283–300.

——. 1992. "Representations of the Rural: A View from Sabaragamuva." In *Agrarian Change in Sri Lanka*, edited by James Brow and Joe Weeramunda. New Delhi: Sage Publications.

Sri Lanka News Bulletin. 1993a. Information Division, Embassy of Sri Lanka, Washington, D.C., 15 January.

——. 1993b. Information Division, Embassy of Sri Lanka, Washington, D.C., 15 February.

Standing, Guy. 1989. "Global Feminization through Flexible Labor." *World Development* 17: 1077–95.

Stanley, Alessandra. 1999. "Ruling on Tight Jeans and Rape Sets off Anger in Italy." *New York Times*, 16 February: A6.

Stokke, Kristian. 1995. "Poverty as Politics: The Janasaviya Poverty Alleviation Programme in Sri Lanka." *Norsk geogr. Tidsskr* 49: 123–35.

Sunday Times (Colombo). 2000. "Susanthika Renews Sex Charge." 1 October: 1.

Tambiah, Stanley J. 1958. "The Structure of Kinship and Its Relationship to Land Possession and Residence in Pata Dumbara, Central Ceylon." *Journal of the Royal Anthropological Institute of Great Britain and Ireland* 88: 21–44.

——. 1992. *Buddhism Betrayed? Religion, Politics, and Violence in Sri Lanka.* Chicago: University of Chicago Press.

Tambiah, Yasmin. 1997. "Women's Sexual Autonomy: Some Issues in South Asia." *Options* 9: 28–32.

——. 2005. "Turncoat Bodies: Sexuality and Sex Work under Militarization in Sri Lanka." *Gender and Society* 19: 243–61.

Taylor, Frederick. W. 1911. *The Principles of Scientific Management.* New York: Harper and Row.

Tennekoon, Ranjith. 2000. "Labour Issues in the Textile and Clothing Industry: A Sri Lankan Perspective." International Labour Office, Geneva, Sectoral Activities Department (SECTOR), Workshop Background Paper. Available at www.ilo.org/public/english/dialogue/sector/papers/tclabor/index.htm.

Tennekoon, Serena. 1986. "'Macho' Sons and 'Man-Made' Mothers." *Lanka Guardian,* 15 June.

——. 1988. "Rituals of Development: The Accelerated Mahavali Development Program of Sri Lanka." *American Ethnologist* 15: 294–310.

Thompson, E. P. 1967. "Time, Work-Discipline, and Industrial Capitalism." *Past and Present* 38: 56–97.

Thompson, Kenneth. 1998. *Moral Panics.* London: Routledge.

Tiano, Susan. 1994. *Patriarchy on the Line: Labor, Gender, and Ideology in the Mexican Maquila Industry.* Philadelphia: Temple University Press.

Trautmann, Thomas R. 1997. *Aryans and British India.* Berkeley: University of California Press.

Tsing, Anna. 2000. "The Global Situation." *Cultural Anthropology* 15: 327–60.

——. 2002. "Conclusion: The Global Situation." In *The Anthropology of Globalization: A Reader,* edited by Jonathan Xavier Inda and Renato Rosaldo. Malden, Mass.: Blackwell Publishers.

Uvais, Ramesh. 2003. "Song and Music Pay Tribute to the 'Daughters of the Nation.'" *Daily Mirror* (Colombo), 11 October: n.p.

Uyangoda, Jayadeva. 1992. "Political Dimensions of Youth Unrest." In *Unrest or Revolt: Some Aspects of Youth Unrest in Sri Lanka,* edited by S. T. Hettige. Colombo: Goethe-Institut, German Cultural Institute, and American Studies Association (Sri Lanka).

van der Horst, Josine. 1995. *'Who Is He, What Is He Doing' Religious Rhetoric and Performances in Sri Lanka during R. Premadasa's Presidency (1989–1993).* Amsterdam: VU University Press.

Voice of Women. 1983. *Women Workers in the Free Trade Zone of Sri Lanka.* Colombo: Voice of Women.

Wallaboda, Jatila. 1993. "PM Inspects 129th Garment Factory." *Island* (Colombo), 9 September: n.p.

Warrell, Lindy. 1990. "Conflict in Hierarchy: Jealousy among the Sinhalese Buddhists." *South Asia* 13: 19–41.

Waters, Malcolm. 2001. *Globalization.* 2d ed. London: Routledge.

Weber, Max. 1958. *The Protestant Ethic and the Spirit of Capitalism.* Translated by Talcott Parsons. New York: Charles Scribner's Sons.

Weerakoon, Bradman. 1992. *Premadasa of Sri Lanka: A Political Biography*. New Delhi: Vikas.

Weerasinghe, Rohini. 1989. "Women Workers in the Katunayake Investment Promotion Zone (KIPZ) of Sri Lanka: Some Observations." In *Women in Development in South Asia*, edited by V. Kanesalingam. New Delhi: Macmillan India.

Weerasuriya, Padmini. 2000. "The Conditions of the Workers in the Free Trade Zones as a Result of Sri Lanka's Open Economy." Women's Group of ASEM 2000 People's Forum conference on Women's Strategies to Challenge Globalization. Last accessed 1 June 2006 at www.women21.or.kr/data/women21/ENGPDS_X/asem2000.doc.

Wijebandara, Krishna. 1996. "First to the Free Trade Zone, Second to Party Culture," *Lakbima* (Colombo), 17 March: 14 (in Sinhala, trans. Rosemary Chunchie).

Williams, Raymond. 1973. *The Country and the City*. New York: Oxford University Press.

Winslow, Deborah, and Michael D. Woost, eds. 2004. *Economy, Culture, and Civil War in Sri Lanka*. Bloomington: Indiana University Press.

Wolf, Diane. 1992. *Factory Daughters: Gender, Household Dynamics, and Rural Industrialization in Java*. Berkeley: University of California Press.

Wolf, Margery. 1992. *A Thrice-Told Tale: Feminism, Postmodernism and Ethnographic Responsibility*. Stanford, Calif.: Stanford University Press.

Wright, Melissa W. 2001. "Desire and the Prosthetics of Supervision: A Case of Maquiladora Flexibility." *Cultural Anthropology* 16: 354–73.

Wu, Hung. 1997. "The Hong Kong Clock—Public Time-Telling and Political Time/Space." *Public Culture* 9: 329–54.

Yalman, Nur. 1963. "On the Purity of Women in the Castes of Ceylon and Malabar." *Journal of the Royal Anthropological Institute* 93: 25–58.

Yuval-Davis, Nira, and Floya Anthias. 1989. *Woman-Nation-State*. New York: St. Martin's Press.

INDEX

Abeysekera, Sunila, 111–13, 157
advertising, 62, 107, 117, 185, 193
agency (*see also* resistance), 9, 22, 33, 36–40, 47, 109, 240
aggression, as male-gendered trait, 26–27, 102, 112. *See also* docility
agriculture. *See* farming, paddy-field work
AIDS, 178, 181
alcohol, 79, 102, 103–05, 110–11, 126, 151, 170, 176
America. *See* United States
Anderson, Benedict, 250 n.11
Anuradhapura, 56, 119
Appadurai, Arjun, 239
Appalachia, 243
apprenticeship, 39–40
Arjuna Sir, 141, 240–41
army, 27, 47, 102, 111, 119, 129, 132, 133, 154–55, 179, 252 n.18; and "period of terror," 137–39; Indian, 65; U.S., 16
Asanka Sir, 45, 206, 211, 220, 225, 231, 238, 254 n.5. *See also* owner
Asoka, ancient Indian emperor, 77–78
assembly line, 17, 35, 249 n.3

backache, 42–43, 169
Bandarage, Asoka, 110, 183
Bandaranaike, Anura, 92, 94
Bandaranaike, S. W. R. D., 60
Bangladesh, 34
bank, 51, 83, 131, 150, 172, 193
bell, 43, 46, 72, 73, 226
Biyanwala, Janaka, 104, 105
boarding house, 88, 102, 107, 109, 140, 148, 150
bodhipūja, Buddhist ritual, 17–18, 179, 213, 248 n.11
body fat, 190, 253 n.7
boredom, 52, 189
botanical gardens, as trysting spot, 146, 148

Bourdieu, Pierre, 82, 215
boyfriend, 14, 27, 46, 47, 108, 109, 119, 133, 143, 146, 149, 154–55, 158–59, 173–80, 192, 208–09, 218, 222
Britain, 114, colonial legacy of, 63, 67, 80, 96, 100, 102, 133. *See also* English, nationalism
Brooks, Shannon, 243–44
Brow, James, 145
Buddha, 56, 60, 69, 77–78, 153, 213. *See also* Buddhism, dhamma
Buddhism, as locally practiced, 2, 3, 17–18, 45, 56, 79, 113, 134, 179, 184, 213, 248 n.11. *See also bodhipūja*, monk, pilgrimage, Protestant Buddhism, Sinhala Buddhism
"bump." *See* hair
Burgher. *See* minority community
bus, 3–4, 13, 17, 33, 44–45, 73, 91, 112, 129, 131, 132, 133, 137, 147, 148, 168, 184–88, 229–31, 254 n.2. *See also* van

canteen, 1, 2, 3, 13, 135, 186, 196, 233. *See also* lunch break
capitalism, 7, 8, 27, 30, 35–37, 47, 61, 65, 68–70, 80, 99, 127, 142, 239, 241, 250 nn.10, 13; as analytic category, 97; global, 31, 35, 37, 56, 70, 93, 95, 108, 120; "welfare capitalism," 203–07; capitalist discipline, 7, 33, 47, 66, 73. *See also* discipline, globalization
cassette, 189; cassette player, 51, 185, 190, 195
caste, 11, 48–49, 67, 93, 97, 131, 134–36, 140, 145, 166, 174, 179, 183, 215, 253 n.4, 254 n.5
Champa, 138
Champi, 210
Chanaka Sir, 210, 211–12
Chandra, 48, 145, 181, 187–89, 192

Chatterjee, Partha, 64, 98–99
China, 31, 237–38
Chinta, 51–53, 187–88, 234
Christian. *See* minority community
Chuti, 136–37
"civic order committee," village political body, 226
cleanliness. *See* hygiene
clerical work. See paperwork, white-collar status
clock tower, 55–56, 72–75, 251 n.16
"Coca-colonization," 24. *See also* homogenization
Cohen, Stanley, 113–15
Collier, Jane, 47, 127–28, 215
Collins, Jane, 28, 255 n.2
Collins, Steven, 250 n.7
Colombia, 206, 222
Colombo, 3, 5, 10, 13, 28, 43, 57, 61, 73, 101–02, 109, 141–42, 146, 170, 182, 207, 219, 220, 224, 230, 233, 240–41, 249 n.4, 250 n.8, 254 n.4; as glamorous, 167, 193, 198–99; as morally problematic, 37, 44, 62, 103–05, 106–07, 110, 112–13, 115, 118, 119, 148–50, 151–52, 154, 157, 159, 189, 225. *See also* Free Trade Zone
community of practice, 33, 39–41, 45–46, 48, 149
competition, between Shirtex and Serendib workers, 216–18, 225–26, 233–35
Constable, Nicole, 9
consumer culture. *See* consumption practices
consumerism. *See* consumption
consumption, 29, 31, 35, 37, 62, 109, 180, 182, 185, 188, 191, 192–99, 238; of media, 110, 156
cosmetics. *See* lipstick, makeup
costume. *See* dress
cotton dust, 34, 115, 169, 186–87, 240–42, 255 n.2
cricket, 13, 105; cricket field, 132, 224, 226
"cut pieces," 133

daham pāsäl, dhamma school, 77, 80
"Daily Code for the Laity," Buddhist pamphlet, 78–79, 101
damage, to garments, 4, 13, 16, 26, 46, 210, 232

dancing, 184, 188; "Western dance contest," 203, 233–35, 241
darkness, of night, 3, 27, 179, 212, 223–24; of skin, 105, 189–92
day labor. *See* paddy field work
Daya, 135–36
de Alwis, Malathi, 79, 101, 143, 171
de Certeau, Michel, 29–30
de Mel, Neloufer, 100
development, 2, 6–8, 17, 24, 27, 31, 37, 56–59, 60–64, 66–67, 69–71, 73, 79–81, 87, 91, 118, 188, 193, 201, 204–05
dhamma, 60, 76–78, 250 n.7. *See also* Buddha, Buddhism, Sinhala Buddhism
dhammadīpa, Sri Lanka as sacred Buddhist land, 60, 63, 69, 78, 250 n.7
Dharmapala, Anagarika, 63, 68, 70, 77, 78–81, 82, 84, 86, 94, 100–02, 152, 188
disappearance, as tactic of state repression, 5, 64–65, 130, 138–39, 150
discipline, 7, 11, 27, 33, 35, 40, 43, 47, 49, 56–57, 59, 62, 66, 68, 95, 109, 118–19, 140–43, 153, 173, 188–89, 204, 206–07, 210, 222, 228, 233, 235, 239, 249 n.6, 250 n.15; and clock time, 71–74; consumption and, 192–98; dhamma and, 77–78; Dharmapala and, 78–81; politics of, 74–77; and social change, 81–86. *See also* capitalism
docility, as female-gendered trait, 26–27, 102, 112. *See also* aggression, discipline
doctor, 46, 47, 61, 212, 230–33
dowry, 51, 113, 154, 174, 188
dress, 6, 15–16, 34, 46, 48, 51, 76, 81–84, 99, 102, 104–05, 109, 112, 115, 117, 122, 126, 131, 133, 143, 147, 153–54, 161, 169–70, 181, 185–89, 192–96, 205, 227–230, 233–234, 240, 255 n.8. See also *salwar kameez*, sari, sandal, underwear, uniform
drinking. *See* alcohol
driver, 1, 132, 137, 176–77, 184, 222–23
Dutch, as colonial and ethnic presence, 100, 102
duty *yutukam*, 127, 212

education, 5–6, 19, 59, 61, 63, 66–67, 79–80, 83–84, 87, 89, 100, 127, 129–30, 131, 133–35, 162, 169–72, 174, 188, 202, 206. *See also* exam, literacy, student, university

election, national, 60, 69, 137, 138; of Workers' Committee, 219
elopement, 180–81. *See also* marriage, virginity
email, 24
English, 6, 10–11, 12, 13, 15, 26, 43, 48, 55, 60, 74, 83, 93, 100, 104, 129, 134, 141, 147, 151, 157, 174, 176, 177, 186, 187, 195, 198, 207, 209–10, 225, 226, 230, 232, 240; as language of elite, 59, 61, 129, 178; language instruction at factories, 13, 43–44, 59–60, 169
Enloe, Cynthia, 35
ethnonationalism. *See* nationalism
Europe, 16, 57, 70, 72–73, 80, 94, 99, 101, 252 n.13
everyday, as anthropological concept, 9, 11, 29, 99
exam, 5–6, 67, 133–34, 152, 155, 169–72, 207. *See also* student, university

Fair and Lovely, skin bleaching cream, 190
farming, 59, 80–81, 86, 127, 129, 132, 134, 190–92, 250 n.6, 252 n.9. *See also* paddy-field work
Farnsworth-Alvear, Ann, 206, 218, 222
father, of worker. *See* parent
feminism. *See* feminist scholarship
feminist scholarship, on Third World women, 34–36
feminization of labor, 26–27, 248 n.1
Fernández-Kelly, Patricia, 34
Fernando, Anthony, 83–84, 188, 251 n.20
Fernando, Sharmini, 181
film, 94, 107, 109, 111–13, 152, 252 n.18; *Pura Handa Kaluwara*, 111, 119. *See also* teledrama
Ford, Henry, 205–06
foreign exchange, 27, 58, 61, 69, 70, 71, 101
Foucault, Michel, 128, 142, 248 n.8, 249 n.6, 250 n.15
Free Trade Zone, 61, 106, 115, 117–18, 125, 141, 148, 166, 183, 198, 209–10, 250 n.8, 251 n.3; Katunayake Free Trade Zone, 61, 106–10, 126, 147, 150, 152–54
FTZ. *See* Free Trade Zone
funeral, 13, 28, 122, 137, 165, 196, 207, 230–31; of Samarakoon Sir's father, 3–

5, 22, 32–33, 36–37, 44–45, 184, 211–213, 220, 225

Gamburd, Michele, 254 n.3
Gamini Sir, 146–47, 195–98
Geeta, 40–41, 108, 121–23, 134, 201–02, 238, 244
Germany, 99
gift, 14–15, 28, 73, 104, 117, 211, 228, 255 n.8
globalization, 8, 10–11, 22, 28–30, 34, 38, 62, 79, 86, 100, 109, 111, 119, 129, 237–39, 241–42, 248 n.1; gender and, 30–33; and localization, 23–25. *See also* capitalism, imperialism, neoliberalism, liberalization
goḍē, "rural" self-presentation, 48, 81–86, 182, 187–89, 191, 199
Goffman, Erving, 114–15
gold. *See* jewelry
Gombrich, Richard, 80, 254 n.4
Good girl, definition of, 10–11, 126, 165. *See also* Juki girl
Goody, Jack, 72
gossip. *See* kaṭakatā
government job, 87, 170–72. *See also* white-collar status
Grahanaya. *See* teledrama
"greenfields practices," 25
grievance, of factory workers, 215, 218–19, 221–22, 226
Grossholtz, Jean, 171
guard, factory security, 2, 132, 220
Gujarati. *See* minority community
Gunasinghe, Newton, 61, 119–20
Gunawardana, R. A. L. H., 191
Guruge, Ananda, 79

habitus, 82
hair, 2, 15, 35, 51, 102, 104–05, 112, 115, 126, 147, 151–53, 165, 170, 172, 182, 185–86, 188, 234, 240–42
Harlem, 165, 182
Hettige, S. T., 109, 251 n.1
Hewamanne, Sandya, 111, 126, 144, 150, 183, 251 n.3, 252 n.16
hierarchy, 166, 222, 241
Hinduism, 78, 132, 134, 247 n.4
homogenization, cultural, 24–25, 56, 237, 242. *See also* "Coca-colonization"
housework, 52–53, 171, 175–76, 184, 189
hygiene, 48, 82, 183, 187–89, 192

identity construction. *See* self-fashioning, subject production
illiteracy. *See* literacy
illness, 43, 46, 47, 52, 176, 201, 211, 213
IMF. *See* International Monetary Fund
imperialism. *See* neoimperialism.
import substitution, 60–61
India, 16, 56, 62, 64, 77, 78, 98–99, 102, 115, 166, 168, 178, 230, 237, 249 n.4, 252 n.13; purported expansionist designs of, 65
Indonesia, 35
Indrani, 183
Industrial Revolution, 72, 250 n.15
industrialization. *See* rural industrialization
innocence (*ahiṃsaka*), as gendered construct, 88–89, 92–93, 105–06, 110, 118, 120, 125, 146, 155, 157, 160, 165, 251 n.2. *See also* virginity
insult, 21–22, 105, 114, 167–70, 202, 215, 221, 242
International Monetary Fund, 23, 29, 57
investor, 12, 14, 26, 28, 30, 32, 33, 49, 57–59, 73, 84, 96, 125, 157, 211, 218, 238; attitude toward village, 140–41, 149; Premadasa's appeal to, 66–71, 203–06; foreign investor, 7, 14, 24, 56, 57, 61, 68, 70–71, 100, 107
Ira Handa Yata. *See* teledrama
ironing, 12, 26, 43, 136

Jackson, Jean, 249 n.4
Janasaviya Program, state poverty alleviation program, 67, 136, 217
Janatha Vimukthi Peramuna, 5–6, 58–59, 64–66, 68, 71, 74, 76–77, 82, 86, 91, 107, 118, 120, 130, 133, 136–40, 211, 250 nn.13, 14, 251 n.1, 252 n.3, 253 nn.4, 5
Japan, 10, 16, 63, 130, 248 n.9
Jayamanne, Laleen, 111
Jayanthi, 155, 169
Jayasinghe, Susanthika, 103–06, 111, 114–15
Jayawardena, Kumari, 101
Jayewardene, J. R., 65
jealousy (*irisāwa*), 108, 138–39
Jeganathan, Pradeep, 224
jewelry, 51, 113, 153, 170, 184–85, 190, 193–94, 234
Juki, Japanese sewing machine brand, 10, 106, 248 n.9

Juki girl, definition of, 10, 106–10. *See also* Good girl, moral panic, stigma
JVP. *See* Janatha Vimukthi Peramuna

kaṭakatā, orally circulated local information, 143, 175, 178
Kabeer, Naila, 34
kadē, small shop, 2, 132, 190, 193, 233
Kamala, 181, 212, 214
Kandiyoti, Deniz, 98
Kandy, 4, 12, 46, 51, 55, 109, 131–32, 137, 146, 148, 172, 175, 176, 188, 234, 254 n.4 (chap. 5), 254 n.4 (chap. 6); as shopping destination, 169, 186, 192–93; Kandyan sari, 112; "Up Country" as opposed to Colombo or "Low Country," 141, 182, 223, 240–41
Kanthi, 158–59, 178–79, 195
Katunayake FTZ. *See* Free Trade Zone
Kemper, Steven, 16, 62
ketchup, 238–39
kin (*näyo*), 145
king, as heroic figure in Sinhala ethnonationalism, 69, 78, 86, 204
knowledge. *See* learning
Korea, 96
Kumari, 1–5, 8–10, 14, 22, 36–37, 41–42, 49, 132, 133, 190, 220, 222–24, 229, 231–232, 234, 238, 244, 249 n.5

läjja-baya, shame-fear, 11, 142–43, 145–46, 153–54, 157, 173, 218, 224
landowner, 34, 61
Latin America, 96
laughing contest, 228
Lave, Jean, 39–40, 45
learning, as analytic category, 23, 33, 38–40, 197–98, 216; as sanctioned or unsanctioned by factory management, 40–49, 169, 249 n.6
Lebovics, Herman, 63
letter: among workers and managers, 3, 211; anonymous, 137, 219; love letter, 133, 179, 229
liberalization, economic, 5, 8, 9–11, 23–24, 30, 38, 56–57, 59, 60–64, 65, 72, 91, 93, 95, 97, 100, 101, 106, 108, 110, 111, 119, 127–29, 130, 138, 140, 174, 185, 193, 204, 210, 216, 233, 237, 241, 250 n.13, 251 n.7, 252 n.9
Liberation Tigers of Tamil Eelam, 9, 24, 27, 59–61, 64–65, 67, 70–71, 99, 102,

111, 115, 118, 120, 121, 168, 179, 253 n.4
linthead, 242–44, 255 n.2
lipstick, 48, 151–52, 183–85. *See also* makeup
liquor. *See* alcohol
literacy, 3, 58, 86, 133
localization, 22–30, 32, 37, 45, 56–67, 68–69, 71, 206
London, 34
love, 15, 52, 68, 88–89, 151, 154–55, 159, 178, 207, 212, 214–15, 230, 232–33, 244; love affair, 174, 176, 177–80, 197, 216, 232. *See also* "love sickness," marriage, romance
"love sickness," 203, 229–33, 241. *See also* love
Low Country. *See* Colombo
LTTE. *See* Liberation Tigers of Tamil Eelam
Lukose, Ritty, 178
lunch break, 13, 37, 43, 132, 135, 210. *See also* canteen

machine, human worker as, 88, 108, 123, 202. *See also* sewing machine
Maddox, Richard, 47
magazine, 110, 126, 133
Mahaweli Development Project, policy of Sinhala resettlement in Tamil-majority areas, 17, 69
Mahmood, Saba, 36, 38
maid. *See* servant
makeup, 149, 152–53, 165, 183. *See also* lipstick
Mala, 5–10, 21–22, 38, 49, 87–89, 94, 96–97, 114, 150, 167–71, 174, 240, 242, 243, 244
Malaysia, 96, 116, 206, 239
Mallika, 210
Manchester, 96
Manel, 229–232, 238, 239
march. *See* walkout
market, local, 4, 59, 133, 176. *See also* Kandy, shopping
marriage, 9, 168, 212; arranged, 154, 162, 165, 170, 178–80; proposal, 10, 107, 144, 170; virginity at, 93, 101, 145–46, 156, 165, 180–81, 207–09; "love marriage," 162, 177–80; marriage prospects of garment workers, 131, 173–77. *See also* elopement, love affair, rape, wedding

Marx, Karl, 122, 250 n. 15
mass media, 11, 29, 31, 34, 58, 71, 84, 86, 88–89, 92, 103–05, 110–13, 114, 155, 157–58, 193, 251 n.16. *See also* cassette, film, magazine, newspaper, radio, television
Massachusetts, 15–16, 96, 239
McDonald's, 238
meditation, 79, 81
Mencken, H. L., 242–43
Mexico, 96, 239
MFA. *See* Multifibre Arrangement
Middle East, 101, 110, 129, 132, 159, 250 n.9, 252 n.9. *See also* Saudi Arabia
migration: overseas, 101, 129, 252 n.9; urban, 5, 32, 35, 37, 44, 95–96, 101, 107, 110, 112, 118, 140, 167, 241
Miles, Emma Bell, 243
military. *See* army
Mills, Mary Beth, 35
Ministry of Labour, 219
minority community, religious and ethnic (*see also* Dutch, Portuguese, Tamil): Burgher, 102; Christian, 12, 60, 132, 247 n.4; Gujarati, 57, 249 n.4; Muslim, 12, 34, 57, 60, 67, 71, 75, 132, 230, 247 n.4; Sindhi, 57, 249 n.4
modernity, 9–11, 22, 29, 31, 56, 62, 63, 80, 167, 178, 180, 189, 191, 198, 203, 216, 232, 239–41, 249 n.4; and fashion, 74, 230; and gender, 98–99; and hygiene, 188–89; and party politics, 223
monitoring, of villagers, 86, 127–28, 137, 142, 146–47; of women, 10, 86, 99, 108, 142, 146–47; of workers, 86, 127–28, 137, 142, 146–47. *See also* panopticon
monk, 6, 61, 73, 76, 78, 211, 222–23, 250 n.7
Moore, Mick, 65, 250 n.14
moral panic, 92, 107, 111, 113–16, 120, 168, 227, 232
Mosse, George, 99
mother, of worker. *See* parent
mother-in-law, 52, 176, 181
Multifibre Arrangement, 238, 249 n.2
Muslim. *See* minority community

nationalism, 7, 9, 22, 27, 62–65, 68–71, 78–79, 86, 91–92, 95, 97–102, 105, 115–16, 149, 175, 188, 193, 195, 234, 240, 250 nn.7, 11; sexuality and, 118–20. *See also* Sinhala Buddhism

nationalization, of private enterprise, 60
neoimperialism, 8, 30, 71. *See also* globalization, neoliberalism
neoliberalism, 8. *See also* globalization, imperialism
New Year's Princess (*avurudu kumāri*),
190, 227, 233
New York City, 96, 238. *See also* Harlem
Newman, Katherine, 165
newspaper, 6–7, 10, 107, 110, 121–22,
135; and 200 GFP, 58, 81, 84, 116,
117, 118, 188, 205, 206, 251 n.20,
253 n.9; marriage proposal in, 10, 107,
144; and Susanthika Jayasinghe, 103–05
"nimble fingers," of female workers, 26.
See also docility
note. *See* letter
Nuwara Eliya, 211–12

Obeyesekere, Gananath, 63, 76, 79, 80,
143, 254 n.4
Ong, Aihwa, 36, 96, 116
"Open Economy" program, 61–62, 68,
111, 204
opening ceremony: for factory, 6, 58, 67,
78, 84, 117, 204; for school, 77
outsourcing, 237
overtime, 1, 6, 9, 47, 132, 162, 172, 209,
223, 225–26, 254 nn. 2, 3
owner, 12–14, 17, 27, 45, 48, 55, 73, 83,
84, 91, 97, 113, 140–41, 154, 156,
193–94, 197, 204, 211, 216, 219, 220,
229–31. *See also* Asanka Sir, investor,
Tissa Sir

PA, *see* People's Alliance
paddy-field work, 19, 33, 132, 136, 174,
189–92
Pajero, Mitsubishi automobile, 130, 132
panopticon, 128, 140–42, 150. *See also*
monitoring
paperwork, 43–44
parent, of worker, 7, 14, 19–20, 45, 46,
48, 51, 53, 81, 82, 87, 96, 107–09,
112, 117, 121, 156, 165–67, 169, 206,
208, 209–10, 212, 214, 218, 224, 228,
234, 240; and Good-girl identity, 181–
85, 188–89, 191, 193–95, 197; and
JVP, 137–39; of Kumari, 1–3; within
"love sickness" skit, 230–32; and marriage prospects, 154, 173–75, 179–80;
of Sita, 161–62; of Teja, 151–55; in vil-

lage context, 11, 135, 140, 142, 144–
49, 225–26
Paris, 96, 239
participant observation, 9, 12
party, 6, 48, 103–04, 133, 135, 179, 183–
85, 194, 230. *See also* wedding
"passing," 115, 186–87, 190
paternalism, 32, 203, 205–10, 218, 222
pay, 6, 20, 43, 48, 51, 58, 72, 113, 119,
129, 153, 161–62, 166, 171, 174, 187,
189–90, 193, 201, 209, 215, 234
People's Alliance, 62, 137, 223, 250 n.10
People's Liberation Front, *see* Janatha
Vimukthi Peramuna
perfume, 48, 187–89
"period of terror" (*bişna kālaya*), 7, 64, 66,
137, 150. *See also* Janatha Vimukthi Peramuna
petite bourgeoisie, 63
photograph, 14, 130, 133, 139, 175, 179
pilgrimage, 184, 249 n.1
pinning, 43, 169
Piyasena, 82, 182–83, 187, 192
pocketbook, 84, 185, 187, 190
Podi Menike, 3
police, 111, 113, 131, 138–39, 220, 228–
29, 254 n.2
Portuguese, as colonial and ethnic presence, 100, 102, 155 n.4
poster, 102, 137, 219–27, 254 n.4
Poya day, monthly national full moon holiday, 226
Prasanga, 131
pregnancy, 113, 117, 145, 159, 199, 208
Premadasa, Ranasinghe, 7–8, 19–20, 25,
31, 41, 49, 55–56, 58–59, 62, 75, 80–
81, 83–84, 86, 132, 166, 188–89, 219,
241, 251 n.16; and discipline, 71–78;
and JVP, 64–67, 136–37; and nationalism, 67–71; and "underwear critique,"
92, 95, 116–18. *See also* 200 Garment
Factories Program, globalization,
Janatha Vimukthi Peramuna, "period of
terror"
Presidential Commission on Youth, 59, 64
Prichard, James Cowles, 191
production quota. *See* production target
production target, 4, 28, 43, 47, 72, 87–
88, 141, 210, 213, 215, 222
progressive bundle system, 28
promiscuity, sexual, 10, 107, 174. *See also*
prostitution, sex

INDEX

INDEX

UNP. *See* United National Party
Up Country. *See* Kandy
urban migration. *See* migration

van, 3–4, 184, 222–23
Van der Horst, Josine, 77–78
victimization, as analytic construct,
Vietnam, 16–17
village, as zone of moral control. *See* monitoring
Violet, 220, 225
virginity, 93, 107, 126, 165, 178, 180–81, 208, 254 n.4
voting. *See* election

wage. *See* pay
walkout, 203, 218–27, 228, 235, 241. *See also* strike
Warrell, Lindy, 138
watch, 73–74, 193; stopwatch, 28, 72
Weber, Max, 80
wedding, 13, 48, 133, 135, 180–81, 183–85, 196, 211, 213, 220, 230, 254 n.5;

wedding planning as career option, 169–70
Weerakoon, Bradman, 81
"welfare capitalism," 203, 205–07
Wenger, Etienne, 39–40, 45
Westernization, 9, 58, 61–63, 94, 99, 102, 111–12, 178, 192, 234
white woman, as nationalist bogey, 92–94, 125, 251 n.4
white-collar status, 109, 131, 172, 186–87, 191. *See also* government job
Wijeweera, Rohana, 64
Williams, Raymond, 63
Wolf, Diane, 34
Workers' Committee, 219
Workers' Council. *See* Worker's Committee
world-making, 5

Yalman, Nur, 144
Yohan Sir, 4, 14, 169, 210, 211–12, 216, 219–26, 254–55 n.6
youth revolt, see Janatha Vimukthi Peramuna